OXFORD WORLD'S CLASSICS

SATIRES AND EPISTLES

HORACE was born in 65 BC. In 44 BC Julius Caesar was assassinated by conspirators led by Brutus and Cassius. Two years later, when they were defeated at Philippi, Horace commanded one of their legions. On his return to Rome he purchased a position in the Treasury and wrote satires and epodes under the patronage of Maecenas, chief adviser of Octavian. With the defeat of Antony and Cleopatra at Actium in 31 BC Octavian became master of the world, taking the name Augustus in 27 BC. After the publication of his three books of lyric *Odes* in 23 BC Horace returned to a form of satire with his first book of *Epistles* (20 BC), poetic letters reflecting on how to live well. In the course of the following decade his association with Augustus grew closer, as he wrote a hymn to be performed at the Secular Games in 17 BC, and even included a letter to the *princeps* in his second book of *Epistles*; the *Ars Poetica*, an epistle to the Pisos, was written around the same time. In 13 BC he produced his fourth book of *Odes*, largely inspired by Pindar, the most daring and sublime of the Greek lyric poets. He died in 8 BC, fifty-nine days after his friend Maecenas.

JOHN DAVIE is former Head of Classics at St Paul's School, London. He is the author of a number of articles on classical subjects and has translated the complete surviving plays of Euripides for Penguin Classics (four volumes). For Oxford World's Classics he has translated Seneca's *Dialogues and Essays*.

ROBERT COWAN is Lecturer in Classics at the University of Sydney, and formerly Fairfax Tutorial Fellow in Latin Literature at Balliol College, Oxford. He has published widely on subjects as diverse as Aristophanes, Columella, Horace, Virgil, and operatic receptions of Euripides' *Bacchae*, but his main areas of research are post-Virgilian epic, Republican tragedy, and Roman satire.

OXFORD WORLD'S CLASSICS

For over 100 years Oxford World's Classics have brought readers closer to the world's great literature. Now with over 700 titles—from the 4,000-year-old myths of Mesopotamia to the twentieth century's greatest novels—the series makes available lesser-known as well as celebrated writing.

The pocket-sized hardbacks of the early years contained introductions by Virginia Woolf, T. S. Eliot, Graham Greene, and other literary figures which enriched the experience of reading. Today the series is recognized for its fine scholarship and reliability in texts that span world literature, drama and poetry, religion, philosophy, and politics. Each edition includes perceptive commentary and essential background information to meet the changing needs of readers.

HORACE

Satires and Epistles

Translated by
JOHN DAVIE

With an Introduction and Notes by
ROBERT COWAN

OXFORD
UNIVERSITY PRESS

OXFORD
UNIVERSITY PRESS

Great Clarendon Street, Oxford ox2 6DP

Oxford University Press is a department of the University of Oxford.
It furthers the University's objective of excellence in research, scholarship,
and education by publishing worldwide in

Oxford New York

Auckland Cape Town Dar es Salaam Hong Kong Karachi
Kuala Lumpur Madrid Melbourne Mexico City Nairobi
New Delhi Shanghai Taipei Toronto

With offices in

Argentina Austria Brazil Chile Czech Republic France Greece
Guatemala Hungary Italy Japan Poland Portugal Singapore
South Korea Switzerland Thailand Turkey Ukraine Vietnam

Oxford is a registered trade mark of Oxford University Press
in the UK and in certain other countries

Published in the United States
by Oxford University Press Inc., New York

Translation © John Davie 2011
Editorial material © Robert Cowan 2011

British Library Cataloguing in Publication Data

Data available

Library of Congress Cataloging in Publication Data

Data available

Typeset by Glyph International, Bangalore, India
Printed in Great Britain
on acid-free paper by
Clays Ltd, Elcograf S.p.A.

ISBN 978-0-19-956328-9

10

CONTENTS

SATIRES

EPISTLES

BOOK 1

BOOK 2

INTRODUCTION

SATIRE is a paradox. It is poetry which denies that it *is* poetry. It is a moralizing rant which is sucked into prurience about and even complicity with the vice and folly it rails against. It is a cutting-edge slice-of-life which is obsessively self-conscious about its own literary traditions. It is free speech which tells it how it is but is always constrained by limitations on its liberty. Yet even by these standards, Horace's satire is exceptionally paradoxical. It is a finely wrought, pared-down form of a genre whose very essence is bloatedness, disorder, rough edges, a literary equivalent of the messy, chaotic world it evokes. It is a gentle, detached take on the genre of ranting, even bigoted invective, and one which advocates the virtues of moderation with fanatical extremism. In order to gain a sense of how Horace fits, or figured himself as fitting, into the traditions of Roman satire, it will be worth reflecting a little on the history and nature of Roman satire,[1] before turning to Horace's engagement—and sometimes his refusal to engage—with various themes and issues.

A brief history of satire

Roman satire has points of contact with various Greek genres— the invective *iamboi* of Archilochus and Hipponax, which Horace remodelled more directly in the *Epodes*; the socially and politically engaged Old Comedy of Aristophanes and his rivals, explicitly cited as a forebear at the opening of *Sat.* 1.4; the philosophical sermons, or diatribes, of Cynic philosophers, particularly influential on *Sat.* 1.1–3—but, unlike epic, tragedy, lyric, and every other genre, it was neither invented by the Greeks nor did they provide its canonical poets. Satire was a quintessentially Roman genre, 'entirely ours' (*tota nostra*), as Quintilian famously called it. This was not merely a paragraph of literary history or a badge of national pride, but suffused the very ethos of satire, linking to its rejection of pretension, luxury, and all the corrupting influences so readily attributed to the Greeks and

---

[1] By satire, I consistently mean verse satire as opposed to the Menippean tradition represented by Varro, Seneca's *Apocolocyntosis*, and perhaps Petronius.

its concomitant assertion of simple Roman values. When the Roman god Quirinus warns Horace not to use Greek words in his satires, he is making a point quite as ideologically loaded as when Juvenal's bigot Umbricius rails against the 'Greek city' which he claims Rome had become.

Satire's self-consciousness extends to a preoccupation with its own name. The alternative etymologies of *satura* given by the fourth-century AD grammarian Diomedes all (except for the improbable link with satyrs) relate to fullness, even bloatedness, and to an ugly, messy heterogeneity: he derives it from either a composite legal bill (*lex satura*), or a plate full of mixed dishes to be offered to the gods (*lanx satura*), or a sort of stuffed sausage or black pudding (*farcimen*). These etymologies seem to reflect much of satire's self-construction as a genre which is stuffed full of humanity with all its fears, desires, vices, and follies, variegated content which denies it the purity and unity associated with more respectable types of literature. Moreover, the connection with food cannot be coincidental, since satire is obsessed with the low bodily functions and desires which find no place in higher genres but which form the very essence, the stuffing of the sausage that is satire. As Alvin Kernan put it in a study of English satire which revolutionized approaches to its Roman predecessor, 'man is caught in his animal functions of eating, drinking, lusting, displaying his body, copulating, evacuating, scratching'.[2] Food in particular is a recurrent motif, especially in Horace's second book of *Satires*. It represents the lowest, most corporeal and sensual part of human nature, while excessive devotion to consuming, preparing, or studying the science of it is emblematic of the decay and false values of society (esp. in *Sat.* 2.2, 2.4, and 2.8); at the other extreme, the honest, simple fare which is the mark of Rome's rustic past, and which Horace still enjoys in the seclusion of his Sabine farm, stands as a marker for a more honest, simple way of life, as Horace recalls Ofellus arguing in 2.2. Satire abounds in images of the bloatedness and excess which it condemns but also embodies. Yet Horace's avowed attempt to compose finely honed, scaled-down satire in accordance with the poetic principles of Callimachus and the Alexandrians presents us with something of a contradiction in terms, though a contradiction

[2] A. Kernan, *The Cankered Muse: Satire of the English Renaissance* (New Haven, 1959), 11.

whose internal tensions reflect many of the wider aesthetic, moral, and political conflicts within the *Satires*.

The earliest satires, such as that of Ennius and Pacuvius, exist only in fragments, but seem to have constituted a very diverse genre, written in a variety of metres on a variety of subject matter. The earlier satires of Lucilius seem to have been very much in the same tradition, until he made the crucial decision to write in hexameters and thus established satire's defining generic relationship, that of being the antithesis of epic. Book 1 of Lucilius' satires presented a council of the gods following the death of the leader of the Senate, L. Cornelius Lentulus Lupus, in 125 BC in which they deliberate on how to punish Rome for his crimes and vices (Horace alludes to this in *Sat.* 2.1). This is clearly a parody of the council of the gods in Book 1 of what was then Rome's national epic, Ennius' *Annales*, where the deification of Romulus was debated. The relationship is not merely one of parody, but of distortion, perversion, and debasement. Everything which is lofty and noble in epic—the auspicious foundation of the city, the apotheosis of its king for his great virtues, the elevated diction, style, and subject matter—is negated, debased, perverted: the proposed destruction of the city, the condemnation of its leading statesman for his terrible vices; low, ugly language describing his face as being like death, jaundice, poison. Crucially, the metre is the same, metre which for a Roman conjured up associations of ideology and ethos as well as aesthetics and genre. By appropriating, deforming, and distorting epic's defining metrical form, Lucilian satire took its place as, in Morgan's phrase, epic's 'evil twin'.[3] Indeed, satire goes further and defines itself as a perversion of all poetry, a sort of anti-genre, and even so far as to deny that it is poetry at all. When Horace writes of his *Satires* (or *Sermones*) as 'conversational prose' (*Sat.* 1.4.42) and of his 'Muse who goes on foot' (2.6.17), he is engaging with a central aspect of the genre's identity, or rather its denial that it has a generic identity at all.

Lucilius' subject matter was extremely diverse, including not only literary criticism but minutiae of grammar and spelling. Unfortunately, the numerous but generally short fragments which survive cannot give more than a very limited sense of what his satire was really like.

---

[3] Ll. Morgan, 'Getting the Measure of Heroes: The Dactylic Hexameter and its Detractors', in M. Gale (ed.), *Latin Epic and Didactic Poetry: Genre, Tradition and Individuality* (Swansea, 2004), 1–26 at 8.

However, for the purposes of studying the later satire which has sur-
vived, that of Horace, Persius, and Juvenal, it is arguably less important
to think about Lucilius himself and his satiric corpus than about the
'Lucilius' his successors constructed, as a founding father and model
to be followed, rejected, or unsuccessfully emulated. Direct engage-
ments with Lucilius abound in Horace's *Satires*, from the small scale
of an individual name or phrase to the polemical imitation of a whole
poem, such as when *Sat.* 1.5, Horace's 'Journey to Brundisium',
trims down and polishes up Lucilius' 'Journey to Sicily'. Many of
these reminiscences are mentioned in the Explanatory Notes, and
we would doubtless identify more if more of Lucilius survived.
However, Horace's 'Lucilius' is most important as a model of literary
style (or its absence!) to be rejected or surpassed, and of freedom of
speech (*libertas*), who cannot be lived up to. The first of these issues is
addressed explicitly in *Sat.* 1.4 and 1.10, and it underpins the whole of
Horace's project of redefining not only the aesthetics of satire but the
ethos of moderation which that new satiric aesthetic both symbolizes
and is symbolized by. The second is directly addressed in *Sat.* 2.1 but
more broadly defines the self-positioning of Horatian and indeed all
post-Lucilian satire, as Persius and Juvenal follow Horace in drama-
tizing their aspiration to Lucilian *libertas* but also in their recognition
that the constraints of their political and social environment make
it impossible. Trebatius in *Sat.* 2.1 may suggest that Horace play
Lucilius to Octavian's Scipio, but no matter how close to the centre
of power Horace gets, he has neither the social standing nor political
autonomy of his satiric predecessor, and the world of triumviral and
Augustan Rome is very different from the Republic of the late second
century. Both these issues will be considered in more detail under the
headings of literary criticism and politics respectively.

   It remains to be said, if indeed it needs to be said, that satire is
funny. Much of its humour derives from the incongruities gener-
ated by its debasement of higher genres, as lofty motifs or figures are
brought jarringly down to the level of the gutter. When Lucretius'
noble personification of Nature urging man to cease clinging
to life is transformed into a talking penis asking why its owner
insists on thrusting it into 'a cunt descended from a great consul'
(*Sat.* 1.2.68–71) or the great seer Tiresias advises the epic hero
Ulysses, not how to achieve his homecoming from Troy to Ithaca,
but how to ingratiate himself into a childless old woman's will, the

effect is amusing as well as dissonant. Humour, particularly cruel, mocking humour, is also a means of stressing the undesirability of the target's behaviour and encouraging the reader and society as a whole to collude in laughing at and condemning him. Yet Horace particularly emphasizes the role of humour in satire as a means of conveying his serious message—'what's the harm in using humour to put across what is true, just as teachers sometimes offer their pupils biscuits to coax them into wanting to learn their ABC?' (*Sat.* 1.1.24–6)—and in palliating satire's potentially bitter invective, as when Trebatius predicts Horace's ultimate escape from the dangers the satirist incurs: 'Then the case will be laughed out of court, and you'll get off scot-free' (*Sat.* 2.1.86). The gentle humour of Horatian satire, in contrast to the bitter invective of Lucilius, is ultimately embodied in the figure of Priapus, who expels the witches, not with his customarily aggressive threat of rape, but with an amusing, but innocuous, fart.

Epistolary moments

The *Epistles* have a great deal in common with the *Satires* and can indeed be considered as falling within the genre of satire. They are written in hexameters whose versification would be too rough round the edges for epic; they are conversational in tone and structure; they deal with moral questions, focused on the antithesis of town and country; and they are marked by the prominence of a fully characterized authorial voice or persona. Yet, as their name suggests, they are also, crucially, letters. The tradition of poetic letters went back to archaic Greece, and many poets, including Catullus, include examples in their oeuvre. However, the composition of an entire collection of poetic epistles seems to have been an innovation by Horace, uniquely in a poet the rest of whose career consisted of being the new Lucilius, or, in the *Epodes* and *Odes* respectively, the Roman Archilochus or Alcaeus. Horace's choice of the letter form is also influenced by other literary antecedents, notably the tradition of philosophical letters, including those attributed to Plato and those actually written by Epicurus, and more recently Cicero's decision to collect and publish his own correspondence with Atticus. But Horace's *Epistles* are far more than an amalgam of these varied antecedents. Many of the themes and features which they share with the *Satires*, above all their preoccupation with ethics, will be discussed below, but it is worth taking a moment to consider the importance to the *Epistles* that they *are* epistles.

Letters are a very private and personal form of communication between two individuals, whose content can be determined by the specific purpose of the correspondence but may also ramble through the topics which the writer wishes to discuss without the concern for formal unity or cohesion that literary texts tend to demand. Horace emphasizes the privacy of letters, so apt for his retreat both from the composition of lyric and from any involvement in public affairs, even when communicating with the powerful, such as Augustus' stepson Tiberius. He is writing in a register which is both appropriate to his epistolary form and to his increasing desire for a life of seclusion and *otium* (leisure) on his Sabine farm. When there is an emphasis on the distance travelled by an epistle, it is not on the separation of lovers (as in Ovid's *Heroides*) or even of friends, but on the gap— philosophical as well as physical—between the countryside and the city, as when Horace the lover of the countryside writes to Fuscus the lover of the city (*Ep.* 1.10), or to his patron Maecenas to explain why he has not returned to the city as promised (1.7), or when, in a pointed reversal, he writes from the city to his city-loving bailiff who is stuck in the countryside (1.14). He also exploits and subverts the conventions of letter-writing, from those which determine the form of the whole letter, like the recommendation Septimius has solicited against Horace's will (1.9) or the charming dinner invitation to Torquatus (1.5), to formal details such as the conventional wish for health which so resonates with Horace's desire for a healthy soul (e.g. 1.6.67), or the identification of where the letter has been written, as when Horace ends his letter to Fuscus in praise of the country-side with a reminder that he is 'dictating these lines to you behind Vacuna's crumbling shrine'. Finally, letters are explicitly written texts, unlike the *Odes* with their fiction of sung performance, or even the conversational *Satires*, and as such share many of the qualities of the written poetry which they actually are. Horace draws attention to this in *Ep.* 1.20, even though in itself it breaks the fiction of epis-tolarity by addressing the poetry book as though it were a slave-boy. The meditation on the uncontrollability of the written word once it has been published and sent out into the world is one which could apply to almost any literary work, but gains particular resonance because the same is also true of letters.

Finding Horace: persona, face, and autobiography

Both the *Satires* and the *Epistles* feature a very strongly characterized personal voice which identifies itself as Q. Horatius Flaccus, reinforcing this impression of a real person not only by the myriad incidental and trivial details which produce an *effet de réalité* through their very triviality, but by making Horace, his life and opinions, the central focus of the poems. This powerfully persuasive presentation, compounded by the particularly post-Romantic tendency to read first-person texts as confessional and autobiographical, led many critics to read the Horace of the *Satires* and *Epistles* (and even to some extent of the *Odes*) as the 'real' Horace. The reaction to this tendency came with the argument that ancient authors tended to construct *personae* (lit. 'masks'), who spoke in the first person and could even be identified by the name of the historical author, but were nevertheless fictional characters constructed through allusive, generic, rhetorical, and other literary means. Thus Horace (or 'the satirist', as the persona might be called to differentiate him from the historical author) is a character derived from allusions to Cynic diatribe, comedy old and new, as well of course as Lucilian satire.

More sophisticated than a straightforwardly autobiographical approach though this unquestionably is, it also has its limitations. It runs the risk of assuming an equally 'real' person behind the mask, whereas even in 'real life', individuals generate (and have generated for them) complex and varying *personae*, which also take their existence from allusion, be it to literary texts or to conventional conceptions of 'types'. For this reason, it may be more useful to think in terms of what Ellen Oliensis calls 'face', the differing aspects and constructions of one's self which one presents to the world, depending in Horace's case partly on the genre in which he is currently writing (so the aggressive iambist will have a different 'face' from the genial lyricist) and partly on the social situation in which he is writing, including, perhaps most importantly, whom he is addressing, whether Maecenas or a young protégé, an old friend or a passing acquaintance, a slave or Augustus.[4]

However, it is not only the general methodological issues which make the use of persona theory problematic when approaching the

---

[4] This is an oversimplified version of the arguments in E. Oliensis, *Horace and the Rhetoric of Authority* (Cambridge, 1998).

Satires and *Epistles*; it is the texts' own insistence on the centrality of Horace's character and autobiography, the very insistence which led to the autobiographical approach in the first place. This is not, of course, to say that we need automatically take passages such as Horace's anecdotes about his father in *Sat.* 1.4 and 1.6 at face value. Rather, Horace emphatically and insistently places an autobiographical approach at the centre of his own satiric project, even going so far as to implicate Lucilius in the same practice when he claims that 'In earlier days he used to entrust his secrets to his books, as if to trusted friends, not turning to any other source at all, whether things went badly for him or well; and so it comes about that the old fellow's entire life lies open to view, as if it were painted on a votive tablet' (*Sat.* 2.1.30–4). Likewise the source of his satiric technique is not his reading of Lucilius but the positive and negative exemplars which his father pointed out to him as a boy. In the *Epistles*, as we have seen, the very form of the poetry emphasizes the private, the personal, and the confessional. Horace plays with such 'fragments of autobiography' and their interplay with his various satiric masks in such a way that certainty about his identity is never possible.

Politics and society

The *Satires* and *Epistles* were written in the course of some of the largest political changes which Rome ever underwent. *Satires* 1 was published around 35 BC, when memories of the civil wars between Caesar and Pompey, and between Caesar's assassins and his 'avengers' were still painfully fresh, especially for Horace, who had fought in the latter on the 'wrong side' with Brutus at the battle of Philippi. At this time Octavian (the future Augustus) was master of Italy, but still only one of three 'triumvirs', in a constant power struggle with Mark Antony which repeatedly swung from reconciliation to the brink of outright war and back again, and the war with Sextus Pompeius, Pompey's surviving son, had only just been concluded. None of these events is referred to; indeed, Philippi and the meetings between Antony and Octavian at Brundisium and Tarentum are glaringly *not* referred to in 1.7 and 1.5, even when the context seems to be crying out for it. By the time of the publication of *Satires* 2 in around 30 BC, Octavian had defeated Antony at Actium and in Alexandria, and was sole master of the Roman world, already beginning to establish himself as *princeps*, or first citizen, with power and influence which, while not without partial precedents, were nevertheless very new at Rome. Horace's silence on this is even more deafening. *Epistles* 1 was published in 20 BC, when Augustus (as he now was) had 'restored the *res publica*' and firmly established his dominance over Roman politics, but the letters flutter around the edges of power, addressing relatively insignificant young men and older friends, men who are in Tiberius' entourage or stewarding the Sicilian estates of Augustus' right-hand man, Agrippa. Their explicit emphasis on retreat, not only from lyric poetry but from public life, adds to their preoccupation with social interactions and, retreating still further, an almost internalized fixation on how to live well. Even when writing an epistle to Augustus himself, Horace's focus is on literary rather than political matters.

This is surprising. Roman satire was a profoundly political genre, or at least it constantly harked back to a time when it had been. Horace cites Eupolis, Cratinus, and Aristophanes, the three great poets of Athenian Old Comedy, as the principal models for Lucilian satire. Many readers (and viewers) of Old Comedy might mainly think of its *political* attacks on figures like Cleon and Pericles. But Horace reinvents them as *social* satirists, figures with freedom (*libertas*), but who attacked 'anyone who deserved to be marked down for his wicked and thieving ways, for being an adulterer or an assassin, or in any other way notorious' (*Sat.* 1.4.3–5). Lucilius himself is portrayed as someone who fearlessly (and with *libertas*) attacked some of the most powerful politicians of his day, such as Metellus and Lupus, and who 'fastened on the leaders of the people, too, tribe by tribe, showing favour to Virtue alone, of course, and to her friends' (*Sat.* 2.1.67–70). Yet for all the flattering parallels drawn between Lucilius' protector Scipio and his friend Laelius, and Octavian and Maecenas, for all the slightly hysterical, protesting-too-much insistence on his satire's power to re-enact Lucilian *libertas*, to strip away the skin of his contemporaries and reveal the rottenness within, it is Trebatius' warnings about the dangers of writing satire, at best being frozen out by the powerful, at worst having a short life, which eventually prevail. For all the countless named characters in the *Satires*, there is no modern-day Lupus or Metellus whom Horace attacks, not even a Mark Antony or a Sextus Pompeius. The reader is left puzzled as to just how political Horace's *Satires* are, and why?

Of course, one need not interpret politics narrowly as concerning only political leaders and the business of government as conducted in the Senate and assemblies (or indeed Augustus' palace). Politics is that which relates to the *polis* (city-state), and can include all aspects of how citizens behave and relate to each other. In an influential article, Ian DuQuesnay argued that the social and moral behaviour which *Satires* 1 in particular promotes and condemns is associated respectively with Octavian, Maecenas, and their political allies, and their opponents, including Sextus and Antony.[5] Certainly Horace depicts a world in which there has been a move from a chaos created by disruptive forces to greater harmony and order, but one which is still at threat from renewed irruption of such forces, whether on a large or small scale.

This model could be used to interpret almost any of the attacks on 'wrong' behaviour, from gluttony to adultery (both charges, incidentally, made elsewhere against Antony), and the concomitant advocacy of its 'correct' antithesis, but it can perhaps be most clearly seen in two of Horace's 'anecdotal' satires. In *Sat.* 1.8, the grisly Esquiline Hill, a cemetery littered with the bones of civil war, has been civilized by Maecenas through the construction of that ultimate symbol of the harnessing of nature by culture, and of regrowth from decay, a garden. Yet this order is threatened by the dark, irrational forces represented by the witches Canidia and Sagana, a threat which is dispelled by an explosive fart by the statue of the god Priapus, a symbol of the power of gently comic Horatian satire. In the next satire, one of Horace's most engaging and enjoyable, his quiet walk through Rome is threatened by an importunate and persistent 'chatterbox'. However, this is not a harmlessly annoying bore, but a social climber determined to wangle an introduction into the circle of Maecenas, which he assumes is full of ambitious, back-biting opportunists like himself, and which he threatens to disrupt and pervert by promising to help Horace rise at others' expense. Again, a sudden and comical intervention—the arrival of the chatterbox's legal opponent—dispels the threat. The overwhelmingly social and moral vices and follies which Horace attacks can thus be read as both aspects and symbols of larger political evils, and satire can play a part in policing them.

Yet for all that, many readers of the *Satires* still have the constant

---

[5] I. M. Le M. DuQuesnay, 'Horace and Maecenas: The Propaganda Value of *Sermones* I', in T. Woodman and D. West (eds.), *Poetry and Politics in the Age of Augustus* (Cambridge, 1984), 19–58.

feeling that Horace is self-consciously *not* writing about politics. On one level, this could be the same picture looked at from the opposite perspective. The mild, integrative approach focusing on moral and social ills replaces the aggressive, scathing Lucilian voice addressing political concerns, not because it reflects the sunny spirit of reconciliation and coalition, the 'new politics' of a (not quite) post-civil war era, but because under the constraints of that new political reality, which is post-civil war because only one man has been left standing, Horace *cannot* write about politics with Lucilian vigour and freedom. This perspective on Horace's reinvention of the political identity of satire—running parallel with his reinvention of its ethics as those of moderation and of its poetics as those of Callimachean polish and restraint—is supported by two pervasive strands of imagery, both relating to the curtailment of freedom (of speech and more generally): poor vision and silence.

Throughout *Satires* 1 in particular, various characters and particularly Horace suffer from defective vision and especially conjunctivitis (*lippitudo*). Sometimes, as with the Stoic philosopher Crispinus (*Sat.* 1.1.120) or the man who is critical of his friends' faults but blind to his own (1.3.25), this is a symbol of limited or distorted perception, an inability to 'see' things as they are. More frequently, however, it marks a convenient but necessary refusal by Horace to see things which it is unsafe or at least unpolitic to see, what we might in similar terms call 'turning a blind eye'. This is most evident in the frustratingly tantalizing description of (or failure to describe) the journey to Brundisium in *Sat.* 1.5. As noted above, Horace cuts the poem short when they reach Brundisium, either before the crucial meeting between Octavian and Antony took place (if the poem is set in 38 BC), or even before they reached their actual goal of Tarentum, where the second meeting was held the next year. Yet even along the way, Horace uses the smokescreen of Callimachean, anti-Lucilian poetics to omit and pass over any events of political interest or importance. Instead of talk about Cleopatra or Sextus, we get lovelorn bargees and pretentious town-clerks. Like the wet dream Horace has at Trivicum when his date fails to turn up, the reader is led on with the promise of fulfilment but, frustrated, has to make do with an empty (anti)climax. One of the reasons for Horace's failure to deliver is that he could not see anything. Early in the journey, at Anxur, we are told 'I apply some black ointment on my eyes, which were giving

me trouble' (1.5.30–1). Both the existing conjunctivitis and the smear-
ing of the ointment give Horace an excuse for not seeing what he
should not, an excuse he notably employs at Capua, when Maecenas
intriguingly goes off 'to amuse himself'; Horace does not join him
because 'ball games don't agree with those who suffer from sore eyes
(*lippis*)' (line 49) and thus both he and his readers are left in frustrat-
ing but safe ignorance of the political games Maecenas is playing.
The fearless Lucilian satirist cannot be expected to describe political
events if he cannot even see them.

Closely related to this imagery of vision is that of speech and
silence. Horace routinely criticizes those who talk or write too much.
Although this is couched in terms of being an aesthetic flaw of
Lucilius, who composed two hundred lines in an hour standing on
one leg, and social ineptitude on the part of the 'chatterbox', who
almost fulfils the Sabine soothsayer's prediction by talking Horace
to death, it can very easily be interpreted as part of Horace's anx-
ieties about the effects of too much free speech and loose talk, and his
emphasis on the need for discretion, especially in dealings with the
great and powerful. In place of the Lucilian *libertas* which not only
enabled but demanded full and abundant, as well as frank and often
venomous, speech, Horace stresses silence. When he does talk, it is
about trivialities and side issues; about important political matters he
maintains that silence. In *Sat.* 1.7, the inconsequential battle of words
(perhaps the closest Horace comes to the venom of Lucilian satire)
between Rupilius Rex and Persius stands in for the much more inter-
esting and important conflict in which Brutus was involved in the late
40s, but about which Horace cannot or will not speak, even though, or
precisely because, he was involved: the battle of Philippi. And instead
of the assassination of Julius Caesar, we get an uncomfortable pun
alluding to it, but simultaneously emphasizing its absence; killing
'Kings' is nothing new to Brutus, but not in this satire, which will not
speak of such things. The unmentionable subject of civil war looms
small even in the *Epistles*, where Horace advises Lollius to fit in with
all his patron's fads but also to find some private time for himself;
only there, in the seclusion of his own estate, away from the con-
straining presence of the powerful, can he and his brother re-enact
the battle of Actium when brother fought brother in bloody civil war
(*Ep.* 1.18.61–4). Horace may make a virtue of his silence on matters
which are, for whatever reason, best left unspoken, and the varied

responses to civic upheaval from the amnesty following the rule of the Thirty Tyrants in classical Athens to modern South Africa's Truth and Reconciliation Commission show that there is no single solution to the trauma incurred. However, in choosing the genre of *libertas* to exercise his restraint and discretion, Horace has drawn troubling attention to what he is not saying.

The example of Lollius in *Ep.* 1.18 also raises one of the most important social and political issues in both the external reality of Horace's life and the constructed world of his *Satires* and *Epistles* (however we want to read the relationship between the two), that of patronage. The reciprocal relationship between a wealthy, powerful, and socially elevated *patronus* and a *cliens* less fortunate in those three respects, in which *officia* (obligatory favours and services) were performed by each party—food, money, dinner invitations, protection from the patron, morning greetings (*salutationes*), accompaniment around the city to increase prestige, political and even violent support from the client—was a central institution of Roman society. Some poets, especially non-Romans such as the Archias made famous by Cicero, were in this dependent position as clients; but many, like Virgil, Propertius, and Tibullus (and indeed many non-poets like Lollius) were of high social status already, and became a different sort of client, certainly receiving gifts like other clients and reciprocating by commemorating their patrons in verse, even if only in a brief address, but without the sense of economic dependency or social inferiority. A very particular example of this scenario came into being during Octavian's rise to prominence, when his ally Maecenas, a cultured equestrian who always refused official political office, became the 'patron' of poets including Virgil, Horace, and Propertius. In many ways, this was a form of political patronage, as Virgil and Horace at least became part of the Augustan establishment and to some extent at least (however far one wishes to read coded subversion into their poetry) wrote works such as the *Georgics*, *Epodes*, *Odes*, and *Aeneid* as *officia* as much for Augustus and his new *res publica* as for Maecenas.

Horace's case was more complex still, since his involvement at Philippi on the side of Brutus and Cassius seems to have led to the confiscation of his property, leaving him in need certainly of political rehabilitation and perhaps of economic support. Horace himself gives a version of his introduction into Maecenas' circle in *Sat.* 1.6, representing it as a kind of religious initiation and even rebirth as he is sent away for nine months before being acknowledged by his new 'father', a parallel figure to his real father whose attention to Horace's education is described immediately afterwards. The relationship with Maecenas is prominent throughout the *Satires* and *Epistles* 1 (as well as the *Epodes* and *Odes*) as Horace constructs a complex combination of grateful obligation and genuine affection (the Latin *amicitia* could mean both 'friendship' and 'patronage'). Maecenas is the man who gave Horace his Sabine farm, source of his leisure and escape from the turmoil of the city, who reintegrated the ranting outsider of the diatribes into the civil society in which he finds himself by the end of *Satires* 1, a group of cultured, like-minded friends such as Horace praises in 1.9 and 1.10. Yet he is also a major player in the high politics of Octavian's Rome, someone whose secrets are not to be allowed to dribble from a 'leaky ear' (*Sat.* 2.6.46), and hence another of the constraints upon Horace's satiric *libertas*. He is a man who can be demanding of his friend's time and presence (*Ep.* 1.7), whose patronage is not like, but must be carefully prevented from becoming like, the disastrous gifts bestowed by the advocate Philippus on the spry auctioneer Mena. Horace's reflections on the appropriate behaviour of a good client, especially when he advises Scaeva (*Ep.* 1.17) and Lollius (1.18) on how to fit in with the wishes and predilections of their patrons, can feel quite unpalatable to a modern reader, which makes it difficult to judge how far Horace in a contemporary context is also challenging the institution. Yet, particularly in the beast fables, when the vixen finds that she has grown too fat to escape from the granary (*Ep.* 1.7.29–33), or when the horse defeats the stag by accepting a rider, but then cannot free himself of his new master (*Ep.* 1.10.34–8), the desire for an unattainable freedom can certainly be heard.

How to live well—philosophy and ethics

Ethics, broadly defined, is arguably the main preoccupation of the *Satires* and certainly of *Epistles* 1. Regardless of how far we see Horace's emphasis on moral issues as either part of a political message or a way of reneging on political engagement, it is undeniable that the issue of how to live well, and how far various philosophical schools can help or hinder that, is at the heart of Horace's hexameter poetry.

The influence of and allusions to various schools of philosophy litter the *Satires* and *Epistles*, and indeed Horace's explicitly denies doctrinaire adherence to any one school, insisting that 'there's no master I'm bound to swear loyalty to' (*Ep.* 1.1.14). The anarchic denial of society embodied in Cynicism, as much an anti-philosophy as a philosophy, offers at least the formal model for the diatribes of *Sat.* 1.1–3, with their debt to the Cynic diatribes of Bion of Borysthenes. Also, the first Cynic, Diogenes, is ridiculed as the type of the boor with a deluded belief in his own independence in contrast to the pragmatic adaptability of Aristippus in *Ep.* 1.17. The presence of Platonic philosophy is mainly felt in the dialogue form of *Satires* 2 and in Horace's new role as, in W. S. Anderson's phrase, 'the Roman Socrates'.[6] Pythagoreanism is only good for a couple of jokes at the expense of the easy target of the transmigration of souls. The principal players in Horace's philosophical circus are Stoicism and Epicureanism.

Stoicism is the main philosophical target of Horace's ridicule. An adapted form of Stoicism was extremely popular at Rome, since many of its ideals of the restraint of emotion, endurance, and public service, and its belief in a providential divine order, fitted well with existing Roman values. Yet its more extreme and unusual tenets were often the object of derision, as when Cicero lampoons Cato the younger for his Stoic beliefs in the *Pro Murena*. Certainly its tendency towards extremes and absolutes rendered it the polar opposite to the relaxed moderation advocated in the *Satires*. Though references are scattered throughout, it is particularly in *Sat.* 1.3, 2.3, and 2.7 that Horace engages in an extended attack on Stoic doctrine. In 1.3, after a complex, loosely structured 'argument' about inconsistency and people's tendency to be soft on themselves but hard on others, the Stoic doctrine that all crimes are equal is exposed to scrutiny and ridicule. In 2.3, the bankrupt dealer in luxury goods, Damasippus, has been saved from suicide and converted to Stoicism by the philosopher Stertinius, whose long diatribe on the doctrine that everyone except the wise man (*sapiens*) is mad he recites. Finally, in 2.7, Horace's slave Davus takes advantage of the licence of the Saturnalia when slaves

[6] W. S. Anderson, 'The Roman Socrates: Horace and his *Satires*', in J. P. Sullivan (ed.), *Critical Essays on Roman Literature: Satire* (London, 1963), 1–37.

were able to speak freely to their masters (the very freedom Horace so notably lacks) to criticize Horace's inconsistency, arguing, on the basis of doctrine he has picked up from a Stoic philosopher's door-keeper, that, since everyone except the wise man is a slave, Horace is the same as him.

As elsewhere in *Satires* 2, Horace's retreat from the foreground to let his interlocutors make their case adds another layer of complication, especially since in both these satires the main speaker is recounting a perhaps garbled version of something they have heard from another source. On a simple level, one might expect the use of a characterized mouthpiece to undermine the message in a more obvious way than the problematic characterization of the first-person satiric persona of *Satires* 1, and indeed Damasippus and Davus are both marked by a self-serving quality intermingled with their fanaticism. However, it is also striking how many of the blows which they aim at Horace hit home, undermining further the moral authority of his constructed persona, and especially how much the rants of these fanatics have in common with the rants of the fanatical diatribist in *Sat.* 1.1–3; in particular, Davus' ridicule of Horace's preference for adulterous sex with aristocratic women over uncomplicated relief with a cheap prostitute is astonishingly similar to Horace's own attack on *others'* similar preferences in *Sat.* 1.2. Both Horace's moral authority and the consistency of his philosophical outlook are undermined.

Epicureanism was much less congenial to Romans with traditional values. Quite apart from the complexities of its atomist physics, it denied that the gods played any part in human affairs, for good or ill, or that the soul had any existence after death, thus opposing traditional Roman religion; it advocated a life of seclusion and non-involvement in politics, antithetical to the Roman ideal of public service and the Roman reality of insatiable political ambition. Yet in a more or less watered down version, it was followed by a number of leading Romans such as the politician Calpurnius Piso and the great survivor of the late Republic, Atticus. Horace himself may have been connected with a group of Epicureans based by the Bay of Naples which was centred on Philodemus and included Virgil, Varius Rufus, and Plotius Tucca (grouped as Horace's friends—friendship was also a key aspect of Epicureanism—at *Sat.* 1.5.40 and 1.10.81). Certainly there is an Epicurean tone to his emphasis on moderation and his rejection of extreme Stoic doctrines, his delight in retreat from the city and its bustling preoccupations with political and commercial business, and his rejection of conventional political ambition; indeed, he signs off his epistle (*Ep.* 1.4) to Albius as 'a porker from Epicurus' herd', though with his tongue firmly in his cheek and more than a glance at the distorted view of Epicureanism as hedonistic. It would be a gross exaggeration to see Horace as an Epicurean poet, but it is a softened version of this philosophy which most closely resembles the dominant tone of his poetry.

Unlike Stoicism, Epicureanism was closely associated with a particular literary text and this influenced Horace's engagement both with that text and with the philosophy it espoused. In the 50s BC Lucretius wrote one of the greatest and most challenging poems in Latin, *On the nature of the universe* (*De rerum natura*), setting out an explanation of Epicurean physics with a view to curing men's wonder at and fear of death, the gods, and natural phenomena, so that they could achieve the Epicurean ideal of *ataraxia* ('freedom from anxiety'). The poem was immensely influential and poets of the next and subsequent generations endlessly engaged with it, whether in concord or opposition. Alluding to Lucretius could serve as a shorthand for endorsing Epicurean ideas (even though Virgil in the *Georgics* used allusion to Lucretius to oppose him) and the *Satires* in particular are full of references, as the Explanatory Notes will show. To give but two examples, the end of *Sat.* 1.1 notes the rarity of a man 'who quits life in contentment when his time is up, like a guest who has dined well', echoing Lucretius' famous image from the diatribe against the fear of death in *De rerum natura* 3 of life as a banquet which we should contentedly leave when sated, while the second half of *Sat.* 1.2 is full of allusions to the diatribe against passionate love at the end of *De rerum natura* 4. Yet allusions even to Lucretian Epicureanism are often more complex and less straightforwardly affirmative, as in the adaptation of Lucretius' condemnation of the use of pet names for the beloved which disguise their flaws to argue that people *should* use such palliating names for their friends. Most puzzling of all is the sustained engagement with Lucretius in *Sat.* 2.4, where the lecture on gastronomy recounted by Catius is full of allusions to *De rerum natura*; this might be part of the ridicule of the science of cooking's aspiration to the level of natural philosophy, a rebuttal of the distorted view of Epicureanism which read its emphasis on pleasure as a call to hedonism, or perhaps an undermining of the privileged position which that philosophy seems to hold elsewhere in the *Satires*.

The philosophy of the *Epistles*, as has been noted, is not drawn in doctrinaire fashion from any particular school, and Horace is explicit about his own inconsistency in this respect: 'Sometimes I become active and take the plunge into civic life, an unwavering guardian and attendant of true virtue [i.e. a Stoic]; sometimes unconsciously I slip back into the rules of Aristippus and I try to place circumstances under my control, not vice versa [a Cyrenaic]' (*Ep.* 1.16–19). Many of the *Epistles*, with their rejection of ambition and embrace of retreat and seclusion, continue the broadly Epicurean tone of the *Satires*, but what is most striking about these very philosophical poems is the way in which they reject formal philosophy as the best means of living well. At the opening of *Ep.* 1.2, Horace tells Lollius that he has been learning about ethics, not from the philosophers Chrysippus and Crantor, but from rereading Homer's *Iliad* and *Odyssey*. Throughout the rest of the collection, Horace consistently uses Homeric exempla, tendentiously interpreted, to support his ethical arguments, as when Ulysses' crew are (unjustly) used as a paradigm of those who put too much emphasis on the pleasures of food, because they killed and ate the cattle of the Sun (*Ep.* 1.6.63–4). Other poems too are similarly employed, using no less tendentious and even distorting interpretations, as when the assertion of Dionysus in Euripides' *Bacchae* that the god will free him is taken as meaning he will die and be liberated from the constraints of human life (*Ep.* 1.16.73–9). In part, of course, this is a self-reflexive exercise, since the *Epistles*, despite a disingenuous claim not to be, are themselves poetry, and poetry which can be used as a means of working out how to live well, part of Horace's wider concern, in the *Odes* as well as the hexameter poems, with the role of the poet in society.

One last issue, which also connects ethics with poetry, is the way in which Horace does not merely argue that reading the didactic content of poetry can help in the quest to live well, but uses poetics and aesthetics as symbols and metaphors for the right way to live. As has been noted before, the Callimachean aesthetic ideals of finely wrought, small-scale poetry, in antithesis to the bloated messiness of Lucilian satire, can be read as parallel to the Horatian insistence on moderation and the avoidance of extremes and excess. The implicit connection between the two comes closest to being explicit at *Sat.* 1.1.54–60:

It's as if, when you needed no more water than a jug or cup holds, you were to say, 'I'd prefer to take what I need from a great river than from this little spring, though the amount is the same.' The result of this is that people who crave more than their fair share are carried off by fierce Aufidus, swept away together with the bank they stand on. However, the man whose small desires match his needs doesn't swallow water thickened by mud or forfeit his life among the waves.

This recalls the famous passage at the end of Callimachus' *Hymn to Apollo*, where the god espouses the virtue of the pure spring, representing small-scale, polished poetry, over that of the great muddy river (there the Euphrates), representing overlong, unpolished epic. The allusion to a symbol of poetics in a passage discussing ethics draws the parallel between the two, a parallel which is reinforced when Horace later uses the image of the muddy river more conventionally to describe the un-Callimachean poetics of Lucilius (*Sat.* 1.4.11 and 1.10.50–1). Ethics, poetics, and indeed politics all intersect, or rather stand as parallel metaphors for each other as Horace—quite literally—espouses moderation in all things.

Literary criticism

Literary criticism was already a feature of Lucilius' satire and it is pervasive in Horace's. In the *Satires* themselves, the principal engagement is with the theory and practice of satire itself, in terms both of the technical manipulation of metre and diction, and the social implications of its moral stance and invective tone, though satire is measured on these criteria against other genres, such as epic and comedy. In all of these areas, Lucilius is held up as the model who is simultaneously to be emulated for his positive qualities but also regarded as falling short in care, technique, and stylistic polish. As has been noted, Horace's rejection of these aspects of Lucilius' poetic technique in favour of the 'Callimachean' approach favoured by the Alexandrians and their imitators at Rome has both a political and ethical dimension alongside the aesthetic.

Horace's second book of *Epistles* (if indeed he intended them to be considered as a book, for which there is no compelling evidence) is overwhelmingly, almost exclusively concerned with literary criticism. The *Epistle to Augustus* is an extended attack on the alleged contemporary vogue for archaic Roman poetry, with all its imperfections of style and form, in preference to the more polished efforts of modern poets. The parallels to the criticism of Lucilius in *Satires*. 1 can clearly be seen, but in the negotiation of old and new, particularly in a letter to the *princeps* who revived the values of the good old days but also boasted of his modernizing building programme, finding Rome made of brick and leaving it made of marble, it is tempting to see a moral and political dimension to this question of aesthetics too. The *Epistle to Florus* contains a more thoroughgoing interweaving of issues of ethics and poetics, as it explores the poet's place in society. Horace affects to justify his failure to reply to Florus' letter or to write more lyric poetry, and his reasons range from the mundane, that he does not need the money he would earn from composition, through a reflection on the gap between what a poet should be and what too often in practice he is, to a position very similar to that of *Epistles* 1, that he must now put away the childish things of lyric and concentrate on the pursuit of more philosophical goals, including once again how to live well.

   The *Epistle to the Pisos: The Art of Poetry* (*Ars Poetica*) is perhaps Horace's most influential work, but also his hardest to appreciate. Its authority and influence on subsequent theories of literary criticism are matched only by Aristotle's *Poetics*, but it is difficult to balance its status as a treatise on poetics with its being a poem and a letter. The presence of the addressees in the letter, (probably) L. Calpurnius Piso and his two sons, is faint and Horace rarely exploits features of epistolary form as he had in *Epistles* 1. According to the ancient commentator Porphyrio, Horace drew on a work by one Neoptolemus of Bithynia and, though this cannot ultimately be proven, it certainly belongs to a long tradition of literary criticism and demands to be read in that context as much as in that of Horace's other satiric works. Its subject matter ranges widely, taking in issues such as unity, structure, the role of the poet in society, and an extensive discussion of the history and nature of drama. No summary can do it justice and it is best appreciated by being read. Yet some remarks can be made about its overall character. It is a conservative work, privileging decorum and canons of acceptable taste over what others might consider the exuberance and energy of baroque fantasy and radical innovation. The famous opening image of the painting with the head of a woman, the neck of a horse, and the tail of a fish is explicitly meant to be absurd and risible, but such iconoclastic hybrids might well appear attractively bizarre to tastes different from Horace's. We might detect yet again in Horace's aesthetics a parallel to the ethics and politics of his earlier *Satires* and *Epistles*, where moderation and the avoidance of extremes is the ideal, an ideal which might also be interpreted as a reluctance to step out of line and cause offence. But before the *Ars Poetica* begins to sound dry and severe, it is also important to stress how close to the spirit of satire it remains, with its exuberant language and imagery, its unexpected and striking transitions, and above all its mordantly ironic tone. This last feature is perhaps best experienced in the astonishing conclusion to the poem (and probably to Horace's entire oeuvre) with the depiction of the mad poet, being teased by children, falling down wells, like Empedocles jumping into Mt. Etna, and finally embracing the reader in a bear hug at a recitation and refusing to let him go. One last time Horace tells the truth while laughing as he depicts this crazed behaviour of the 'wrong' sort of poet at the very moment when he himself—decorously and sanely—lets his reader go.

NOTE ON THE TEXT

THE critical edition used as a basis for the translation of the complete satires and epistles in this volume is the Oxford Classical Text of Horace's works by Edward C. Wickham, second edition by H. W. Garrod (Oxford, 1901). Marginal line numbers and references to line numbers refer to the original Latin text.

SELECT BIBLIOGRAPHY

Editions with commentary

Brink, C. O. (ed.), *Horace on Poetry II: The Ars Poetica* (Cambridge, 1971).
—— (ed.), *Horace on Poetry III: Epistles Book II. The Letters to Augustus and Florus* (Cambridge, 1982).
Brown, P. M. (ed.), *Horace: Satires I* (Warminster, 1993).
Kiessling, A., and Heinze, R. (eds.), *Q. Horatius Flaccus, Briefe* (4th edn., Berlin, 1914).
—— (eds.), *Q. Horatius Flaccus, Satiren* (5th edn., Berlin, 1921).
Lejay, P. (ed.), *Horace: Satires* (Paris, 1911).
Mayer, R. (ed.), *Horace: Epistles. Book I* (Cambridge, 1994).
Muecke, F. (ed.), *Horace: Satires II* (Warminster, 1993).
Palmer, A. (ed.), *The Satires of Horace* (London, 1883).
Rudd, N. (ed.), *Horace: Epistles. Book II and Epistle to the Pisones ('Ars poetica')*, (Cambridge, 1989).

Roman verse satire

Anderson, W. S., *Essays on Roman Satire* (Princeton, 1982).
Braund, S. H. (ed.), *Satire and Society in Ancient Rome* (Exeter, 1989).
—— *Roman Verse Satire*, Greece & Rome New Surveys in the Classics 23 (Oxford, 1992).
—— *The Roman Satirists and their Masks* (Bristol, 1996).
Coffee, M., *Roman Satire* (London, 1976; 2nd edn., Bristol, 1989).
Freudenburg, K., *Satires of Rome: Threatening Poses from Lucilius to Juvenal* (Cambridge, 2001).
—— (ed.), *The Cambridge Companion to Roman Satire* (Cambridge, 2005).
Gowers, E., *The Loaded Table: Representations of Food in Roman Literature* (Oxford, 1993).
Henderson, J., *Writing down Rome: Satire, Comedy, and Other Offences in Latin Poetry* (Oxford, 1999).
Hooley, D. M., *Roman Satire* (Blackwell, 2007).
Keane, C., *Figuring Genre in Roman Satire* (Oxford and New York, 2006).
Kernan, A., *The Cankered Muse: Satire of the English Renaissance* (New Haven, 1959).
Morgan, Ll., 'Satire', in S. J. Harrison (ed.), *A Companion to Roman Literature* (Oxford, 2005), 174–88.
Plaza, M., *The Function of Humour in Roman Verse Satire: Laughing and Lying* (Oxford, 2006).

Richlin, A., *The Garden of Priapus: Sexuality and Aggression in Roman Humor* (New Haven, 1983; 2nd edn., Oxford, 1992).
Rudd, N., *Themes in Roman Satire* (London, 1986).

Horace

Armstrong, D., *Horace* (New Haven, 1989).
Costa, C. D. N. (ed.), *Horace* (London, 1973).
Davis, G. (ed.), *A Companion to Horace* (Oxford, 2010).
Fraenkel, E., *Horace* (Oxford, 1957).
Harrison, S. J. (ed.), *Homage to Horace: A Bimillenary Celebration* (Oxford, 1995).
—— (ed.), *The Cambridge Companion to Horace* (Cambridge, 2007).
Hills, P. D., *Horace* (Bristol, 2004).
Houghton, L. B. T., and Wyke, M. (eds.), *Perceptions of Horace: A Roman Poet and his Readers* (Cambridge, 2009).
McNeill, R. L. B., *Horace: Image, Identity, and Audience* (Baltimore, 2001).
Oliensis, E., *Horace and the Rhetoric of Authority* (Cambridge, 1998).
Rudd, N. (ed.), *Horace 2000: A Celebration. Essays for the Bimillennium* (Ann Arbor, 1993).
Woodman, A. J., and Feeney, D. C. (eds.), *Traditions and Contexts in the Poetry of Horace* (Cambridge, 2002).

Satires

Anderson, W. S., 'The Roman Socrates: Horace and his *Satires*', in J. P. Sullivan (ed.), *Critical Essays on Roman Literature: Satire* (London, 1963), 1–37.
DuQuesnay, I. M. Le M., 'Horace and Maecenas: The Propaganda Value of *Sermones* I', in T. Woodman and D. West (eds.), *Poetry and Politics in the Age of Augustus* (Cambridge, 1984), 19–58.
Fiske, G. C., *Lucilius and Horace: A Study in the Classical Theory of Imitation* (Madison, Wis., 1920).
Freudenburg, K., *The Walking Muse: Horace on the Theory of Satire* (Princeton, 1993).
—— (ed.), *Horace: Satires and Epistles*, Oxford Readings in Classical Studies (Oxford, 2009).
Gowers, E., 'Horace, *Satires* 1.5: An Inconsequential Journey', *Proceedings of the Cambridge Philological Society*, 39 (1993), 48–66.
—— 'Blind Eyes and Cut Throats: Amnesia and Silence in Horace *Satires* 1.7', *Classical Philology*, 97 (2002), 145–61.
—— 'Fragments of Autobiography in Horace *Satires* 1', *Classical Antiquity*, 22 (2003), 55–91.

—— 'The Restless Companion: Horace, *Satires* 1 and 2', in K. Freudenburg (ed.), *The Cambridge Companion to Roman Satire* (Cambridge, 2005), 48–61.

Harrison, G., 'The Confessions of Lucilius (Horace, *Sat.* 2.1.30–34): A Defense of Autobiographical Satire?', *Classical Antiquity*, 61 (1987), 38–52.

Henderson, J., 'Be Alert (Your Country Needs Lerts): Horace, *Satires* 1.9', *Proceedings of the Cambridge Philological Society*, 39 (1993), 67–93 = *Writing Down Rome: Satire, Comedy, and Other Offences in Latin Poetry* (Oxford, 1999), 202–27.

—— 'On Getting Rid of Kings: Horace, *Satire* 1.7', *Classical Quarterly*, 44 (1993), 146–70 = *Fighting for Rome* (Cambridge, 1998), 73–107.

Muecke, F., 'Horace the Satirist: Form and Method in *Satires* I.4', *Prudentia*, 11 (1979), 55–68.

—— 'The *Satires*', in S. J. Harrison (ed.), *The Cambridge Companion to Horace* (Cambridge, 2007), 105–20.

Rudd, N., *The Satires of Horace* (Cambridge, 1966).

Schlegel, C., 'Horace and his Fathers: *Satires* 1.4 and 1.6', *American Journal of Philology*, 121 (2000), 93–119.

—— *Satire and the Threat of Speech: Horace's Satires Book I* (Madison, 2005).

Zetzel, J. E. G., 'Horace's *Liber Sermonum*: The Structure of Ambiguity', *Arethusa*, 13 (1980), 59–77.

Epistles 1

Armstrong, D., 'Horace's *Epistles* 1 and Philodemus', in D. Armstrong, J. Fish, P. Johnston, and M. B. Skinner (eds.), *Vergil, Philodemus, and the Augustans* (Austin, Tex., 2004), 267–98.

Ferri, R., 'The *Epistles*', in S. J. Harrison (ed.), *The Cambridge Companion to Horace* (Cambridge, 2007), 121–31.

Freudenburg, K., '*Solus sapiens liber est*: Recommissioning Lyric in *Epistles* I', in A. J. Woodman and D. C. Feeney (eds.) *Traditions and Contexts in the Poetry of Horace* (Cambridge, 2002), 124–40.

Johnson, W. R., *Horace and the Dialectic of Freedom: Readings in Epistles 1* (Ithaca, NY, 1993).

Kilpatrick, R. S., *The Poetry of Friendship: Horace, Epistles I* (Edmonton, 1986).

MacLeod, C., 'The Poetry of Ethics: Horace, *Epistles* I', *Journal of Roman Studies*, 69 (1979), 16–27 = *Collected Essays* (Oxford, 1983), 280–91.

Mayer, R., 'Horace's *Epistles* I and Philosophy', *American Journal of Philology*, 107 (1986), 55–73.

Moles, J. L., 'Cynicism in Horace *Epistles* 1', *Papers of the Liverpool Latin Seminar*, 5 (1985), 33–60.

Moles, J. L., 'Poetry, Philosophy, Politics and Play: *Epistles* I', in Woodman and Feeney (eds.), *Traditions and Contexts*, 141–57.

Morrison, A., 'Advice and Abuse: Horace, *Epistles* 1 and the Iambic Tradition', *Materiali e Discussioni*, 56 (2006), 29–61.

Porter, D., 'Playing the Game: Horace, *Epistles* 1', *Classical World*, 96 (2002/3), 21–60.

Epistles 2 *and* Ars Poetica

Brink, C. O., *Horace on Poetry. I: Prolegomena to the Literary Epistles* (Cambridge, 1963).

Feeney, D. C., '*Vna cum scriptore meo*: Poetry, Principate and the Traditions of Literary History in the Epistle to Augustus', in A. J. Woodman and D. C. Feeney (eds.), *Traditions and Contexts in the Poetry of Horace* (Cambridge, 2002), 172–87.

Freudenburg, K., 'Writing to/through Florus: Criticism and the Addressee in Horace *Epistles* 2.2', *Memoirs of the American Academy in Rome*, 47 (2002), 33–55.

Kilpatrick, R. S., *The Poetry of Criticism: Horace, Epistles II and Ars poetica* (Edmonton, 1990).

Laird, A., 'The *Ars Poetica*', in S. J. Harrison (ed.), *The Cambridge Companion to Horace* (Cambridge, 2007), 132–43.

Rutherford, R. B., 'Horace, *Epistles* 2.2: Introspection and Retrospective', *Classical Quarterly*, 31 (1981), 375–80.

—— 'Poetics and Literary Criticism', in Harrison (ed.), *Cambridge Companion*, 248–61.

Russell, D. A., '*Ars poetica*', in C. D. N. Costa (ed.), *Horace* (London, 1973), 113–34 = A. Laird (ed.), *Oxford Readings in Ancient Literary Criticism* (Oxford, 2006), 325–45.

Spencer, D., 'Horace and the Company of Kings: Art and Artfulness in *Epistle* 2.1', *Materiali e discussioni*, 51 (2003), 135–60.

Wiseman, T. P., 'Satyrs in Rome? The Background to Horace's *Ars poetica*', *Journal of Roman Studies*, 78 (1988), 1–13.

Further reading in Oxford World's Classics

Aesop, *Aesop's Fables*, trans. Laura Gibbs.

Classical Literary Criticism, trans. D. A. Russell and Michael Winterbottom.

Horace, *Odes and Epodes*, trans. David West.

Juvenal, *Satires*, trans. Niall Rudd.

Lucretius, *On the Nature of the Universe*, trans. Ronald Melville, ed. Don and Peta Fowler.

Petronius, *The Satyricon*, trans. P. G. Walsh.

CHRONOLOGICAL SURVEY

BC	(Early dates traditional)
1090	Fall of Troy.
753	Foundation of Rome by Romulus.
510	Expulsion of the Tarquins.
509	Creation of Roman Republic.
264–241	First Punic War.
218–201	Second Punic War.
218	Hannibal crosses the Alps.
202	Scipio Africanus Maior defeats Carthaginians at Zama.
149–146	Third Punic War.
146	Scipio Africanus Minor destroys Carthage.
70	Birth of Virgil.
65	Birth of Horace.
63	Birth of Octavian.
59	First Triumvirate: Caesar, Crassus, and Pompey.
53	Crassus defeated by Parthians at Carrhae.
44	Caesar assassinated.
43	Second Triumvirate: Antony, Lepidus, and Octavian.
42	Defeat of Brutus and Cassius at Philippi.
39	Virgil, *Eclogues*.
38	Virgil introduces Horace to Maecenas.
37–36	War against Sextus Pompeius.
35	Horace, *Satires* 1.
33?	Horace receives Sabine farm.
31	Octavian defeats Antony and Cleopatra at Actium.
30	Death of Antony and Cleopatra in Alexandria.
30?	Horace, *Epodes*.
	Horace, *Satires* 2.
29	Virgil, *Georgics*.
	Triple triumph of Octavian.
28	Temple of Palatine Apollo dedicated.
	Propertius, *Elegies* 1.
27	Octavian takes the name Augustus.
26	Tibullus, *Elegies* 1.
26–5	Augustus campaigns in Spain.
23	Horace, *Odes* 1–3.

SATIRES

BOOK 1

SATIRE 1

How come, Maecenas, that no man lives satisfied with his own lot, whether given to him by his own choice or thrown his way by fortune, but looks enviously on those who follow different careers? 'How lucky merchants are!' says the soldier, feeling the years weigh on him, his frame now worn out by long years of service. But listen to the mer- 5 chant in turn, when his ship is being tossed by southern gales: 'I'd rather have a soldier's life. And why, do you ask? Two armies suddenly close in battle: in the blink of an eye it comes, speedy death or the joy of victory.' The farmer attracts the envy of the expert in law and its statutes, when a client knocks on his door before cockcrow, with 10 questions to put. The fellow has been hauled up to town from the country to show himself in court, and claims in a loud voice that only town-dwellers know happiness. The other examples of this kind are so numerous they'd exhaust that windbag Fabius. So as not to bore you, let me tell you the moral of this, as I see it. Suppose some god 15 should say, 'Look! Here I am, ready to carry out your wishes: you, a soldier before, will now be a merchant; you, a lawyer just now, shall be a farmer: off you go now, the pair of you, with your roles reversed! What's this? Still standing there?' They would refuse. And yet they are being given the chance to be happy. Give me a reason why Jupiter 20 wouldn't be justified in puffing out both cheeks in a rage and tell-ing them he won't be so obliging as to lend an ear to their prayers in future?

Another point, not to dash over the topic with a laugh, like someone telling jokes—and yet what's the harm in using humour to put across what is true, just as teachers sometimes offer their pupils biscuits to 25 coax them into wanting to learn their ABC?—just the same, joking aside, let's turn our attention to serious matters: our friend who turns over the heavy soil with his stubborn plough, this cheating innkeeper here, the soldier, and the sailors whose course takes them boldly over every sea declare they have only one reason for enduring their 30 toil: they want to retire to a life of secure leisure after piling up for

themselves enough to live on; just as the tiny ant who works with such energy—their model—hauls along whatever her mouth can carry and adds it to the heap she is building, for she knows the future well
35 and keeps it in mind. But as soon as Aquarius makes the year wheel round and wear a gloomy face, she doesn't venture out anywhere and makes wise use of her previously gathered store; not like you, letting nothing deter you from making profit, not scorching summer heat or winter cold, not fire, sea, or sword, and moving heaven and earth to
40 stop another man becoming richer than yourself.

What's the good to you of a vast weight of silver and gold, if you stealthily dig a hole in the earth to bury it there in your nervousness? 'But should you start whittling it away, a worthless penny would be all that was left.' But if you don't spend it, what's the attraction in a piled-up heap? Your floor may thresh out a hundred thousand bush-
45 els of grain, but this won't help your stomach hold any more than mine: imagine you were in a gang of slaves and happened to be the one shouldering the heavy bread-bag, you wouldn't get a crust more than the slave with no load to carry.

Or, tell me, what difference does it make to a man who lives within
50 nature's limits whether he has a hundred or a thousand acres to plough? 'But there is the appeal of drawing from a big supply!' Provided you allow me to draw the same amount from my little pile, why should you praise your granaries above my bins? It's as if, when you needed no more water than a jug or cup holds, you were to say, 'I'd prefer to
55 take what I need from a great river than from this little spring, though the amount is the same.' The result of this is that people who crave more than their fair share are carried off by fierce Aufidus, swept away together with the bank they stand on. However, the man whose small desires match his needs doesn't swallow water thickened by mud or
60 forfeit his life among the waves.

But a good many people are taken in by a desire that makes them blind to reality. 'Nothing is enough,' they say, 'since a man is rated according to his possessions.' What can you do with such a fellow? Tell him to be miserable; that's what he enjoys doing. He resembles the
65 wealthy Athenian in the story, a miser, who was in the habit of taking no notice of what the people said about him, declaring, 'The people boo me, but I give myself the applause in my own home the moment I clap eyes on all the cash in my chest.' The thirsty Tantalus snatches at the water that eludes his lips—why do you laugh? The name has

been changed but you're the one the story is about; you sleep, open- 70
mouthed, on top of moneybags piled up all around, compelled to keep
your hands off them as though they are sacred, or to take the pleasure in
them as you would if they were paintings on canvas. Don't you know
the purpose of money, the enjoyment it provides? Use it to buy bread,
vegetables, a pint of wine, and the other things whose absence would
make human life less easy to bear.   75

Or is it more to your taste to stay awake at night half dead with
fear, and day and night to live in dread of wicked thieves, of fires, or
of slaves stealing your goods and then deserting your house? When it
comes to blessings like these my own wish would always be to plumb
the depths of poverty. 'But if you go down with some feverish chill or 80
are stuck in bed through some other misfortune, you have someone to
sit at your bedside, prepare poultices, and summon a doctor to bring
you back to health and restore you to your children and loving family.'
But your wife doesn't want you to get well, and neither does your
son; all your friends and neighbours, young and old, men and women,
hate you. Are you surprised, when you put money before everything 85
else, that no one shows you affection? Have you earned it? Or, should
you wish to keep and retain the affection of relatives given to you by
nature with no effort on your part, would it be as pointless and fruit-
less an ambition as a man trying to train a donkey to run in the races 90
on Mars' Field, obedient to the reins?

So let's put an end to the race for wealth. As you become more
prosperous, let your fear of poverty subside, and having gained what
you desired, you should make a start at bringing your struggle to an
end. You don't want to end up like a certain Ummidius, whose story 95
can be briefly told: so rich that he weighed, not counted, his cash, so
miserly that he never dressed better than one of his slaves, he was
afraid right up to the hour of his death that he would die of starva-
tion. In fact he was split in two by an axe wielded by one of his freed-
women, the boldest of Tyndareus' daughters. 'Well, what advice *are* 100
you giving me? Should I live my life like a Naevius or Nomentanus?'
Ah, now you are seeking to put together things that are completely
opposed to each other. When I tell you not to become a miser, I'm
not advocating that you turn into a worthless spendthrift. There's a
halfway house between Tanais and Visellius' father-in-law. A measure 105
exists in all things, as do, in short, prescribed limits; go beyond or fall
short of them and you cannot be right.

I return to my starting point: how it is that greed makes no one
satisfied with his lot and encourages a man to envy those in differ-
ent careers, pining away if his neighbour's she-goat has udders
110   more swollen, and, rather than comparing himself with the larger
crowd of poorer men, striving to surpass now this man, now that?
In a race like that there's always someone richer blocking your path.
It's like a chariot race when the teams break from their stalls, swept
on by the animals' pounding hoofs, and the driver presses hard on
115   the horses outstripping his own, caring nothing for the rival he has
passed and left at the back of the track. And so it happens that we
seldom can find a man who claims to have lived a happy life, who
quits life in contentment when his time is up, like a guest who has
dined well.

That's enough now. I won't add a word more, in case you think I've
120   ransacked the writings of Crispinus with his myopia.

SATIRE 2

The Honourable Companies of flute-girls, purveyors of quack medi-
cines, beggars, 'actresses', clowns, and all belonging to that tribe
are in grief and distress at the death of the singer Tigellius. 'What a
generous soul he was!' By contrast, we have a fellow who, for fear of
5   being described as a spendthrift, would refuse to give a needy friend
enough to keep at bay the cold and hunger's pangs. Should you ques-
tion another as to why out of thankless gluttony he shamelessly strips
away a father's or grandfather's splendid estate, borrowing money
to buy all the delicacies for his appetite, he answers that he wouldn't
10   like to be thought tight-fisted and mean in spirit. His reward for this
is praise from one side and criticism from the other. Fufidius, rich in
land and rich in money loaned at interest, fears the reputation of a
worthless spendthrift: he slices away five times the interest from the
principal and, the closer the borrower gets to ruin, the more relent-
15   lessly he presses him to repay; those he targets for entry in his books
are young fellows with stern fathers at home, who have just newly put
on the toga of manhood. 'Jupiter Almighty!' goes up the general cry
when this is heard. 'But presumably he spends money on himself to
match his gains.' No he doesn't! You'd scarcely believe how poor a
20   friend he is to himself: why, not even the father in Terence's play who

is shown to have lived a life of misery after booting out his son put himself through worse torments than he does.

Suppose someone should now put the question, 'Where is all this leading?' well, here's my point: in seeking to avoid one fault fools rush to embrace its opposite. Maltinus strolls along with his tunic trail- 25 ing; another with his hoisted up so high it exposes his private parts, the height of fashion, he thinks. Rufillus smells of mouth lozenges, Gargonius of a billy-goat. There's no middle course. Some men will have nothing to do with women whose ankles are not concealed by a low-hanging flounce; another, by contrast, will only lay hands on a 30 woman who stands for sale in some foul-smelling brothel. When a well-known person was emerging from a brothel, 'Bravo! Keep on that track!' was the godlike verdict of Cato, 'for the moment that foul lust makes their members swell, it's right for young men to come down here, instead of grinding away at other men's wives.' '*That's* not 35 the sort of praise *I'd* like to have,' says Cupiennius, who gets his kicks from cunts wearing white.

It's worth your while to lend an ear, you who wish good fortune to keep distant from adulterers, how on every side they fare badly, how their pleasure is marred by considerable pain, and, seldom coming, 40 is often accompanied by cruel perils. One man flings himself from the roof of a house; another is flogged to death; another while run- ning away falls into a fierce band of robbers; another parts with cash to save his life; another gets himself irrigated by stableboys; once it actually happened that a husband hacked off with his sword his 45 victim's balls and lustful prick. 'That's what the law prescribes,' is the general cry; Galba begged to differ.

But how less dangerous are the wares you get in the second class— freedwomen, I mean—those Sallust goes as crazy for as any adulterer. Yet, if Sallust wanted to be courteous and generous, so far as his means 50 and reason dictated, and allowing him to be liberal without excess, he would part with a sum that was sufficient and would spare him the shame of financial ruin. But no; on this one point he prides himself, because of this he basks in self-admiration and praise: 'I keep my hands off all married women.' It reminds me of what Marsaeus said 55 once, the celebrated lover of Origo, who presented an actress with his ancestral hearth and home: 'I'd never get involved with other men's wives.' But you *are* involved with actresses, yes, and with prostitutes, too, and this damages your reputation more seriously than it does

60 your resources. No doubt you're perfectly happy to avoid the role of
    adulterer rather than what actually does the harm, whatever the cir-
    cumstances! To destroy your good name, to squander an inheritance
    from your father is bad behaviour at all times. What difference does
    it make whether you offend with a married woman or with a maid
    dressed in a toga?
        Villius, Sulla's 'son-in-law,' was punished richly and more than
65 enough because of his weakness for Fausta; falling, poor fool, for this
    name alone, he was beaten up and attacked with the sword while the
    door was shut against him yet opened wide for Longarenus. Suppose,
    as he faced these indignities, he imagined his tool saying these words
    to him: 'What are you up to? Do I insist you supply me with a cunt
70 descended from a great consul and wrapped in a matron's robe, when
    my passion boils over?' What would his reply be? 'The girl is born
    of a noble father.' But how much better, how at variance with these
    notions, is the advice of nature, rich in her own resources, if only you
    would manage them properly and not confuse what is desirable with
75 what should be avoided. Do you think it is immaterial whether your
    problems stem from your own fault or circumstance? And so, in case
    you live to regret it, put a stop to chasing after married women, for
    they'll give you more pain and misery than any real satisfaction from
80 the experience. This lady may be draped in pearls and emeralds but,
    though the jewellery is your creation, Cerinthus, this doesn't make
    her thigh any softer or her leg any straighter, and very often a tart
    in her toga is even better. What's more, she struts her stuff without
    disguise and displays quite openly what she has for sale, and, if she
85 has some attractive feature, she doesn't flaunt and parade it, or seek
    some means of hiding blemishes. Kings have this habit: when they
    are buying horses they have them covered before examining them, so
    that if, as frequently happens, the animal's elegant form is supported
    by a soft hoof, it may not take in the onlooker as he gapes in admir-
    ation at the splendid haunches, the small head, the imposing neck.
90 They are right in this respect: don't study the best physical details
    with the eyes of a Lynceus, while turning an eye on the faults that
    is blinder than poor old Hypsaea. 'What a leg! What arms!' you cry,
    but she hasn't any buttocks, her nose is long, her back of no length,
    and her feet huge. In a matron's case you can't see anything except
95 her face, for, unless she's a Catia, she conceals everything else under
    a full-length robe. If it's forbidden delights you're after, hedged by

a rampart—for this is what robs you of all reason—many things will
then block your progress, attendants, her litter, hairdressers with
curling-tongs, hangers-on, her robe dropping to the ankles and pro-
tected by her mantle, all sorts of things to grudge you a clear, unim-   100
peded view. But with the other, nothing gets in your way: in her Coan
silk you can see her virtually naked and make sure she doesn't have
bad legs or ungainly feet; you can measure with your eye her length
from waist to shoulder. Or would you rather have a trick played on
you and payment snatched from your hand before you get a sight of
the merchandise? Our friend sings of how the hunter pursues a hare   105
amid deep snow but won't touch it once stretched out at his feet,
adding 'My love is just like this: what lies to hand it flits past and
chases what runs away.' Do you imagine verses of this quality can
drive from your heart the pain, the tides of passion, the burden of   110
care? Wouldn't it benefit you more to enquire what limit nature sets
upon desires, what she can supply for herself if denied her, what, to
her sorrow, she cannot, and to separate void from substance? When
your throat is parched by thirst, you don't ask for a golden cup, do
you? When you're hungry, do you turn your nose up at everything   115
except peacock and turbot? When your groin swells up and a maid
or slave-boy of your household is available to get stuck into there and
then, do you prefer to burst with lust? I don't: it's love that's available
and easy to come by that I like.

The woman who says, 'A bit later! Well, it'll cost you more! Only   120
if my huband's left the house!' is for the Galli, says Philodemus, who
prefers for himself the type who doesn't sell her wares too expen-
sively or waste time once she's been summoned. Let her be tall, and
with good skin; smartly presented but without wishing to create
the appearance of greater height or a paler complexion than nature
has given her. When such a girl has slipped her left side under my   125
right, she is Ilia and Egeria: I give her whatever name I like and don't
worry while screwing her in case her husband comes dashing back
from the country, the door is broken down, the dog starts barking,
the house is stormed and echoes to an almighty din on every side,
the woman (horrors) leaps out of bed, white as a sheet, her guilty   130
maid screams she is wretched, she fearing for her legs, her mistress,
caught *in flagrante*, for her dowry, and me for myself. Barefoot,
I have to run for it, tunic undone, to avert disastrous consequences
to bank-balance or backside, or, at least, to reputation. To be caught

would be misery; I could make that case even if Fabius were sitting
in judgement!

SATIRE 3

All singers have this fault: when asked to perform among friends
they're never so inclined, when not invited, they never stop. Tigellius,
the well-known son of Sardinia, was like this. Caesar, who could have
compelled him, would have got nowhere at all, had he asked him to
5 remember his father's friendship and his own; but if it took his fancy,
our friend would sing out, 'Ho, followers of Bacchus, come!' from
hors d'oeuvre straight through to dessert, now in a treble voice, now
in the one resounding lowest on the lyre's four chords.

   The fellow lacked all consistency; often he would tear along like a
10 man trying to escape from the enemy, very often proceed like some-
one carrying Juno's sacred baskets; often he would keep two hun-
dred slaves, often just ten; sometimes he would speak of kings and
tetrarchs, nothing but grand affairs, sometimes he'd say, 'All I ask is
a three-legged table, a shell of clean salt and a toga that can keep out
15 the cold, however coarse the material.' Imagine you'd given a million
sesterces to this man of thrift, contented with so little, five days later
his pockets were bound to be empty; each night he would be awake
until dawn, then spend the whole day snoring; never was a man so full
of contradictions. Now someone may say to me, 'What about you?
20 Are you entirely free from faults?' Well, no, but they are different
ones and perhaps not as great. When Maenius was having a go at
Novius behind his back, 'Hang on there,' said someone, 'don't you
know yourself, or do you think you are taking us for fools as though
we don't know you?' 'I know all right, but I'm forgiving myself,' said
Maenius. This sort of self-love is stupid and shameless and deserves
condemnation.

25   When you examine your own faults with eyes that are inflamed
and covered with ointment, why in the case of friends' faults is your
eyesight sharper than an eagle's or an Epidaurian snake's? But, on
the other hand, what happens to you is that they also in turn start
examining *your* faults. He's a little too liable to lose his temper, not
30 particularly in tune with the fastidious standards of modern society;
he might be laughed at because his haircut is less than fashionable,

his toga trails to one side and his ill-fitting shoe barely stays on his foot: but he's a good man, none better, and beneath that unpolished exterior lurk considerable gifts. In short, give *yourself* a shaking and 35 see if nature or instead bad habit has at any time planted in you the 35 seeds of any faults; for it's in neglected fields that ferns take root and need to be burnt away.

Let's turn our minds to the following fact: a lover in his blindness fails to note his girlfriend's unattractive defects, or even is actually charmed by them, as Balbinus was by Hagna's polyp. My wish would 40 be that friendship caused us to make the same mistake, and virtue had given an honourable name to this error. But when dealing with a friend we should imitate a father's treatment of his son, and not show disgust at any defect he may have: if a boy is cross-eyed, his father describes him as 'having a cast', and if a man has a son who's 45 embarrassingly stunted, like the midget Sisyphus in earlier days, he calls him his 'wee chick'; another, with crooked legs, receives the pet-name 'pigeon toes', while the boy whose deformed ankles can barely support him becomes 'raw-bones'. This friend lives in a somewhat penny-pinching fashion: let's call him 'careful with money'. Another is tactless and a little too prone to showing off: he's expecting his 50 friends to regard him as 'amusing company'. This one, on the other hand, is rather aggressive and outspoken: let him be thought of as 'frank and not afraid to speak his mind'. Another is a bit of a hothead: let's count him among the men of spirit. It's this attitude, I reckon, that binds friends together and keeps their friendship intact. But we 55 turn actual merits upside down and are eager to tarnish a container that's clean. If someone sharing our circle is a decent fellow and entirely modest, we give him the nickname 'slowcoach' or 'dense'. Another evades every trap and doesn't leave a flank exposed to any shaft of malice, as he's involved in the type of life where envy has 60 an edge and slanderous criticisms are rife: instead of calling him 'entirely sensible' and 'a prudent fellow' we speak of his 'insincerity' and 'crafty ways'. If someone is rather open in manner, the sort of impression I would hope you have often formed of me, Maecenas, so that he interrupts a person when he's reading, perhaps, or engaged in quiet thought, and makes a nuisance of himself with some chat- 65 ter or other, 'He's quite lacking in consideration for other people,' we declare. But, ah, how foolishly we are establishing an unforgiving precedent against ourselves! For no one is born free from faults: the

best fellow is the one who is burdened by the least. A kindly friend
should, in fairness, balance my good points against my bad ones, and,
70 if he wants to keep my affection, he should turn the scales in favour
of the former as being more numerous—assuming, of course, that my
good points *are* in the ascendancy: if he follows this principle he'll be
weighed on the same scale. Someone who expects a friend to turn a
blind eye to his own boils will view with tolerance the other's warts;
when a person asks for forgiveness for failings, it's only fair that he
75 grants it duly in return.

Again, given that it's impossible to cut out the fault of anger com-
pletely, and likewise all the other faults that attach themselves to
fools, why does reason not employ her own weights and measures,
and bring to bear on offences the punishments that are appropriate
80 to each? Should a man's slave lick up some half-eaten fish and its
lukewarm sauce when told to take away a dish, and then be cruci-
fied for this, men of sanity would brand the master as less sane than
Labeo. How much crazier and more offensive a transgression is this!
85 A friend has been guilty of some peccadillo that you would be con-
sidered ungracious not to forgive: you react with bitter hatred and
give him as wide a berth as someone owing money to Ruso gives him,
for, unless he manages to scrape up interest or principal from some
source or other by the time the gloomy Kalends have overtaken him,
90 poor devil, he's bound to present a captive audience, as if his throat is
bared to the knife, for Ruso's boring histories. Suppose a guest, when
drunk, has wet the couch or knocked off the table a cup worn thin
by Evander's hands, should I regard him as a less agreeable friend
on this account, or because, in a moment of hunger, he picked up
95 before me a chicken set down on my side of the dish? What am I to
do if he commits a theft, or betrays confidences, or reneges on a legal
agreement?

Those who have established as their view that all transgressions
are much on a par find themselves in difficulty when it comes to
actual instances; instinct and convention are armed against them, as
is expediency itself, the virtual mother of justice and fairness. When
100 living creatures crawled forth from the earth in its infancy, dumb
beasts without moral sense, their desire for acorns and lairs made
them fight with nails and fists, then with clubs, and so in time with
weapons that experience had later forged, until they discovered verbs
and nouns with which to give meaning to their cries and emotions;

that was when they began to cease from war, to build towns, and 105
to establish laws whereby no one should be a thief or robber, or
commit adultery. For a good time before Helen a cunt was the
most terrible cause of war, but an unrecorded death was the fate of
those who, clutching at random love like wild beasts, fell victim to
one of superior strength, like bulls in a herd. If you wish to unroll 110
the annals and calendar of the world, you are bound to admit that
fear of injustice caused the discovery of justice. And nature has not
the power to draw between justice and injustice the distinction she
draws between things helpful and harmful, what should be shunned
and what pursued; and reason will never prove the case that a man 115
is guilty of one and the same offence whether he breaks off young
cabbages in a neighbour's garden or steals the gods' holy emblems
under cover of night. Let us make use of a scale for imposing penal-
ties that are a just reflection of crimes, in case you flog with the fear-
some scourge one who merits only the strap. For I've no worries about 120
you caning someone who deserves a more serious flogging, since
you say that stealing and acts of highway robbery are equal crimes,
and threaten to prune back minor offences with the same hook you
would use for major ones, should men bestow on you the power of a
king.

If the wise man is rich, and a good cobbler, and if he alone is hand-
some and a king, why do you long to have what you already possess? 125
'You do not understand father Chrysippus' meaning,' comes the
reply; 'the wise man has never made shoes or sandals for himself;
and yet the wise man is a cobbler.' How can this be? 'In the sense
that Hermogenes, although silent, is nonetheless the best of singers
and musicians; in the sense that the shrewd Alfenus, despite throw- 130
ing away every tool of his art and closing up his shop, was a barber,
the wise man, and he alone, is the best exponent of every craft, and
so is a king.' Naughty boys are plucking at your beard; unless you
keep them under control with your stick, you are surrounded and
jostled by a crowd of them, and in your wretchedness burst your 135
lungs in barking, most mighty of mighty kings. Let me be brief:
while you, a king, make your way to bathe for your farthing, with no
escort to attend upon you except the ridiculous Crispinus, my genial
friends will pardon me, if in my folly I commit some offence, and I, 140
in turn, will gladly tolerate their transgressions, and in my private
station shall live a happier man than Your Majesty.

SATIRE 4

The poets Eupolis and Cratinus and Aristophanes, and other authors
of the Old Comedy, satirized with considerable freedom anyone
who deserved to be marked down for his wicked and thieving ways,
5 for being an adulterer or an assassin, or in any other way notorious.
Lucilius depends entirely on these men, following in their foot-
steps and changing only the metres and rhythms they used; he was
witty, with a sensitive nose, but unpolished in the composition of his
verses: for this was his area of weakness: in one hour, as a sign of
10 his talent, he would often dictate two hundred lines on one leg: as
he flowed along like a muddy river, one wished to remove some of
the material: words poured from his lips and he was too idle to put
up with the effort of writing, that is, of writing correctly: for I'm not
at all impressed by the volume of his output. Here's Crispinus now,
making me a challenge at long odds: 'Take up your notebook, please,
15 take it up now; let a place be appointed for us, a time, and judges; let's
see which one of us can write more.' I thank the gods for fashioning
me with a feeble and poverty-stricken intellect that rarely expresses
itself, and then only in very few words; but feel free, as it's what you
prefer, to copy the air shut up in goatskin bellows, constantly strain-
20 ing away until the fire softens the iron. What a lucky man Fannius
is, delivering his books and a bust of himself to libraries without
being asked, whereas no one reads my work and I'm afraid to read it
in public, for the reason that there are some who take a dim view of
this type of writing, seeing that most of them deserve censure. Select
25 from a crowd anyone you please: either greed or wretched ambition
makes him suffer: one fellow's crazy with love for married women,
another for boys; here's a third who's captivated by the lustrous sheen
of silver; bronze statuary makes Albius gape with desire; another bar-
ters his wares from the rising sun to regions warmed by its evening
30 rays, even rushing headlong through perils like dust gathered by a
whirlwind, in his fear that he may lose something from his capital or
fail to get a return on his investment. All these fellows dread verses
and hate poets: 'He has hay tied to his horns; keep a good distance
from *him*: provided he raises a laugh, he won't show mercy to himself,
35 or to any friend; whatever he has scribbled once on his pages he'll be
dying for everyone returning from the bakehouse or water-tank to

know, every slave and old woman.' Come now, listen to a few words
in reply to this.

In the first place I would exclude myself from the number of those
to whom I would give the name of poet. You would not describe it as   40
sufficient to produce a metrical line; and if, as I do, a man should write
what's more akin to conversational prose, you wouldn't consider him
a poet. The honour of this name you should confer upon one who
possesses genius, whose intelligence the gods have inspired, whose
voice is capable of an impressive resonance. It is for this reason that   45
certain people have raised the question whether comedy is poetry or
not, since neither its diction nor its content contains the fiery power
of inspiration, and, apart from the fact that it differs from prose by
its fixed metre, it is unadulterated prose. 'But the father shows pas-
sion when he rages because his extravagant son, mad with love for his
courtesan girlfriend, turns down a wife with a good-sized dowry, and,   50
creating a mighty scandal, walks the streets before sunset, drunk, sur-
rounded by torches.' Would Pomponius come in for a lecture any less
harsh than this, were his father still alive? It isn't enough, then, to pen
a line of verse in plain language such that, should you break it up, any   55
father would express his anger just like the one in the play. Suppose
you stripped the regular quantities and rhythm from the verses I write
now and those Lucilius wrote in earlier days, altering the sequence of
the words and transposing first and last, it would not be the same
as breaking up 'When once loathsome Strife the iron-clad posts and   60
portals of War broke asunder': even when he was dismembered you
would find there the limbs of a poet.

Enough of these questions: another time I'll consider whether this
kind of writing is true poetry or not, but for the present this is the
only point I mean to investigate, whether you are justified in view-
ing it with scepticism. The implacable Sulcius and Caprius stalk the   65
streets, with throats horribly hoarse and indictments in hands, the
pair of them a great terror to robbers; but should a man spend his
days honourably, with hands unstained by guilt, he may hold them
both in contempt. Even supposing *you* are like Caelius and Birrius,
I can never be like Caprius or Sulcius; why should you be afraid of   70
me? My writings can never be found in any shop or dangling from
a pillar outside to absorb the sweat from the mob's hands or those
of Hermogenes Tigellius. I don't give readings from them to anyone
except my friends, and only when they press me hard, not anywhere

75 or before any old audience. There are plenty who recite their works
in the middle of the forum, or at the baths: the enclosed space gives a
pleasing resonance to the voice. This delights the empty-headed, who
fail to ask the question if their performance lacks tact or timing.

'You enjoy hurting people's feelings,' says someone, 'and you do
80 it deliberately, from malice.' Where have you found this charge to
hurl at me? Is there anyone at all among my close friends to back it
up? The man who runs a friend down behind his back, who doesn't
defend him from another's accusations, who wants the public to laugh
loud and long at his remarks, and to be thought of as a wit, who can
make up what he hasn't seen but can't keep a confidence, he has a
85 black heart; good Roman, keep not his company. Often at dinner-
parties you can see four persons on each of the three couches, one of
whom is in the habit of casting all kinds of aspersions on every guest,
excluding the man whose party it is; later even he is mocked by our
friend in his cups, when the truthful god who makes men free unlocks
90 the secrets of the heart. You think this fellow agreeable, sophisticated,
and frank, you who have no time for the black-hearted. If I laughed
because silly Rufillus smells of lozenges or Gargonius of a billy-goat,
do you regard me as spiteful and back-biting? If some reference was
95 made in your presence to the thefts of Petillius Capitolinus, you'd
defend him in your usual way: 'I have been an associate and friend
of Capitolinus since childhood, and he has done a great deal to assist
me when asked. I am delighted that he lives without recriminations
here in Rome; just the same, it amazes me how he got off at that trial.'
100 This is the ink of the black cuttlefish, this is unadulterated venom:
this fault, I promise, will be far from my writings and my mind, as it
has been in the past, if there is any promise I can truthfully make.

If something I say is too outspoken, perhaps too calculated to raise
105 a laugh, you'll be forgiving and grant me this measure of justifica-
tion: my excellent father taught me the habit, by marking out the
various vices by examples, so that I should steer clear of them. When
he encouraged me to live with thrift and frugality and to be content
with what he had personally provided for me, he would say, 'Don't
you see what a miserable existence Albius' son has, and how Baius
110 lacks for everything? A powerful lesson that no one should wish to
squander his inheritance'; when he sought to deter me from an igno-
minious passion for a prostitute, it would be, 'Don't be like Scetanus';
and to discourage me from pursuing adulterous wives, when I might

enjoy a permissible affair, 'Trebonius was caught in the act,' he'd say, 'and his reputation wasn't a pretty one. A philosopher will give you theories for avoiding or pursuing this or that: it's enough for me if I'm able to preserve the rule our ancestors have handed down, and, while you need a guardian, to protect your life and good name from harm; as soon as the years have put some strength into your body and mind, you won't need cork to swim.' This was how he tried to mould me in my boyhood with his words; and if he was telling me to do a particular thing, he'd say, 'You have an authority for doing this', and he would point to one of the selected jurymen; or if he was telling me not to, it would be, 'Can you be at all uncertain whether this action would bring discredit and disadvantage when so-and-so roasts in the fire of notoriety?' As a neighbour's funeral terrifies gluttons who are not in good health and makes them take care of themselves for fear of dying, so the shame attaching to others often deters impressionable minds from faults.

This training has made me free from the faults that bring destruction, and those that do have their grip on me are not too serious and the sort to earn pardon. Perhaps even these will be substantially diminished by advancing years, the frankness of a friend and self-counsel; for whenever I find the welcome of a sofa, or stroll in the colonnade, I do not let myself down. 'This is the more honourable course,' I say; 'if I do this, I'll have a better life; this will bring a smile of pleasure to my friends when I meet them; that wasn't a nice thing for so and so to do. I hope I'll never be so inconsiderate as to do anything like that one day.' These are the thoughts I keep turning over in my head, with lips sealed fast; whenever I'm granted any leisure, I waste writing paper. This is one of the less serious failings I mentioned; should you be unwilling to allow me this, make way for the great company of poets that would come to my aid (for we're easily in the majority), and, like the Jews, we'll force you to make your way into our swelling band.

SATIRE 5

I'd left great Rome and Aricia gave me welcome in a modest inn: Heliodorus the teacher of rhetoric was sharing my journey, by far the most learned of the Greeks; from there we came to Forum

Appii, which was crammed full of boatmen and tight-fisted inn-
5 keepers. Being lazy types we split this journey, which travellers more
energetic than ourselves do in a single stretch; slowcoaches find the
Appian less hard work. Here, because of the water, which was dread-
ful, I declared war on my stomach as I waited impatiently for my
fellow travellers to finish their dinner.

10 Now night was preparing to draw her shadowy veil and to sprin-
kle the heavens with stars. That was when the slaves began hurling
insults at the boatmen and the boatmen at the slaves. 'Put in here!'
'You're cramming hundreds on board: stop, that's enough now!' What
with collecting fares and harnessing the mule, a whole hour goes by.

15 Damned mosquitoes and marsh-frogs banish sleep, while our boat-
man, sozzled on amounts of sour wine, sings of the charms of the
girlfriend he left behind, as one of the passengers gives him some
competition: finally the passenger, worn out, starts sleeping, and the
lazy fellow of a boatman, having sent the mule out to pasture, ties his
reins to a stone and, falling on his back, begins to snore.

20 Now day had dawned when it comes to us that the boat was
making no progress, until one fellow, something of a hothead, jumps
out and, with willow-branch in hands as a cudgel, starts laying
into the back and head of mule and boatman. We'd scarcely landed
two hours before noon. We bathed faces and hands in your waters,
25 Feronia. Then after taking breakfast we crawled three miles and
drew near to Anxur, perched on its rocks, gleaming far and wide.
My fine friend Maecenas was due to meet us here, together with
Cocceius, both of them sent as envoys on important business, no
30 strangers to reconciling friends who had quarrelled. Here I apply
some black ointment on my eyes, which were giving me trouble.
Meanwhile Maecenas arrives, and Cocceius, together with Fonteius
Capito, a man of flawless nature and unrivalled in his friendship
for Antony. Without regret we left Fundi with Aufidius Luscus as
35 its praetor, laughing at the regalia of this crazy clerk, his bordered
toga, his tunic with broad stripe and pan of charcoal. Then, worn
out, we rested in the city of the Mamurrae, where Murena put his
house at our disposal and Capito his cuisine. The next day's dawn
was the most joyful by far, for we were met at Sinuessa by Plotius
40 and Varius and Virgil, the purest souls the earth has produced,
and men whose friendship no man values more deeply than I. Ah,
how we clasped one another, how happy we were together! Never

while I keep my senses would I compare anything with the pleasure of friendship.

Then we were given shelter by the lodge that lies close to the 45 Campanian bridge, and, as their duty required, the state suppliers provided fuel and salt. Next, at Capua, our mules laid aside their saddlebags in good time. Maecenas went off to amuse himself, Virgil and I to get some sleep, as ball games don't agree with those who suffer from sore eyes and poor digestion. Our next source of hospital- 50 ity was the well-stocked villa of Cocceius, which overlooks the inns of Caudium.

Now, Muse, I would have you relate to me in brief words the battle of Sarmentus the jester and Messius Cicirrus, and the lineage both men claimed when they entered the fray. The pedigree of Messius was distinguished—the Oscans; the mistress of Sarmentus is still 55 living: sprung from such ancestors they met to do battle. Sarmentus issued the first challenge: 'I declare that you resemble a wild horse.' We laugh, and Messius for his part responds: 'And so I do,' toss- ing his head. 'Oh,' continued his adversary, 'what would you do if your forehead didn't have its horn cut off, seeing how you threaten 60 in this hornless state?' In point of fact the left side of his hairy fore- head had been disfigured by an unsightly scar. After a good number of jokes about his Campanian disease and his looks, he resorted to asking him to dance the shepherd Cyclops' dance, adding 'You've no need of a mask or tragic buskins!' Cicirrus made plenty of ripostes 65 to this, enquiring several times if he had already fulfilled his vow and presented his chains to the household gods; he may have been a clerk, but this was no reason why his mistress' claims over him were any the less. Finally, he asked him why he had ever run away, when a pound of meal was enough to fill the belly of such a scrawny little runt. It was a 70 real delight to make that dinner-party last longer.

Next we headed straight for Beneventum, where our painstaking host almost reduced his home to cinders while turning some lean thrushes on the fire: Vulcan's blaze left its grate, and the wandering flames, as they spread through the old kitchen, made haste to lick the roof. Then you could have seen the starving guests and terrified slaves 75 snatching up the dinner, and everyone trying to quench the blaze.

After this Apulia began to show me her familiar mountains, scorched as they are by the Atabulus. Never would we have crawled our way over these, had we not found shelter in a villa near Trivicum

80 that supplied eye-stinging smoke as well, when damp branches, foli-
    age and all, were being burnt by the stove. Here, like a total idiot,
    I waited right up to midnight for a lying girl to turn up; but sleep
    carried me off, eager though I was to make love; as I lay on my back
85 dreams then turned to obscene fantasies that made a mess of my
    nightclothes and stomach.

        From here we are whirled along in carriages for twenty-four miles,
    to stay in a little town whose name can't be fitted into verse, though
    it's no problem to identify by its features: water, nature's most access-
    ible gift, is charged for here, but the bread is easily the best, so that
90 the traveller in the know is in the habit of carrying it further on his
    shoulders, as it is full of grit at Canusium, the place which isn't a
    jugful richer in water and was founded in early days by the brave
    Diomedes. Varius here takes his sorrowful leave, to the tears of his
    friends.

        From there we came to Rubi, worn out from covering a lengthy
95 stage of the road that heavy rain had made less passable. The next
    day's weather was better but the road worse all the way to the
    walls of Barium, the fish-town; then Gnatia that was built when
    the water nymphs were angry gave us the chance to laugh and have
    some fun, as it tried desperately to convince us that incense melts
100 without fire at the entrance to the temple. Apella the Jew may
    believe this, but not I: I've learnt that the gods live lives that are free
    from care, and that, if some miracle is caused by nature, it is not sent
    down by the gods from their lofty dwelling in the sky to show their
    unhappy mood. Brundisium marks the end of a long story and a long
    journey.

                              SATIRE 6

    Although, Maecenas, of all Lydians who inhabit Etruria's lands no
    one is of nobler birth than you, although your ancestors on your
    mother's and father's side alike held power over mighty legions in
5   days gone by, you do not follow most men's habit and turn your nose
    up at those of unknown birth, such as myself, a freedman's son.
    When you say it makes no difference what kind of parent each man
    has, if only he's a gentleman himself, you are rightly acknowledg-
    ing that, before Tullius held royal power from humble origins, many

men descended from ancestors of no account often lived virtuous 10
lives and were honoured with high office; but you also are conced-
ing that Laevinus, scion of the Valerius who drove the proud Tarquin
from his throne into banishment, was never considered to be worth
tuppence, and it was that judge you know so well, the people, that 15
gave him a black mark, that in its stupid way often bestows honours
on the unworthy and is foolishly enslaved to renown, that gapes in
admiration at titles of honour and ancestral busts. What is the right
course for *us* to take, who are far, far removed from the common herd?
For let's allow that the people would rather give office to a Laevinus
than to an unheard-of Decius, and that Appius the censor would 20
strike my name from the senatorial roll, if I was not the son of a
free-born father—I couldn't object either, seeing that I hadn't kept
quiet and stayed in my own hide! But Glory draws all in her train,
bound to her gleaming chariot, unknowns no less than high-born.
What did you gain, Tillius, by assuming once more the stripe you 25
had doffed and becoming a tribune? Envy battened on you again,
which would have been less if you were not in office. For the moment
anyone has so lost his wits that he binds the black leather thongs
halfway up his leg and lets the broad strip fall down his chest, straight
away he hears: 'Who's this fellow? Who's his father?' It's just like
someone suffering from the same disease as Barrus and longing to 30
be thought a beauty: everywhere he goes, he makes the girls eager
to ask about details—what his features are like, his calves, his feet,
his teeth, his hair: so the man who promises to care for his fellow
citizens, for the city, for Italy and empire, for the shrines of the gods, 35
compels every living Roman to take an interest and to ask who his
father is, whether he carries the shame of an obscure mother. 'Have
you, the son of a Syrus, a Dama, a Dionysius, the effrontery to cast
citizens of Rome from the rock, or to deliver them up to Cadmus?'
'But,' you reply, 'my colleague Novius sits one row behind me, as 40
he's what my father was.' 'Do you think this makes you a Paulus or
a Messalla? But in this fellow's case, even supposing two hundred
wagons and three funerals should clash in the forum, he'll make a
noise to drown the horns and trumpets; this at least makes him claim
our attention.'

Now I return to myself, the son of a freedman, the man everyone 45
snipes at for being the son of a freedman, and these days for being
one of your associates, Maecenas, but in earlier days for commanding

a Roman legion as tribune. The two cases are different, since it
might perhaps be justified for anyone to grudge me that office, but it
wouldn't be in the case of your friendship as well, especially as you
are careful to admit as friends only those who merit it and have no
interest in disreputable self-seeking. I couldn't say that luck played
a part in that an accident assigned me to you as a friend, for it was
in no sense chance that presented me to you: the excellent Virgil
some time ago, and after him Varius, told you what kind of man I was.
When I came before you, I uttered a few faltering words, for a shy-
ness that tied my tongue was keeping me from speaking further, and
I told you, not that I was the son of a famous father, not that I rode
round my estates on a Tarentine nag, but the reality of my life. Your
response was brief, as is your habit: I took my leave; nine months later
you called me back and invited me to join the circle of your friends.
I consider it a great thing that I found favour with you, who can dis-
tinguish between a man of honour and one of none, not because of a
distinguished father but because of integrity of life and morals. Yet
if my nature is marred by faults that are not too serious or numerous
and is otherwise sound, as you might criticize moles scattered over
an admirable body, if no one will be justified in accusing me of greed
or meanness or frequenting disreputable brothels, if (to give myself
praise) I live my life with integrity and free from guilt, and have the
love of friends, this is all due to my father. A poor man he was, with a
meagre plot of land, but he didn't want to send me to Flavius' school,
attended as it was by the imposing sons of imposing centurions, their
satchels and slates dangling over their left shoulders, and carry-
ing their eightpenny fee to be paid on each Ides. No, he was brave
enough to transport his young son to Rome, to receive instruction
in the same accomplishments as any knight or senator would teach
offspring of his own. Had anyone seen the clothes I wore and the
slaves attending me, as was habitual in a populous city, he'd have sup-
posed those expenses were paid for me from an ancestral estate. My
father was there in person and served as a guardian beyond reproach
while I went the rounds of all my teachers. I need not expand: he
kept me uncorrupted, which is virtue's foremost grace, free not only
from every shameful action but from every shameful accusation as
well; and he wasn't afraid that sometime later a man might find fault
with him if I earned a paltry wage advertising auctions, or, like him-
self, a commission from collecting the buyers' money; nor would

I have complained, but, as things stand, because of this I owe him the greater praise and thanks.

In no way, as long as I'm in my right mind, could I be ashamed of such a father, and so I wouldn't defend myself as a great number 90 do, saying that it's not through any fault of their own that they don't have freeborn or famous parents. Both what I say and what I think are far different from this: for if nature ordered us after we'd reached a certain age to retrace the span of time experienced, and if each of 95 us chose any other parents he might wish to have in keeping with his pride, I would be satisfied with my own and decline to take parents ennobled by the rods and chairs of high office, a madman in the judgement of the mob but rational enough, I suspect, in yours, for not wanting to carry a troublesome burden my shoulders have never been used to supporting.

For straight away I'd have to increase my means, to give and receive 100 more morning calls, and, when I went to the country or abroad, I'd have to take one or two companions, to avoid travelling on my own; I'd have to maintain more grooms and nags, and take along wagons. As things are, if it suits me, I may ride a gelded mule even as far 105 as Tarentum, his hindquarters galled by the saddlebag's weight, his withers by the rider's. No one will accuse me of meanness the way they do you, Tillius, when you travel as praetor to Tibur with five slaves in attendance carrying a chamber pot and wine-container. In this way and a thousand others I live a more comfortable life than 110 you, renowned senator. I stroll out alone, wherever the fancy takes me; I enquire as to the price of greens and meal; many a time as evening draws on I wander through the Circus, where hucksters gather, and the Forum; I mingle with the fortune-tellers; then I make my way home to a dish of leeks and chickpeas and fritters; my dinner 115 is served by three slave-boys, and a white slab of marble supports two cups with a ladle; next to them stands an inexpensive cruet, and an oil-flask with its saucer, Campanian ware. Then I go off to sleep, untroubled by any thought of having to rise early the next day, or having to appear before Marsyas, who declares he can't bear the 120 sight of the younger Novius' face. I lie in bed until four hours after sunrise; after this I take a stroll, or, after reading or writing something for my own private pleasure, I have oil applied, though not the sort used by the filthy Natta, stolen from lamps. But when I 125 get tired and the sun, grown fiercer, has warned me to go to the baths,

I shun the Field and the game of ball. I have a light lunch, as much
as keeps me from having to last the day on an empty stomach, and
then take my ease at home. This is the life of men who are not the
130 prisoners of wretched and oppressive ambition; in these ways I
comfort myself with the thought that I'll live more agreeably than if
my grandfather had been a quaestor, and my father and his brother
likewise.

SATIRE 7

How the cross-breed Persius avenged himself on the foul and poi-
sonous Rupilius Rex, outlawed from the state, is known, I fancy, to
everyone suffering from poor vision and every barber. This Persius,
5 a man of wealth, had a very large business at Clazomenae and was
also engaged in a troublesome lawsuit with Rex. A tough character
and capable of outdoing Rex in offensiveness, he was overbearing and
bombastic, with such an acid tongue that he could leave a Sisenna or a
Barrus standing. I return to Rex. After the pair of them failed to come
10 to any terms (for great warriors who clash in battle are as aggressive
as their bravery dictates; between Hector, Priam's son, and the fiery
Achilles such a deadly anger existed that in the end death alone parted
them, and this was entirely because each man's valour was supreme:
15 should two cowards come to blows, or an ill-matched pair meet on the
battlefield, as Diomedes and Lydian Glaucus, the one of fainter heart
quits the field, and sends gifts into the bargain), well, when Brutus
was commanding as governor the rich province of Asia, Rupilius and
20 Persius locked horns, a pair every bit as well matched as Bacchius
and Bitho. With fire in their hearts, they sally forth to court, the pair
of them a sight to thrill the eye. Persius sets forth his case; laughter
breaks out from the entire assembly; he praises Brutus, he praises
his staff: he calls Brutus 'sun of Asia', and his suite 'health-bringing
25 constellations', all except Rex; he had come, he said, like the Dog-star
hated by farmers. He was rushing on like a winter torrent where the
woodman rarely takes his axe. That was when the scion of Praeneste
in answer to this rich stream of wit hurled back insults squeezed
30 from the vineyard, as tough and invincible as any vine-dresser who,
on hearing the wayfarer's loud cries of 'Cuckoo!', has often made him
take to his heels.

But Persius the Greek after his drenching in Italian vinegar cries out, 'Tell me, Brutus, in the name of the mighty gods, why don't you cut this Rex's throat, when regicide is nothing new to you? The job is 35 right up your street, believe me.'

SATIRE 8

Once I was a fig-tree's trunk, a useless piece of wood, when a carpenter, unsure whether to make a pedestal of me or a Priapus, chose that I should be a god. A god, then, I became, causing complete terror in thieves and birds; for thieves are kept in check by my right hand and by the red stake that protrudes indecently from my crotch; as 5 for annoying birds, the reed attached to my head gives them a fright and keeps them from landing in the new gardens. Before now a slave would pay to have the corpses of his fellows carried here in a cheap coffin, once they'd been thrown out from their narrow cells; this was the communal burial place appointed for Rome's wretched poor, for 10 Pantolabus the scrounger and good-for-nothing Nomentanus: here a pillar prescribed for a frontage of a thousand feet and a depth of three hundred: 'the monument not to pass on to heirs.' These days one may inhabit an Esquiline that is healthy, and stroll on the sunny Mound, 15 which of late presented the melancholy sight of ground disfigured by bleaching bones; and as for myself, I'm not troubled and worried by the thieves and beasts that haunt this place so much as I am by the hags who bend people's minds with their spells and deadly potions; 20 as soon as the wandering moon has lifted up her lovely face, I can in no way destroy these creatures or prevent them from gathering bones and pernicious herbs.

With my own eyes I have seen Canidia walking with black cloak hitched up, her feet bare and hair let loose, and shrieking with the elder Sagana: their pallid skin had made the pair of them a ghastly 25 sight. They began to dig up the earth with their nails and to tear a black lamb to pieces with their teeth; all its blood was poured into a ditch so they could entice spirits from there, ghosts that would give them answers. One effigy was made of wool, the other of wax: 30 the woollen one was bigger so as to gain control over the smaller by inflicting punishment; the waxen one stood there in an attitude of submission, as if about to suffer death as a slave would. One hag called

on Hecate, the other on savage Tisiphone; you could see snakes and
35 hell-hounds roaming about and the blushing Moon hiding behind
the tall tombs so she could not witness these deeds. No, if I'm telling
any lie here, may my head be spattered with white crows' droppings,
and may Julius, the softy Miss Pediatius, and the thief Voranus come
to piss and shit on top of me.

40   What need have I to tell of every detail, in what manner, as they con-
versed with Sagana, the ghosts returned a melancholic, shrill sound,
how they stealthily buried in the ground a wolf's beard and the fang
of a dappled snake, how the waxen image made the fire blaze higher,
45 how I shuddered at the words and actions of the two Furies, though
in witnessing these I did not go without vengeance? For I farted and
my fig-wood buttocks split with a crack as loud as the sound of a bal-
loon bursting: off they ran, those two, into town. Then you'd have
50 laughed loud and long with merriment to see Canidia's false teeth and
Sagana's high wig falling off, and the herbs and enchanted love-knots
tumbling from their arms.

SATIRE 9

As chance would have it, I was walking along the Sacred Way, in my
usual fashion turning over in my mind something of no importance
whatever, completely absorbed in this. Someone I know only by name
comes running up and seizes me by the hand. 'How are you, dear
5 old thing?' he says. 'Pretty well, for the time being,' I reply, 'and I
wish you all the best.' When he continued to keep up with me, I got
in first with 'Anything more I can do for you?' But he came back,
'You should get to know the man you see before you; I'm literary.'
To this I say, 'I'll value you the more for this.' Desperately trying to
get away, I now increased my pace, then sometimes stopped, mut-
10 tering something or other in my slave-boy's ear, while the sweat
dripped all the way down to my ankles. 'Bolanus, how lucky you are in
having a short temper,' I kept saying under my breath, as he gabbled
away about whatever took his fancy, praising the streets and the city
itself. When I was making him no reply, he said, 'You're desperately
15 keen to get away; I've noticed this for quite a while now: but it's no
good; I'll hang on to you all the way; I'll stick close to you from here

to your destination.' 'There's no need for you to be taken out of your
way: I want to visit someone you don't know: he's confined to bed a
long way away from here across the Tiber, near Caesar's gardens.'
'I've nothing to do and plenty of energy: I'll accompany you the whole
way.' I let my poor ears droop, like a bad-tempered donkey when it   20
receives a load too heavy for its back.

'If I don't deceive myself,' he begins, 'you won't regard Viscus or
Varius as more important friends: for who can write more verses, or
more quickly? Who can cut a trimmer figure dancing? My singing   25
would make even Hermogenes envious.' Here was a chance to inter-
rupt: 'Do you have a mother or relatives who depend on your contin-
ued health?' 'Not a single one: I've laid them all to rest.' 'How lucky
for them! Now I'm the one left. Finish me off; for it advances upon
me now, the gloomy fate the Sabine woman foretold for me when a   30
boy, as she shook her divining urn:

> 'This youth no deadly poison shall consign to death,
> No foeman's sword in battle wielded rob of breath,
> No wracking pleurisy, nor halting gout, nor cough;
> A chatterbox shall one day see him off.
> So, if he's wise, then talkers he should shun,
> When once, his childhood o'er, mature years have begun.'

Vesta's temple had been reached, with a quarter of the day already   35
gone, and at that time by chance he had to give answer to a plaintiff;
failure to do this would mean forfeiting his case. 'Just oblige me,' he
says, 'and lend me your support here for a while.' 'Damn me if I have
the strength to stand, or know the laws of the land,' say I, 'and I'm
hurrying off to that place you know about.' 'I just don't know what to   40
do,' comes his reply, 'whether to lose your company or my case.' 'Oh,
my company, please!' 'I won't,' he replies, and starts forging ahead.
As for yours truly, I follow on, since it's hard to do battle with one
who's stronger.

'How do you get on with Maecenas?' he resumes after this. 'There's
a man with few friends and a very sound mind; no one has ever made   45
shrewder use of his luck. You'd have an able assistant, one who could
play a minor role, if you saw fit to introduce your acquaintance here;
damn me if you wouldn't send all the rest of them packing!' 'The
relations we live under there are not as *you* suppose them to be: no

household is as unsullied as that one, or less accustomed to distaste-
50 ful behaviour such as that; it is no disadvantage to me whatever that
someone is richer than I or has more literary talent; each one of us
has his own position.' 'That's extraordinary, scarcely to be believed.'
'Well, that's the way things are.' 'You're fuelling my appetite for get-
ting really close to him.' 'You need only wish it, and, such is your
55 prowess, you'll take him by storm. What's more, he's the sort of man
one can win over, which is why he makes initial approaches so dif-
ficult.' 'I won't sell myself short; I'll bribe his slaves; if I'm denied
60 access today, I won't give up: "On mortals nought doth life bestow,
save through toil untold." '

   As he was holding forth in this fashion, Aristius Fuscus suddenly
bumps into us, a close friend of mine and one who knew the fellow all
too well. We stopped. He asked me my destination and told me his. I
started plucking at his sleeve and clutching his arms, which showed
65 no response whatsoever, nodding my head and rolling my eyes for
him to come to my rescue. But he smiled, practising a cruel joke, and
pretended not to notice; rage made my heart seethe. 'You definitely
said there was something you wanted to discuss with me in private,'
I said. 'I remember it well,' he replied, 'but I'll tell you about it at
70 a better time: today's a thirtieth Sabbath: you don't want to offend
bob-tailed Jews, surely?' 'I don't have any religious qualms,' I replied.
'Well, *I* do,' said he; 'I'm a bit too weak-minded, one of the many;
forgive me, but I'll speak to you another time.' To think so black a day
could have dawned on me! Without compunction the creature fled,
leaving me at the mercy of the executioner's blade.

   By chance the fellow's legal opponent came face to face with him
75 and shouted loudly, 'Where are you off to? Have you no principles
at all?' Then, turning to me, he asked, 'May I call upon you as a wit-
ness?' At once I extended my ear towards him. He marched his man
away to court. Shouting broke out on all sides; everywhere there was
running this way and that. In this way Apollo saved me.

SATIRE 10

It's true I said that Lucilius' verses ran along with unpolished rhythm.
Who is so undiscriminating a devotee of Lucilius as not to concede
this? And yet on the same page you will find praise for the same poet

for having given the city a good scouring with the rich salt of his wit.
But in granting him this merit I would not allow him all others as 5
well: for on this principle I'd admire Laberius' mimes also as beau-
tiful poems. It's not sufficient, then, to make the listener grin from
ear to ear: yet even in this there is some merit: one needs to be suc-
cinct, so that the thought may run on and not become entangled in
wordiness that weighs upon weary ears; and a style is needed that is 10
sometimes grave, often merry, maintaining the role now of orator or
poet, sometimes of the sophisticated person who deploys his powers
sparingly and deliberately underplays them. A jocular approach often
cuts through more forcefully and effectively than one that is earnest. 15
This is where those writers of Old Comedy had success, this is where
they deserve to find imitators: they haven't been read either by the
pretty Hermogenes or by that ape whose training fits him to drone
only the lines of Calvus and Catullus.

'But his blending of Greek and Latin words was a considerable 20
achievement.' Ah, you late learners! Is it really, do you think, a task of
amazing difficulty to do what Pitholeon of Rhodes achieved by luck?
'But a style that happily combines both languages gives more pleas-
ure, as when the Falernian brand is blended with Chian.'

Is this the case only when you write verse, I put the question to 25
you, or is it also true when you have to plead the lengthy and challen-
ging case of the defendant Petillius? Do I take it you'd rather forget
fatherland and father, and while Pedius Publicola and Corvinus
work up a sweat pleading their cases in Latin, you'd prefer to mingle
with your native vocabulary words imported from abroad, like the
Canusian who speaks two languages? I, too, though born this side 30
of the sea, once took to writing little verses in Greek, but Quirinus
appeared to me after midnight, when dreams are true, and in such
words ordered me to refrain: 'It is just as mad to carry timber to a
forest as to wish to swell the teeming ranks of the Greeks.' So while 35
the bombastic Alpman slays Memnon and fashions a muddy head
for the Rhine, I amuse myself with these diversions, which aren't
meant to echo in the temple in competition for Tarpa's verdict or
to return to be seen again and again in the theatre. Fundanius, you 40
alone of living poets can rattle off charming volumes that show the
cunning courtesan and Davus fooling old Chremes; Pollio in triple-
time beat sings of the deeds of kings; Varius unequalled in spirit spins
the heroic epic; on Virgil the Muses whose delight is the countryside 45

have bestowed tenderness and charm. This was the kind of writing
I could perform more successfully, a form that Varro of Atax and cer-
tain others had attempted in vain, though I fell short of its inventor;
and it would be sheer presumption on my part to snatch from him the
garland that clings with such distinction to his head.

50   But I did say that his style resembles a muddy stream, often carry-
ing along more you would prefer to remove than to leave behind.
Come, I ask you as a man of literary taste, do you find nothing to
criticize in great Homer? Does Lucilius, engaging though he is, wish
to change nothing in Accius' tragedies? Doesn't he laugh at Ennius'
55   verses when they fall short in dignity, while describing himself as
no greater than those he censures? What's to stop me also, as I read
Lucilius' work, from asking if it was his own nature or the unfavour-
able conditions of his day that denied him verses more finished and
smoother in rhythm than a writer's who was content simply to round
60   off something in six feet per line, and prided himself in having writ-
ten two hundred lines before dinner, and the same number after it,
just like Etruscan Cassius, whose inspiration had more energy than
a river in spate and who, as we're told, was cremated on a pyre of his
65   own books and their cases. Granted, I say, that Lucilius was engaging
and urbane in his wit. Granted also that he had more refinement than
the author of unpolished verse untouched by the Greeks and more
than the crowd of older poets: but that man, had fate postponed his
life until this present day of ours, would smooth away much of his
70   work and prune everything that trailed beyond the right limit, often,
as he composed verse, scratching his head and gnawing his nails to
the quick.

     Often must you use the eraser, if you're going to write what deserves
a second reading, and you mustn't worry about being admired by the
crowd, but satisfy yourself with a few readers. Or are you mad enough
75   to prefer that your poems be dictated in worthless schools? That's
not for me: 'I am satisfied if the knights give me their applause,'
as the dauntless Arbuscula said when she was booed off the stage,
showing contempt for the rest of her audience. Should I be worried
by that louse Pantilius or tormented that Demetrius does me down
behind my back, or that the foolish Fannius, who sits at table with
80   Hermogenes Tigellius, stabs me in the back? I wish for my work to
have the approval of Plotius and Varius, of Maecenas and Virgil, of
Valgius and Octavius, of Fuscus, best of men, and how I wish for the

commendation of both Viscus brothers! With no fear of flattery I can
mention you, Pollio, and you, Messalla, together with your brother; 85
also you, Bibulus and Servius; along with these also yourself, honest
Furnius, and several others, men of literary taste and friends, whose
names I deliberately omit here; they are the men I should like to be
delighted by these compositions, such as they are, and it would upset
me if they gave less pleasure than I'd hoped. As for you, Demetrius, 90
and you, Tigellius, I bid you go and whine among the easy chairs of
your female students.

Off you go, boy, and lose no time in adding these lines to this little
book of mine.

BOOK 2

SATIRE 1

There are some who think I hit too hard in my satire, and that I stretch my work beyond a legitimate point; the other half reckons all my writing is insipid, and that verses like mine can be spun a thousand a day. Trebatius, give me advice on what to do. 'You should take
5 a rest.' Not write verses at all, you mean? 'Correct.' Damn me utterly if that wouldn't be the best course! But I can't get to sleep. 'Let those who need deep sleep oil themselves three times and swim across the Tiber, and, as night draws on, let them steep themselves in wine with
10 no water in it. Or, if so strong a desire for writing has you in thrall, have the courage to tell of the deeds of unvanquished Caesar, and many a reward you'll win for your efforts.' I have the desire, my excellent and worthy friend, but my strength fails me: not anyone you like can portray columns of men bristling with spears, or Gauls falling in
15 death with spear heads shattered, or wounded Parthian sliding off his horse. 'But you might take as your theme his justice and greatness of heart, as wise Lucilius did of Scipio's scion.'

I will not let myself down, when the moment presents itself; unless the time is right, Flaccus' words will not find Caesar's ear attentive,
20 and should you flatter him clumsily, he'll kick out all round to guard against trouble. 'How much more sensible that would be than laying into 'Pantolabus the scrounger and good-for-nothing Nomentanus' with verse that stings, making every man fear for himself, though not made a target, and hate you!'

What am I to do? Milonius starts dancing once the heat has reached
25 his wine-struck head and he sees twice as many lighted lamps; Castor delights in horses, his brother, born from the same egg, in boxing; for every thousand living souls there are just as many fads: what gives me pleasure is rounding off words in feet as Lucilius did, a better man
30 than both of us. In earlier days he used to entrust his secrets to his books, as if to trusted friends, not turning to any other source at all, whether things went badly for him or well; and so it comes about that the old fellow's entire life lies open to view, as if it were painted on

a votive tablet. This is the man I follow, unsure whether I hail from
Lucania or Apulia, as the settlers of Venusia plough land close to the 35
borders of each. To this region they were sent, so the old story goes,
when the Samnites were driven out, so that no enemy might ever
attack Romans through an open frontier, whether Apulia's sons or
the fiery men of Lucania were hammering on the anvil of war. But
this pen will never attack any living soul without provocation, and, 40
like a sword sheathed in its scabbard, it will keep me safe; why should
I try to draw it, while robbers' assaults can do me no harm? O Jupiter,
father and king, I pray that this weapon be discarded and perish from
rust, that no man may do me harm, as what I desire is peace! But
the fellow who makes my temper rise (keep your hands right off, I'm 45
warning you) shall be sorry for it, and become a marked man, his
name on every citizen's lips.

Cervius threatens those who earn his anger with laws and the urn,
Canidia her enemies with the poison of Albucius, Turius with 'big
trouble', should you find yourself engaged in a lawsuit when he's a
judge. How each man uses his own source of strength to frighten those 50
he suspects, and how much this depends on all-powerful Nature's
command, you must conclude with me from this: the wolf attacks
with his teeth, the bull with his horns. From where did they receive
this instruction if not from instinct? Put his long-lived mother in
the care of spendthrift Scaeva: no crime will his dutiful right hand
commit (not really surprising that the wolf attacks no one with a hoof 55
or the ox with a fang!), yet dangerous hemlock in poisoned honey will
carry the old lady off. Let me be brief: whether a peaceful old age
awaits me or Death flits around me with her black wings, rich or poor,
at Rome or in exile, should chance so determine, whatever hue my life 60
takes on, I will be a writer.

'My poor lad, I'm afraid your life may be short, and that one of
your high-placed friends may strike you down with a deadly chill.'
Really? When Lucilius first dared to write poetry of this kind and to
strip off the skin in which each man strolled along, a splendid sight
to all onlookers but rotten within, did Laelius take offence at his wit, 65
or the man who took his well-deserved name from the conquering of
Carthage, or were they hurt when Metellus was injured or Lupus was
swamped by scurrilous verses? Yet he fastened on the leaders of the
people, too, tribe by tribe, showing favour to Virtue alone, of course, 70
and to her friends. What's more, when the gallant scion of Scipio and

the wise and forbearing Laelius withdrew from the crowd, abandon-
ing the public stage for a private place, it was customary for them to
indulge in frivolity with Lucilius, and, changing their formal clothing,
to play games with him until the vegetables came to the boil.

75   Whatever my own qualities, however much I fall short of Lucilius
in terms of wealth and natural ability, yet Envy will always admit in
spite of herself that I have lived with the great, and, when she tries to
grind her teeth on something weak, she'll come up against something
solid; but learned Trebatius, you may not entirely agree. 'For my own
80 part, I can take no exception to this; but just the same, be warned and
mind you don't let ignorance of the sacred laws bring you into any
trouble: right of action and legal redress are lying in wait for anyone
who writes bad verses against another.' Fair enough, if he writes bad
verses; but what if a man produces good verses, that Caesar's judge-
85 ment finds praiseworthy? If he has barked his criticisms at someone
who deserves to be abused, and is himself blameless? 'Then the case
will be laughed out of court, and you'll get off scot-free.'

SATIRE 2

What the virtue of frugal living is, and how great (and this is no talk
of mine but the teaching of the countryman Ofellus, a man of self-
taught wisdom and rough learning) you should learn, my friends,
5 not at rich tables with lavish dishes, when the eye is spellbound by
senseless splendour and the mind, inclining to worthless attractions,
rejects what is of greater worth; no, here, before we take dinner, exam-
ine the question together with me. 'Why this subject?' I will say, if
I can.
    Every judge who has accepted a bribe weighs truth badly. A man
10 who has been hunting the hare, or is worn out from failing to break
a horse—or if you're used to playing the Greek and training for the
Roman army exhausts you, or you get exercise from the fast ball, when
passion for the game pleasantly beguiles the hard effort, or from the
discus, send that discus spinning through the yielding air—when work
has blunted the edge of your fussy tastes, and your throat is dry, your
15 stomach empty, *then* despise plain food, *then* drink only mulled wine
whose honey from Hymettus has been mixed with Falernian. The
butler has gone out of doors, the sea is dark and stormy, protecting its

fish: bread and salt will be enough to pacify your growling stomach. What is the cause of this, do you think, how does it come about? The greatest pleasure resides not in an expensive aroma but in yourself. So make yourself sweat to earn your sauce; someone pale and overweight from self-indulgence won't be able to benefit from oysters or trout or exotic grouse. And yet if a peacock is served up, I'll not find it easy to rob you of your desire to brush your palate with this rather than with a chicken, seduced as you are by the outward show, since the bird is rare and costs gold, and makes a fine show with the palette of its outspread tail; as if this had anything to do with the matter. You don't eat the feathers you so admire, do you? Is the bird such a fine sight once it's cooked? To think that you prefer the one to the other, taken in by their different appearances, when in their meat there's nothing to tell them apart!

Very well: what leads you to suppose that this pike with gaping jaws was caught in the Tiber or out at sea, whether it was tossed about between the bridges or at the mouth of the Tuscan river? Have you taken leave of your senses, praising a three-pound mullet that you have to cut up into single portions? The appearance is what attracts you, I see; what, then, is the point of disliking lengthy pikes? It is, of course, because Nature has given pikes size and mullets lightness of weight. Only a stomach that rarely feels the pangs of hunger is scornful of everyday sustenance. 'What I'd like to see is a big fish stretched out on a big dish,' says the gullet worthy of the greedy Harpies. Now is the time for you to come in all your strength, you winds from the south, and make their side dishes inedible, even if their boar and fresh turbot already give off a smell, as too much of a good thing troubles the sick stomach, when, full up, it would rather have radishes and tart pickles. Not yet has the poor man's food been wholly banished from the banquets of kings; for eggs, that cost little, and black olives still have their place these days. It's not so long ago that a sturgeon brought disgrace on the table of Gallonius the auctioneer. Was the sea, we ask, less productive of turbots in those days? The turbot was safe, and safe the stork's nest, until you were taught to acquire this taste by a praetor who showed the way. So if anyone now proclaims that roasted gulls are delicacies, the young men of Rome, not slow to learn bad habits, will fall into line.

In Ofellius' judgement a mean style of living will differ from a plain one; for it will be pointless if you shun one fault only to embrace

55 another by going off at a tangent in your weakness. Avidienus, who
quite rightly has the nickname 'Dog' attached to him, eats olives that
are five years old and cornel-berries from the forest, and he only opens
wine that has already gone off, while his oil has such a smell that you
60 couldn't endure it; but even though he may be celebrating a wed-
ding or a birthday-feast or some other holiday in freshly cleaned toga,
he pours the rancid stuff on the cabbage with his own hands from a
two-gallon jar, and shows no stinginess when it comes to his aged
vinegar. What manner of lifestyle, then, will the wise man adopt, and
which of these two will he imitate? It's just as the saying goes: a wolf
65 attacks on one side, a dog on the other. He will show refinement to
the extent that he gives no offence through meanness, and his way
of living will not become wretched through following either direc-
tion. He will not, like old Albucius, show cruelty to his slaves while
assigning them tasks, or follow the example of unthinking Naevius
in offering greasy water to his guests; this, too, constitutes a serious
faux pas.

70   Let me tell you now what advantages accompany plain living, and
how considerable they are. First and foremost, there is good health: for
you may believe the harm that a variety of dishes brings upon a man
when you recall the simple food that pleased your stomach well enough
in earlier days; but the moment you mix boiled and roasted, or shellfish
75 and thrushes, sweetness will turn to bile, and thick phlegm will play
havoc with your stomach. Do you see how pale each guest is as he rises
from a 'What should I choose' dinner? What's more, the body, weighed
down by the previous day's excesses, drags down with it the mind as
80 well, and nails to the earth a portion of the divine spirit. The other man,
after surrendering his body to sleep sooner than you can say, his appe-
tite unsatisfied, rises up with vigour to carry out his appointed tasks.

    But there will be times when he can turn his attention to better
entertainment, whether the year's cycle brings round a holiday or he
wishes to put some vigour back into his shrunken body, and when the
85 years mount up, and feeble old age wishes to be treated with more
indulgence: but in your case, if ill health strikes or debilitating old
age, what on earth will be added to that indulgence you enjoy prema-
turely while young and strong? Our forefathers used to praise boar
90 that was rank, not because they had no sense of smell, but with this
thought, I imagine, that, should a guest arrive a bit late, it would be

more appropriate for him to eat it tainted than for the master to eat it up greedily when it was fresh. Oh, if only the earth in its earliest years had given me birth to live among these heroes!

You set some store by a fine reputation, which, more welcome than song, charms the ear of man: big turbots on big dishes bring big dis- 95 grace, not just heavy expense: add to the mixture an angry uncle, angry neighbours, and your own hostility to yourself, cheated of your longing to die, when you're so hard up you can't afford the penny to buy a rope to hang yourself. 'It's fair enough to scold Trausius in such terms,' comes the reply, 'but *I* have large revenues and wealth 100 enough to please three kings.' Is there, then, nothing better for you to spend this surplus on? Why does anyone undeservedly suffer from poverty, while you are rich? Why are the ancient temples of the gods collapsing? Why, you selfish creature, don't you measure out some-thing for your beloved country from that great heap? You alone, 105 of course, will always enjoy the prosperous life. What a laughing stock you will be to your enemies in days to come! Which of these two will rely on himself with more confidence when chance blows hot and cold? The one who has made his scornful mind and body accustomed to excess, or the one who, happy with little and fearful of the future, 110 has in time of peace, like a wise man, prepared what is required in war?

To make you put more trust in these words of mine, I know, from the time I was a small boy, that this Ofellus made no greater use of his means when untouched than he does of them now that they have been pruned back. You could see him on his plot of land after the surveyors had done their work, a sturdy tenant-farmer with his cattle 115 and his sons, giving this account: 'On a working day it wasn't my way to eat, without good reason, anything more than greens with a foot of smoked ham. And if ever, after a long interval, a guest came to see me, or, when rainy weather had given me a respite from work, a neighbour appeared as a welcome companion at table, we had a good time of it, 120 not with fish fetched from town, but with a chicken and a kid; then our second course was set off by hung-dried grapes, nuts and split figs. Next we'd play a game of serious drinking, with a forfeit to rule our feast, and, once we'd made our prayers to Ceres, "so might she rise on lofty stalk", she smoothed away with wine the worries of a 125 frowning brow.

'Let Fortune rage and stir up fresh turmoil, how much will she take
away from these pleasures? How much less prosperous, my sons, have
130 you or I looked since this new settler came here! For Nature hasn't
established him or me or anyone else as owner of his own land: he has
driven us out, and he in turn will be driven out by his own useless-
ness or ignorance of the law's quirky ways, or finally at any rate by
an heir with time on his side. For the moment the land goes under
Umbrenus' name, not long ago it was called Ofellus', and no one will
own it for good but instead it will pass now into my use, now into
135 another man's. And so live on with courage, and with courage in your
hearts stand up to fate's buffetings.'

SATIRE 3

'You write so infrequently that in a whole year you don't call for parch-
ment, unweaving the web of all your writing and angry with yourself
for being generous with wine and sleep but writing no poetry worth a
mention. What will come of this? But just when the Saturnalia came
5 along, you say, you fled here for refuge. Well then, sober as you are,
give us some poetry worthy of your promises: begin. Not a jot: in vain
you blame your pen, and the poor undeserving wall, that was born
when the gods and poets were angry, suffers from your poundings.
And yet you had the look of one who threatened to produce no short-
10 age of brilliant material, once you had some free time and had found
welcome under the warm shelter of your little country house. So what
was the point of packing Plato with Menander, and of taking out of
the city Eupolis and Archilochus, such impressive companions? Do
you mean to appease envy by abandoning your own excellence? You'll
be treated with contempt, poor fellow; you must turn your back on
15 that shameless Siren, laziness, or resign with equanimity all that
you've achieved in a more fruitful time of life.'
  Ah, Damasippus, for this true counsel may the gods and goddesses
bestow on you—a barber! But how come you know me so well? 'Ever
since all my fortunes foundered at the central Janus, I've been look-
ing after other people's business affairs, now I've been flung over-
20 board and lost my own. There was a time, you see, when I used to
love trying to find out in what bronze piece cunning old Sisyphus had
washed his feet, which work had been unskilfully carved, which cast

too rigidly; having an expert's eye, I would value this or that statue at a hundred thousand; when it came to gardens and fine houses, I was unique in knowing how to do business profitably; this gave rise 25 to the crowds at street corners giving me the nickname "Mercury's pal".' I know, and it amazes me you've been cleared of that disease. 'But what's really amazing is the way a new disease has displaced the old, as normally happens when the pain of an aching side or head has transferred itself to the stomach; it's like when your lethargic man turns into a boxer and starts punching his doctor.' As long as you 30 don't do anything like that, let it be as you please. 'My good friend, don't deceive yourself; you are mad, and so are virtually all stupid people, if there's any truth in Stertinius' loud pronouncements.

'I myself took a note of these wonderful lessons from him in my eagerness to learn, at the time when by way of consolation he told 35 me to cultivate a philosopher's beard and retrace my steps from the Fabrician bridge, no longer sad. For when my business had failed and I'd covered my head in preparation for throwing myself into the river, he stood at my right hand and said, "Mind you don't do anything unworthy of yourself; what's torturing you is a false sense of shame, since you're afraid to be thought mad among madmen. Now, let me 40 start by examining the question what it is to be mad: if this quality is found in you alone, I'll add not one word more to stop you dying bravely. Every man who is driven blindly on by perverse folly and ignorance of the truth Chrysippus' portico and flock maintain is mad. This is a general rule that applies to the masses and to mighty kings 45 alike, with only the wise man as an exception.

' "Now let me tell you the reason why all men who have labelled you mad are just as crazy as you. Just as in a forest, when some mistake drives men from the proper path, so they wander off this way and that, one going off to the left, another to the right, both of them 50 victims of a single error but led astray in different directions; so you must only to this extent believe you are mad, that the one who laughs at you has a tail dragging behind him, and is not a jot the wiser man. One class of folly is when a man fears things that give no cause at all for fear, so that he complains that his way across an open plain is blocked by fire, by precipices, by rivers; the other type, diverging 55 from this but none the wiser, would show a man rushing through fires and rivers right in his path. Though his dear mother, respected sister, father, wife, relatives may shout, 'There's a huge ditch here, there's

60 an enormous precipice, watch out!' he'll hear no more than drunken
    Fufius did once, when he slept through the role of Iliona and twelve
    hundred Catienuses were shouting, 'Mother, I implore you!'
         '"I shall now demonstrate that the whole crowd suffers from a
    madness that resembles this derangement. Damasippus' madness
65 consists in buying up old statues. Damasippus' creditor is sound of
    mind. Fair enough! Suppose I say to you, 'Take this loan which you
    needn't ever pay me back,' will you be mad to accept it? Or are you
    more out of your wits to reject the profit that propitious Mercury
    offers? Make a record of ten thousand sesterces paid out on loan
70 through Nerius; the security isn't sufficient: add a hundred bonds of
    the cunning Cicuta, add a thousand fetters: the blasted crook will still
    escape these chains, a regular Proteus. Drag him to court and he'll be
    laughing with other men's jaws, then he'll turn himself into a boar,
    sometimes a bird, sometimes a rock, and, when he wants, a tree. If a
    man's madness appears in managing his affairs badly, and his sanity,
75 by contrast, in managing them well, then, believe me, Perellius' brain
    is much more addled, when he dictates that you are at liberty never
    to pay back.
         '"Now I invite to listen and arrange his toga anyone who is pale
    from sordid ambition or from love of silver, or who is feverish with
80 the desire for gratification or depressing superstition, or any other
    disease of the mind; come closer to me here in due order, while
    I demonstrate that you are all mad.
         '"Lovers of wealth must be given by far the largest dose of hel-
    lebore, and I'm inclined to think Reason would administer all of
    Anticyra to them. The heirs of Staberius engraved on his tomb the
85 total sum he had bequeathed, as, if they hadn't done so, they would
    have been legally bound to provide for the people's entertainment
    a hundred pairs of gladiators and a public feast that would satisfy
    an Arrius, together with as much corn as Africa's harvest yields.
    'Whether this wish of mine is right or wrong, don't play the uncle
    with me': this, in my view, is what Staberius in his wisdom foresaw.
90 'Well, what did he mean by requiring his heirs to engrave the total
    sum of his legacy on the stone?' For as long as he lived, he believed
    poverty was a massive fault and there was nothing he guarded against
    more keenly, so that, if he had happened to die less rich by a single
    farthing, he would think himself so much the more worthless a man:
95 you see, everything, virtue, a good name, beauty, things human and

divine give way to the loveliness of wealth; the man who has amassed this will be famous, brave and just. 'And will he be wise?' Yes, that too; he will also be a king, and all that he wishes to be. He expected that great renown would come to him from this wealth, as if he had won it through merit.

' "Did the Greek Aristippus do anything like him? He was the man who in the middle of Libya told his slaves to throw away gold, on the ground that they were making too slow progress, weighed down by their load. Which of these two is madder? There's nothing to be said for an example that seeks to solve one puzzle by means of another.

' "Should a man purchase lyres and then, once bought, stock them together when he feels no interest in the lyre or any Muse, should he do likewise with cutting tools and lasts, though not a cobbler, or with ships' sails when he strongly dislikes the life of a trader, everyone would describe him as a raving lunatic, and with good reason. Now, if a man hides away his cash and gold, not knowing how to use his store and fearing to touch it as if it were sacred, how does he differ from these others? Should a man lie outstretched beside a huge heap of corn, keeping constant watch over it with a long stick, without ever daring to touch one grain of this though owning it and feeling the pangs of hunger, but preferring to feast, miser-like, on bitter leaves; should he have laid down in his cellar a thousand jars—that's nothing, three hundred thousand—of Chian and old Falernian, and quaff sharp vinegar; look, should he lie on a bed of straw when a year short of his eightieth birthday, though fine coverlets lie mouldering in his chest, a banquet for moths and grubs, not many, believe me, would think him mad, since the self-same fever robs the vast majority of mankind of sleep. Tell me, god-forsaken old man, are you guarding these for a son, or even a freedman, to drink up as his inheritance? Are you afraid of running short? I mean, what a trifling amount will each day clip off the total, if you begin using better oil to dress your vegetables, yes, and that head of yours, so unsightly with its uncombed scurf? Why, if the slightest thing meets your needs, do you resort to breaking oaths, to indiscriminate thieving and plundering? This is proof of your sanity, is it?

' "Should you start to pelt the crowd with stones, or your own slaves for whom you paid hard cash, everyone, young and old, would call you mad: when you hang your wife and poison your mother, no

harm comes to your head. Why is this? It's not at Argos you're doing
it, you're not killing the mother who gave you birth with a sword
like mad Orestes. Or do you suppose madness came upon him after
135 he'd killed his mother, and he wasn't driven insane by the fearsome
Furies before he warmed his sharp blade in his mother's throat? No,
from the time Orestes was reckoned to be of unsafe mind, there is no
action whatever he took that you can criticize: he didn't dare to attack
140 with his sword Pylades or Electra, his sister, simply insulting both of
them by calling her a Fury and him some other name prompted by
his glittering black bile.

'"Opimius, a poor man for all the silver and gold he had stored
in his house, who on holidays was in the habit of drinking wine
from Veii out of a Capuan ladle, and on working days sour wine,
145 fell once into a lethargy so profound that his heir was already run-
ning around his keys and coffers overjoyed and jubilant. He was
brought round by his doctor, a quick-witted and dependable fellow,
in the following way: he gave instructions for a table to be set up
and bags of coin to be poured out, and for a number of people to
150 come forward to count it, adding this remark: 'If you fail to guard
what's yours, a greedy heir will soon be off with it.' 'What, while
I'm alive?' 'So, to continue living, keep your eyes open: take care!'
'What should I do, then?' 'You are weak, and your veins won't provide
enough blood if your collapsing stomach doesn't get the strong but-
155 tressing of food. Are you hesitating? Come on, take this rice gruel.'
'What did the rice cost?' 'Nothing much.' 'How much, then?'
'Eightpence.' 'Oh, dear! What's the difference if I'm ruined by illness
or theft and pillage?'

'"Who, then, is sane?" "The man who is not a fool." "What about
the man in love with riches?" "He's a fool and a madman." "Well,
160 if someone were not in love with wealth, would he automatically be
sane?" "Far from it." "How come, good Stoic?" "I will tell you. It's
not dyspepsia (imagine Craterus was speaking) that this patient has:
is he well, then, and will he get up? No, will be Craterus' reply, since
the chest or kidneys are under attack from an acute disease. He is
165 not a cheat or miser: let him sacrifice a pig, in that case, to the benevo-
lent Lares; but he is ambitious and a risk-taker: let him take ship
to Anticyra. For what difference does it make, whether you commit
everything you have to a bottomless pit or never use what you have
accumulated?

'"The story goes that Servius Oppidius, a wealthy man by the reckoning of early times, divided his two farms at Canusium between his two sons, and said this to the youngsters when he had summoned them to his deathbed: 'From the day I saw you, Aulus, carrying your knucklebones and nuts in a loose fold of your tunic, giving them away and gambling with them, and you, Tiberius, counting them with a frown of concentration and hiding them in holes, I started to fear that the pair of you would be driven by madness of opposing kinds, that *you* would follow Nomentanus, and *you* Cicuta. And so I beg you both by our household's gods, *you* beware of reducing and *you* of increasing what your father considers sufficient and nature prescribes as a limit. What's more, in case ambition tickles your fancy, I shall bind you both by an oath: whichever one of you becomes aedile or praetor, let him be outlawed and under a curse. Would you squander your wealth on chickpeas and beans and lupins, so that you can strut for all to see in the Circus and stand in bronze, stripped of the land, stripped, madman, of the money your father left you? All, no doubt, so that you may receive the applause that Agrippa gets, you the cunning fox striving to be like the noble lion.'

'"'Son of Atreus, why do you give the order that no one bury Ajax?' 'I am king.' 'I am a mere commoner, so ask no more.' 'And this my edict is a just one; but if any man considers me unjust, I give him leave to voice his thoughts freely.' 'Mightiest of kings, the gods grant that you take Troy and bring your fleet back home! Am I, then, permitted to ask a question and respond in turn?' 'Put your question.' Why is Ajax, the hero next to Achilles, and famous for rescuing the Greeks so many times, mouldering in death? Is it so that Priam and Priam's people may delight in burial being denied the man who caused so many of their warriors to go without a grave in their native soil?' 'The madman slaughtered a thousand sheep, crying out that he was killing renowned Ulysses, Menelaus and myself at the same time.' 'And you, when at Aulis you set your own sweet daughter at the altars in a heifer's place, sprinkling her head with salt and grain, you shameless man, are you keeping your mind on the path of right?' 'What point are you making?' 'Well, what did the madman Ajax do when he laid the flock low with his blade? He withheld violence from his wife and child; many were the curses he hurled at the heads of Atreus' sons, but he brought no harm to Teucer or even to Ulysses.' 'But to free the ships stuck fast on the unfriendly shore

I showed sense in winning back the gods' favour with blood.' 'Yes, you maniac, with blood that was your own.' 'My own blood, I grant, but I was no maniac.' The man whose mind grasps presentations that differ from the true and are confused by the turmoil caused by crime will be thought deranged, and it will make no difference whether folly
210 or anger makes him go astray. When Ajax puts harmless lambs to the sword, he is insane: when you deliberately commit a crime for the sake of empty distinctions, are you in your right mind, and is your heart, when swollen with ambition, free of fault? Should someone wish to
215 carry about in his litter a sleek lamb and provide it, like a daughter, with clothes, maidservants and gold, calling it Rufa or Posilla, and planning to marry it off to a gallant husband, the praetor would place him under an injunction and remove all his legal rights, and guardianship of him would pass to relatives in their right mind. Tell me, if someone offers up his own daughter for a sacrifice as if she were a
220 dumb lamb, is he sound of mind? Don't say so. And so, where folly is perverse, there is the height of madness; the man who has committed crime will also be a maniac; the one who has been captivated by fame's glittering mirror has thundering about his head Bellona who delights in bloody deeds.

'"Come now, join me in hauling up for judgement self-indul-
225 gence and Nomentanus: For Reason will prove that spendthrifts are fools and madmen. This man no sooner received an inheritance of a thousand talents than he decreed like some praetor that the fisherman, the fruiterer, the fowler, the perfumer, the vile rabble of the Etruscans' street, the sausage-maker and the idle scroungers, too,
230 the whole market and Velabrum, should come to his house next morning. What was the result? They came in big numbers. The brothel-keeper opened the business: 'Whatever I have, whatever any of these men has at his disposal, believe me, is yours; send for it today or, if you like, tomorrow.' Hear the reply that the generous young
235 man gave to this: 'You sleep with leggings on in the Lucanian snow so that I may have a boar for dinner: you sweep fish from a stormy sea. I am the idle one, unworthy of possessing so much: take it away: you take a million sesterces for yourself; you the same; and you, whose wife comes running from the house after midnight when
240 I send for her, take three times as much.' Aesopus' son, no doubt wanting to swallow a solid million, dissolved in vinegar a wondrous pearl he had taken from Metella's ear: how is he saner than

if he were to toss that same thing into a fast-flowing river or sewer?
The offspring of Quintus Arrius, a famous pair of brothers, twins in
depravity and frivolity and a love of the perverse, were in the habit   245
of breakfasting on nightingales that had cost them a huge sum. What
category are they to go into? Marked with chalk as sane, or with
charcoal?

'"Should a man with a beard show delight in building toy houses,
in harnessing mice to a tiny cart, in playing at odds and evens and
riding a hobby horse, he would be afflicted by madness. If Reason   250
proves beyond doubt that being in love is more childish than these
things, that it makes no difference whether you build in play in the
sand, as before you did at the age of three, or you whine in torment for
the love of a prostitute, then, I ask, would you behave like Polemo who
was once converted? Would you abandon the emblems of your illness—
the leg-bands, arm-wrap, scarves—just as, we are told, when he was   255
drunk that man surreptitiously plucked the garlands from around
his neck, the moment he was brought up short by what the teacher
said before *he* had eaten lunch. When a child is sulking and you offer
him apples, he turns them down: 'Take them, pet!' He says no: if you
weren't to give them, he'd crave them: how does the locked-out lover   260
differ from this, when he debates whether or not to go where he meant
to return to, though not invited, and hangs about the doors he hates?
'Shall I not go even now, though she asks me without my prompting?
Or should I rather think about putting a stop to my suffering? She
has shut me out; she calls me back: should I return? No, not even if
she begs me.' Now, listen to his slave, wiser by far: 'O sir, something   265
that has no measure or judgement in it, can't be treated with reason
or measure. Love contains these evils, first war, then peace: these are
things that drift about by blind chance, almost as unpredictable as the
weather, so if a man should strive to impose some rule on them in his
life, he would no more sort them out than if he aimed to go mad by   270
means of reason or measure.' Tell me, when you squeeze the pips out
of apples from Picenum and are delighted if you happen to have hit
the ceiling with one, are you all right in the head? Again, when you
strike out baby-talk from an adult's palate, how does this make you
saner than one who builds toy houses? Add bloodshed to folly and   275
poke the fire with the sword. The other day, I say, when Marius ran
Hellas through and then flung himself headlong, was he possessed,
or will you acquit the man of having a disordered mind and find

280 him guilty of crime, applying to things words that are related, as we often do?

'"There was a freedman who in old age would run around the street-corner shrines in the early morning before he had touched breakfast, his hands washed, and utter this prayer, 'Save me from death, me alone' ('Just me, it's a small enough request,' he would add); 'It's an easy task for gods!' The fellow was sound enough in
285 ears and eyes; but as for his mind, his owner would exclude that from warranty when selling him, unless he enjoyed lawsuits. This crowd, too, Chrysippus will find a place for in the prolific clan of Menenius. 'Jupiter, who send and take away grievous pains,' cries the mother of the child whom sickness has kept bedridden for five months, 'if
290 the shivering quartan fever leaves my boy, early on the morning of the day you appoint for fasting he will stand, naked, in the Tiber.' Whether chance or a doctor rescues the sick lad from the point of danger, his deranged mother will kill him, bringing back his fever
295 by planting him on an ice-cold river bank; what evil has shaken her mind? Fear of the gods."

'These were the weapons put in my hand by Stertinius my friend, eighth of the sages, so that henceforth I should not be called names without exacting my revenge. Whoever calls me mad shall hear as much said about him, and he shall learn to look behind at what hangs from his back but escapes his notice.'

300 My Stoic friend, as you hope to sell everything at a profit after any loss, what folly is it that causes my madness, since there is more than one type? For in my own mind I am sane. 'Look, when Agave in her madness is carrying her poor son's head that she has torn off, does she
305 at that moment think herself to be crazy?' I'm stupid, I admit it, let me yield to the truth, and I'm mad as well: but expound this only, what mental disorder do you think is the cause of my sickness? 'Listen: first you are engaged in building, that is, you are trying to measure up to the high-headed, even though from top to toe your full height is two
310 feet; and yet you laugh at Turbo's confident swagger in his armour as though it's too big for his physique: how do you cut a less laughable figure than he does? Or is it right that, whatever Maecenas does, you too should do, when you are so unlike him, and so unfitted in importance to compete with him? When a mother frog was away from home,
315 a calf squashed her young with his hoof. One of them got away and tells her the whole story, how a huge monster crushed his sisters and

brothers to death. "What size was it?" asked the mother; "as big as
this?" as she puffed herself out. "Half as big again." "As big as this,
then?" As she blew herself up more and more, he said, "Not even if
you burst yourself, will you be as large." This picture comes close to 320
capturing you. Add your poetry now, that is, add fuel to the flame, for
if any man has composed poetry when sane, then you are sane when
you write yours. I say nothing of your frightful temper.'

Stop there! 'And your lifestyle that goes beyond your means.' Just
mind your own business, Damasippus. 'The thousand passions you 325
have for girls, the thousand for boys.' O greater madman, please spare
a lesser one!

SATIRE 4

Catius, where have you been and where are you off to? 'I've no time
to stop, I'm so keen to make notes of some new teachings that are
of a kind to outdo Pythagoras and the man Anytus put in the dock
and learned Plato.' I admit my fault in interrupting you at so propi-
tious a moment; but be a good chap and accept my apologies, please. 5
If any detail has slipped from your memory now, you'll recover it
soon. Whether this skill you have is due to nature or to art, you're
a wonder either way. 'No, I was just worried about how I could keep
the whole lecture in my head, as its arguments were subtle and subtly
expressed.' Make known the man's name. Is he a Roman or a stranger? 10
'The teachings themselves I will recite from memory, their author's
name will be kept a secret.

'Be mindful to serve up eggs of an oblong shape, as they have a
better flavour and are whiter than round ones; for they have hard
skins and contain a male yolk. Cabbages that have grown in dry fields 15
are sweeter than those from plots near the city; nothing is more lack-
ing in taste than the produce of a watered garden. If a guest suddenly
surprises you in the evening and you fear a tough fowl may answer
badly to his taste, you will not miss a trick by plunging it alive into
diluted Falernian; this will make it tender. Mushrooms picked in a 20
meadow are best in quality; you do not put your trust wisely in the
others. A man will get through summers in good health who con-
cludes his lunches with black mulberries that he has picked from the
tree before the sun becomes oppressive.

'Aufidius used to mix his honey with strong Falernian, and here he
25 was in error, as only what is mild should be put into veins that are
empty; you would better soak the lungs in mild honeyed wine. If con-
stipation afflicts your bowels, limpet and inexpensive shellfish will
dispel the blockage, and low-growing sorrel, but don't forget to add
30 white wine from Cos. New moons fill up the slippery shellfish; but not
every sea produces the choicest kind. Mussels from the Lucrine are
better than cockles from Baiae, oysters come from Circeii, sea urchins
from Misenum, and luxurious Tarentum boasts of her broad scallops.

35 'Not anyone may lightly lay claim to knowledge of the art of dining,
without having first mastered the subtle system of flavours. And it is
not enough to sweep away fish from an expensive counter if one does
not know which are better with sauce and which, when grilled, will
40 make the jaded guest rise up on his elbow once more. Umbria is home
to the boar that, fed on holm-oak acorns, makes the round serving-
dishes buckle, when the host will have no truck with tasteless meat, for
the Laurentian beast is poor fare, fattened as he is on sedge and reeds.
Roe deer bred in vineyards are not always suitable for eating. The con-
45 noisseur will hunt the forelegs of a hare that carries young. As regards
fish and fowl, what their qualities and best age should be, no palate
before mine has investigated and made clear to anyone.

'Some there are whose talent lies only in producing new forms of
biscuit. It is in no way sufficient to devote one's attention to a single
detail of the menu; it would be like a man striving only to ensure that
50 his wines are not substandard while not caring about the quality of oil
he pours on his fish.

'If you expose Massic wine to a cloudless sky, any thickness it
possesses will evaporate in the night air, and the scent that harms
the sinews will pass off; but that wine when strained through linen
55 is spoiled and loses its flavour. A shrewd fellow mixes Sorrento's
wine with lees of Falernian, and carefully collects the sediment with
a pigeon's egg, as its yolk sinks to the bottom and draws with it all
foreign matter. If a drinker is flagging you will revive him with fried
60 prawns and African snails; for lettuce rises on the dyspeptic stomach
after wine; ham and sausages are what it craves to be pricked and
freshened by; in fact, it would rather have any kind of meat brought
piping hot from dirty cookshops.

'It's worth your while getting to know properly the nature of the
two types of sauce. The simple consists of sweet olive oil, which

should be mixed with thick, undiluted wine and sea water, just like 65
the brine that makes your barrel of tunny from Byzantium smell so
strong. Once this has been mixed with chopped herbs and has come
to the boil, then has been sprinkled with Corycian saffron and left to
stand, you should add besides some juice produced from the pressed
berry of the Venafran olive.

'Tibur's apples yield to Picenum's in flavour; I make this point, 70
since the former are of better appearance. Venuculum's grape suits
the preserving jar; the grape of Alba you would do better to dry in the
smoke. You'll find that I was first to serve this last grape round the
table with apples, as I also invented the serving of wine-lees and
fish-pickle paste, and of white pepper sifted with black salt in clean 75
little bowls. It's a gargantuan error to spend three thousand at the
fish-market, and then to confine the sprawling fish in a narrow dish.
It fairly turns the stomach if a slave has handled a wine-cup with
hands greasy from a mouthful of snatched food, or if unsightly mould
clings to your antique wine-bowl. What's so expensive about ordinary 80
brooms, napkins, and sawdust? But neglect them and how scandal-
ous is the disgrace! Think of it—you sweeping the mosaic floor with
a dirty palm-broom, or putting unwashed valences round covers of
Tyrian purple, forgetting that the less care and expense these things 85
involve, the more justified someone is in blaming you for neglect-
ing them rather than for the absence of things only the tables of the
wealthy can afford!'

O learned Catius, in the name of our friendship, in the name of the
gods, I beg you, don't forget to take me to listen to the next lecture,
wherever you go to it. For though you report everything to me with a 90
retentive memory, yet by merely interpreting you wouldn't give me as
much pleasure. And then there are the man's expression and bearing
to consider; you don't think much of having seen these, you lucky
fellow, because the good fortune came your way; but I have no moder-
ate longing to be able to draw near to those sequestered springs and to 95
drink deep the teachings of the happy life.

SATIRE 5

Answer me this, too, Tiresias, in addition to what you have told me,
by what ways and means I can regain my lost wealth. Why do you

laugh? 'Is it no longer enough for the man of many wiles to sail back
5 to Ithaca and set eyes on his ancestral home?' O you who have never
uttered falsehood to any man, you see how, as you prophesied, I am
returning home, naked and needy, and there neither wine-cellar nor
flock has been left untouched by the suitors; yet neither a man's birth
nor his courage is worth any more than seaweed if he lacks posses-
sions. 'Since, to put it in plain terms, poverty is what you dread, hear
10 by what means you can become rich. Suppose you are given a thrush
or anything else for yourself, let it fly off to where great wealth shines
and the owner is old. Your sweet fruit and all the glorious produce
your tilled farm yields, let the rich man taste before your Lar does,
15 the Lar who deserves less reverence than the rich man; however much
he may be a breaker of oaths, of no family, stained with the shed-
ding of a brother's blood, a runaway slave, you must still not refuse
to walk beside him on his outside, if he asks you.' What? Cover the
side of some filthy Dama? I acted in no such fashion at Troy, always
20 taking the fight to better men. 'Then you will be poor.' I will bid my
hardy soul endure this; in former days even greater trials did I bear.
But lose no time, seer, tell me from where I am to rake up riches and
piles of cash. 'I have told you, I say, and am telling you: you must
hunt craftily in every place for old men's wills, and, if one or two
25 are cunning enough to escape the fisherman after nibbling the bait
from your hook, don't abandon hope or give up the practice because
you've been baffled. If one day a case is argued over in the forum,
big or small, make yourself the advocate of the man who is rich and
childless and has the shameless audacity to summon the better man
30 into court; have nothing to do with the citizen whose case and reputa-
tion are superior, if he has a son or fruitful wife at home. "Quintus,"
let's say, or "Publius" (sensitive ears delight in hearing first names),
"your excellent character has made me your friend; I know the
35 complications of the law, I can defend cases; I'll let any man pluck
out my eyes sooner than he should hold you in contempt and make
you a nutshell the poorer; what concerns me is that you don't lose a
penny or give people cause to laugh at you." Tell him to go home and
look after his precious skin; become his attorney yourself, stand fast
and show endurance, whether the red Dog-star causes unspeaking
40 statues to split or Furius, stomach crammed with rich tripe, bespatters
with white snow the wintry Alps. "Don't you see," someone will say,
nudging a neighbour in the crowd with his elbow, "what tolerance he

has, how accommodating he is to his friends, how energetic?" More
tunny will swim up, and your fish-ponds will swell. What's more, if 45
someone has a son who keeps poor health but has been acknowledged
by him and is being raised in wealthy circumstances, then to avoid
being exposed by flagrant servility to one who is childless, by means
of your attentiveness towards him creep unobtrusively into the hope
that you may be named as his second heir, and, should some mis-
chance consign the boy to Orcus, that you may occupy the empty 50
place: it's most unusual for this game to fail. If ever a man gives
you his will to read, be sure to decline and to push the documents
from you, but in such a way that a sidelong glance steals for you the
contents of the second line on the first page; swiftly run your eye 55
across to see if you are sole inheritor or you share with many others.
Quite often a public clerk cooked up from a humble magistrate
will make a fool of the raven with its gaping beak, and Nasica the
fortune-hunter will give Coranus cause for laughter.'

  Are you raving? Or are you in your senses and mocking me by your
oracular responses? 'O son of Laertes, all that I say shall be or not be:
for prophecy is great Apollo's gift to me.' Nevertheless, if I may be 60
told, tell me the meaning of this story of yours. 'At that time when a
youth whom the Parthians dread, scion descended from lofty Aeneas,
shall be mighty by land and sea, the stately daughter of Nasica shall
marry the brave Coranus, who is reluctant to pay back his debt in full. 65
Then shall the son-in-law do this: he shall give his will to his father-
in-law and beg him to read it; long shall Nasica refuse but then shall
he take the will at length and read in silence, and he shall find nothing
bequeathed to him and his but to go hang.

  'Here is another piece of advice: if by chance a crafty woman or 70
freedman has influence with an old man whose wits have left him,
join up with them as a partner; pay them compliments, so that they
may compliment you in your absence. This too helps; but far better
than this is to storm the chief stronghold himself. If he's a lunatic
writing bad poetry, praise it. If he chases after women, make sure 75
he doesn't have to ask you; without prompting hand over Penelope
obligingly to your better.' Do you think her services can be bought,
a woman of such honesty and virtue, whom the suitors could not
turn away from the right track? 'Yes, for it was young men who came,
who were frugal in giving a lot, and were more interested in the 80
kitchen's offerings than those of Venus. This is why your Penelope

is virtuous; give her just one taste of a nice bit of profit from one
old man, having you as her partner, and she'll be just like the dog
that can never be scared away from the greasy hide. When I was old
what I'm going to tell you did happen: a wicked old woman at Thebes
85 was carried out for burial in the following way, by the terms of her
will: her corpse, generously anointed with oil, was carried by her heir
on his bare shoulders, no doubt since she wished to see if she could
give him the slip in death; when she was alive, he had pressed her
too hard, I suppose. Be careful in making your approach: don't fall
90 short in service or overflow with it, losing all proportion. Someone
who is bad-tempered and peevish will find a chatterbox offensive;
but at the same time you shouldn't be silent beyond due measure. Be
Davus in the comedy and stand with head to one side, looking very
much like one who is overawed. Make your advances with flattery;
warn him, if the breeze has grown stronger, to be careful to cover
95 his precious head; use your shoulders to get him clear from a crowd;
when he becomes talkative, make your ears prick up attentively. If he
insatiably loves being praised, give it to him strong, until, with hands
raised to the sky, he cries, "That's quite enough!" and blow up the
swelling bladder with hot air. When he has set you free from long
100 slavery and worry, and, convinced you're wide awake, you hear the
words, "Let Ulysses inherit one quarter", scatter continually such
phrases as, "So is my old friend Dama now no more? Where shall I
find a man so brave, so loyal?" and, if you can shed a few tears, drop
105 in some: it's possible to hide the expression that betrays joy. If the
tomb has been left to your discretion, build it without meanness; let
the neighbourhood praise a funeral managed especially well. If one
of your fellow heirs, older than yourself, happens to have a bad
cough, tell him that, should he wish to buy a farm or house from your
share, you would happily knock it down to him for a pittance. But
110 Proserpina drags me away, and she brooks no resistance; live long and
fare well.'

SATIRE 6

This was what I prayed for: a piece of land of no great size, where
there would be a kitchen garden, and next to the house a spring of
ever-flowing water, and a little woodland above them. Larger and

better than this has been my gift from the gods. I am satisfied. O
son of Maia, I ask for nothing more except that you make these gifts 5
of yours for ever mine. If I have neither made my wealth greater by
wicked means nor intend to make it smaller by excesses or careless-
ness, if I make no such foolish prayers as these: 'Oh, if only that little
corner nearby were added on, which now spoils the shape of my little
farm! Oh, if only some piece of luck would show me a jar full of silver, 10
as it did the man who found a treasure and purchased and ploughed
the self-same fields he had worked for hire, made rich by the favour
of Hercules!'—if what I have makes me content and happy, then this
is the prayer I make to you: make my flocks fat for their master, and
everything else apart from my wits, and, as is your custom, stay by my 15
side as chief protector!

And so, once I have forsaken the city for my citadel in the moun-
tains, what should I celebrate first in my satires with my Muse who
goes on foot? Here no wretched desire for advancement makes my
life death, no leaden sirocco or unhealthy autumn, from which heart-
less Libitina makes profit. Father of the Morning, or 'Janus', if that 20
title pleases you more, from whom men take the beginnings of life's
work and toil, for so is heaven's will, be the prelude of my song. At
Rome you hurry me off to stand surety for a friend: 'Come on, stir
yourself or someone else will answer duty's call before you.' Whether 25
the north wind sweeps the earth, or winter drags out the snowy day
in a narrower circuit, go I must. Later, once I've stated loud and clear
what may do me harm, I must battle in the crowd and shove out the
way the slowcoaches. 'What's your problem, you lunatic, and what's
your business?' So some rude fellow accosts me with angry curses; 30
'do you have to batter anything in your way, if you're running back to
Maecenas, thinking of nothing else?'

This delights me and is like honey, I'll not pretend otherwise. But
the moment I reach the gloomy Esquiline, a hundred concerns of
others dance on top of my head and all around me. 'Roscius begs you 35
to meet him at the Well tomorrow before the second hour.' 'Treasury
officials beg you, Quintus, to remember to return today on some new
and important matter of business of common interest.' 'Make sure
that Maecenas puts his seal to these papers.' Say to this, 'I'll try,' and
his insistent response will be, 'You can, if you want to.'

The seventh year, no, closer to the eighth, will soon have sped by 40
since Maecenas began to count me among his friends, only to the

extent that, when making a journey, he might want to take me along
in his carriage and entrust small-talk to me such as 'What time is it?
45 Is Chicken the Thracian a match for Syrus? The morning frosts are
nippy now for those who don't take enough care'; and such things
as are safely dropped in a leaky ear. Throughout all this time, every
day and every hour, our friend has been more and more the victim of
envy. If he'd watched the games with him or played ball with him in
the Campus, every mouth would cry, 'Some people have all the luck!'
50 A chilly rumour runs from the Rostra through the streets: any man
who meets me asks my opinion: 'My good sir, for as one who comes
into closer contact with the gods you ought to know, have you heard
any news about the Dacians?' 'Not a thing, I assure you.' 'Ah, what
a joker you will always be!' But may all the gods drive me to distrac-
55 tion if I've heard a word. 'Tell me now, is it in Sicily or in the land of
Italy that Caesar means to give the veterans the farms he has prom-
ised?' When I declare on oath that I know nothing, they marvel at me
as, believe it or not, the one man on earth in possession of a silence
extraordinarily profound.

With occupations like these I waste my day pitifully, while I utter
60 prayer after prayer: 'O my country estate, when shall I set eyes on
you? When shall I be free to drink sweet forgetfulness of life's wor-
ries, now with books of ancient authors, now with sleep and hours
of idleness! Oh, when shall beans, Pythagoras' kinsmen, be served
65 to me, and with them greens well oiled with fat bacon! O nights and
feasts of the gods! When I myself and my friends dine before my own
household god and feed my cheeky house-bred slaves, after making
a food-offering. Just as each of them pleases, the guests drain the
cups, well watered or not at all, not bound by mad laws, whether one
70 brave fellow takes his cups strong or grows mellow more happily with
moderate ones. And so conversation arises, not about other people's
villas or town houses, or whether Lepos dances badly or not; rather
our discussions are about matters that concern us more, and which it
would be bad not to know: whether it is wealth or virtue that makes
75 men happy; or what attracts us to friendships, self-interest, or an
upright character; and what is the nature of goodness and what its
highest form.

My neighbour Cervius on such occasions prattles on with old
wives' tales that fit the case. For if someone praises the wealth of

Arellius, not realizing the anxiety it causes, he begins in this fash-
ion: 'They say that once upon a time a country mouse welcomed a 80
town mouse into his humble hole, host and guest both old friends.
A rough fellow and careful with his store he was yet capable of
relaxing his tight nature with acts of hospitality. Let me not detain
you. He did not grudge his hoard of chickpeas or long oats, and,
bringing in his mouth a dried raisin and half-eaten scraps of bacon, 85
he served them, wishing by such variety of fare to overcome the dis-
dain of his friend, who with lordly tooth was barely touching each
item; meanwhile the father of the house himself was stretched out
on fresh straw and eating emmer wheat and darnel, leaving the
better parts of the feast to his guest. Finally the city mouse said to 90
him, "What pleasure can you have, my friend, in living in such hard
conditions on the ridge of a steep wood? Put your trust in me and
take to the road with me as your companion; since earthly creatures
live with mortal souls as their lot, and there is no escape from death 95
for great or small, therefore, my good fellow, while you may, live a
happy life amid joyful things; live mindful of how brief your time
is." When these words had struck home with the countryman, he
leapt light-footed from his house; then the pair of them carried on
to the end of the journey they had planned, eager to creep under
the walls of the city by night. And now night held the mid-space of 100
heaven, when the two planted their footsteps in a wealthy mansion
where covers dyed with rich scarlet blazed on top of ivory couches,
and many dishes were left over from a dinner of the previous night, 105
lying in baskets that were piled up aside. So when the townsman had
made his guest seated, stretched out on purple covers, he bustled to
and fro like a servant with tunic tucked up, serving one course after
another and performing all the duties of a home-bred slave, first lick-
ing everything he serves. His friend lay back, delighted by his change 110
of fortune, and in his prosperous state played the happy guest, when
suddenly a monstrous banging of the doors sent both of them tum-
bling from their couches. Terrified, they ran the length of the room,
and still more they panicked, blood deserting their cheeks, when the
lofty dwelling rang to the baying of Molossian hounds. Then the 115
countryman said, "I don't need this kind of life; goodbye to you: my
wood and hole, secure from alarms, will keep me content with simple
vetch."

SATIRE 7

'I've been listening for a while now and wanting to say a few things to
you but as a slave I've been afraid to.' Is that Davus? 'Yes, it's Davus,
a bought slave but one who's a friend to his master and an honest
fellow, that is, honest enough not to be considered too good to live.'
5 Come, make use of the freedom December allows, as our forefathers
wanted it so; say your piece.

   'Some men persist in delighting in vice and eagerly pursue their
chosen course; most waver, at one time aiming at the right, at others
yielding to the wrong. So Priscus, who often got noticed for wear-
10 ing three rings but sometimes for keeping his left hand bare, lived so
unpredictably that he would change his stripe each hour, emerging
from a stately mansion only to bury himself suddenly in some dive
that a fairly respectable freedman could barely come out of without
tongues wagging; now choosing to be a philanderer in Rome, now to
live as a man of letters in Athens, he was a fellow born when every
15 single Vertumnus was against him. The jester Volanerius, after the
gout he had earned had crippled his finger-joints, kept a man hired at
a daily wage to pick up the dice for him and put them in their box; the
more persistent he was in pursuing the same vices, the less unhappy
20 he felt and the more well-off than the man who struggles with rope
now taut, now slack.'

   Won't you tell me today what all this gibberish is aiming at, you
con-man? 'At you, I say once more.' How's that, you rogue? 'You
praise the fortune and character of the people of old, and yet you'd
also refuse every time, were some god suddenly to take you back to
25 those times, either because you don't really feel that what you pro-
claim is the sounder course or because you are shaky in defending
what's right and stick fast in the mire while longing vainly to pluck
the sole of your foot out of it. In Rome you yearn to be in the country,
in the country you praise the distant city to the stars without a sec-
30 ond's thought. If it happens that no invitations to dinner come your
way at all, you praise your carefree greens and, as though you wore
chains when going anywhere, call yourself so lucky and hug yourself
at not having to go out boozing somewhere. But should Maecenas bid
you to join him for dinner late, just as the lamps are about to be lit,
35 it's "Won't someone fetch me oil quicker? Isn't anyone listening?" as

you rant in a loud voice before scurrying away. Mulvius and his fellow
parasites take their leave, cursing you in language not to be repeated.
"It's true," he would say, "I admit it, I'm an inconstant fellow, led by
his stomach, my nose leans back at a savoury smell, I'm weak, lazy,
and, if you like, call me a greedy-guts into the bargain. But when 40
you're the same as me or maybe worse, why should you presume to
attack me as if you are superior and seek to cover up your vice with
fine words?" And what if you're found out to be a greater fool than
even I, who cost you five hundred drachmas? Don't try to scare me
with a look; keep your hand and temper in check while I unfold the 45
lessons taught me by Crispinus' doorkeeper.

'You are captivated by another man's wife, Davus by a whore:
which one of us is more deserving of the cross for his sin? When in-
sistent nature has made me stiff, whatever woman, naked in the lamp's
bright light, has taken my swollen tail's blows, or, entering into the
spirit, with bouncing bottom has ridden me on my back as her horse,
she lets me go with no harm to my reputation and no worry that some- 50
one richer or more good-looking may piss in the same place. As for
you, once you've thrown off your badges of rank, your knight's ring
and Roman dress, and reveal yourself, not as a juror, but as a Dama,
a fellow of no breeding, your scented head concealed by your cloak, 55
aren't you what your disguise suggests? With fear in your heart you are
let into the house, trembling to your bones as panic contends with lust.
What difference does it make whether you sell yourself as a gladi-
ator to be scorched with whips and killed by the sword, or, shut up
in a demeaning chest where the maid who shares her mistress' guilty 60
secret has stowed you away, you squat with crouched head touching
your knees? Does the erring lady's husband have lawful power over
both parties? His power over her lover is still more justified. It's not
the woman, after all, who changes her clothes or position, or who lies
on top as she sins. Because the woman is afraid of you and doesn't 65
trust you, her lover, will you deliberately shove your head in the
stocks and put in the hands of a furious master, not just your body,
but all your fortune, your life, your reputation? Suppose you escape:
you'll be afraid, I don't doubt, and take care having learned your
lesson: no, you'll look for chances of being able to know fear again and
again to come to ruin, you slave time and again! What wild beast that 70
has once broken its chains and escaped has the perversity to return
to them?

' "I'm no adulterer," you say. And I'm no thief, believe me, when I wisely pass by silver plate: remove the risk and in no time at all our nature will leap out, the reins once removed, and go where it will. Are
75 you my master, someone who is subject to the rule of so many men, so many things, whom a magistrate's rod of liberty, laid on three or even four times, would never rid of wretched fear? Consider this point, too, no less valid than those I've stated: for whether the man who does a slave's bidding is a "deputy", as you free men put it, or a "co-slave",
80 which am I to you? It's clear enough that you, who give me orders, are the miserable servant of another and, like a wooden puppet, are moved by strings that other hands pull.

'Who, then, is the free man? The wise man, who wields authority over himself, who has no fear of poverty or death or chains, who is bold
85 enough to stand up to his passions and to hold honours in contempt, who is a whole in himself, smooth and round, so that nothing from outside can get a purchase on his polished surface, and who makes any attack of Fortune fall ineffectually away. Can you recognize any of
90 these virtues as your own? A woman asks you for five talents, harasses you, drives you away from her door and drenches you in cold water, then summons you back again: wrest your neck from this shameful yoke; "I'm free, free," come on, say it. You can't; for your mind is driven hard by a pitiless master and he applies the sharp spurs when you are weary and urges you on when you resist.

95 'Or when you languish, you lunatic, in admiration of a paint-ing by Pausias, how is it you offend less than I, when with strain-ing knees I stare in wonder at battles involving Fulvius and Rutuba or Pacideianus, painted in red ochre or charcoal, just as if they were really fighting, striking out and parrying as they brandish their weap-
100 ons, proper heroes? A "good for nothing dawdler", is what they call Davus; but you yourself get described as a discriminating judge of old masters, a true aficionado. I'm a wastrel if I'm seduced by the smell of a hot cake: does your strength of character, your heroic virtue, resist the allure of rich dinners? Giving way to the belly's demands
105 is more dangerous to me. Why? My back gets a beating, you see. But don't you get punished just as much when you hunt out those fine foods that cannot be bought cheaply? Take my word for it, an endless succession of banquets begins to turn to gall, and the feet that have been duped refuse to support the weight of the over-indulged body. Or is it the fault of the slave-boy who as night falls swaps for grapes

the body-scraper he has stolen? Does the man who sells his estates 110
to comply with his stomach's demands have nothing of the slave
in him?

'Then there's the fact that you can't bear your own company for an
hour, you can't make proper use of your leisure-time, and you try to
shun yourself like a runaway or truant slave, seeking to baffle anxiety
now with wine, now with sleep: all for nothing; for the black compan- 115
ion dogs your steps and gives pursuit when you run away.'

Where can I get hold of a stone? 'What do you need that for?'
Where can I get arrows? 'Either the man is crazy or he's composing
verse.' Clear off from here double quick or else you'll make up the
ninth labourer on my Sabine farm.

SATIRE 8

How did you like your dinner with the wealthy Nasidienus? For when
I sought to have you as my own dinner-guest I was told you were
drinking there yesterday from midday. 'So much so that never in my
life have I had a more enjoyable time.' Tell me, if it's no trouble, what
tasty dish first won round your angry stomach.

'To start with, boar from Lucania; it was caught, as the father of 5
the feast kept telling us, when a gentle wind from the south was blow-
ing. Around it were sharp-tasting things, turnips, lettuces, radishes,
such condiments as give the edge to a jaded appetite, parsnip, fish-
pickle, lees of Coan wine. When these had been cleared away, a slave 10
with his tunic tucked up high wiped the maple table thoroughly with
a crimson cloth, and a second gathered up anything that lay useless
and might cause the guests offence; then, like a maiden of Attica with
the sacred vessels of Ceres, dusky Hydaspes steps forward, carrying
Caecuban wine, and Alcon, carrying Chian wine without sea water. At 15
this point our host said, "If Alban or Falernian wine is more to your
taste than what has been served, Maecenas, we have both."' 'Ah, how
the rich should be pitied! But I'm keen to know, Fundanius, who your
table-companions were with whom you passed a lovely time.

'I was at the top and next to me was Viscus of Thurii, while below, 20
if I recall, was Varius; with Servilius the Jester was Vibidius, the extras
brought along by Maecenas. Above our host was Nomentanus, below
him the Hog, who made us laugh by swallowing entire cheesecakes at

25 one go; Nomentanus was there to point out with his forefinger any-
thing that should happen to escape our attention: for the rest of the
crowd, ourselves, I mean, were dining on fowl, oysters, fish, which
harboured a taste far different from any we knew; this was apparent
30 right from the start, when he passed me livers of plaice and turbot
that I hadn't tasted before. After this he informed me that honey-
apples are red if they're picked when the moon is on the wane. What
difference that makes you would better hear from the man in person.
Then Vibidius says to Jester: "Unless we drink him bankrupt, we'll
35 die unavenged," and he calls for larger cups. Then did paleness invade
the features of the caterer, who feared nothing as much as hard drink-
ers, either because they're too free with their insults or because strong
40 wines dull the refined palate. Vibidius and Jester, with all following
suit, upend whole jugs of wine into Allifanian cups; but no harm was
done to the flagons by the guests on the bottom couch.

'Then is served a moray eel, outstretched on a platter, and sur-
rounded by swimming scampi. At this point the master says: "It was
caught with the roe still inside, as after spawning it will deteriorate
45 in the flesh. These are the ingredients of the sauce: oil from the first
pressing of the Venafran cellar; sauce from the juices of fish from
Spain; five-year-old wine, but produced this side of the sea, while it
is being warmed (after heating Chian suits better than anything else);
50 white pepper, with vinegar made from the fermenting of grapes from
Methymna. I was first to demonstrate the need to boil in the sauce
fresh green rocket and bitter elecampane, while Curtillus advocated
sea urchins, unwashed, as the yield of the seashell is better than fish-
brine."

'This was the moment that the tapestries spread above fell heavily
55 on to the plate, bringing down more black dust than the north wind
blows up from Campania's fields. We feared worse to come, but on
realizing there was no danger, we recovered ourselves. Rufus lowered
his head and began to weep, as if at the death of a son before his
60 time. What would the end have been, if Nomentanus had not, like a
philosopher, raised his friend's spirits like this? "Alas, Fortune, what
god shows us more cruelty than you? How you always enjoy making
sport of men's affairs!" Varius could scarcely suppress his laughter
with his napkin. Jester, who looks down his nose at everything, was
65 saying, "These are the terms of life, and this is why your effort will
never be equalled by your fame. To think that, just to ensure grand

entertainment for me, you should be racked and tortured by all manner of anxiety, that the bread should not be served burnt, or the sauce badly seasoned, that all the slaves should be properly dressed 70 and have smart hair when they serve! Then there are these accidents to consider, the curtains falling down, as they just have, or a stable-boy tripping up and smashing a plate. But someone who entertains guests is like a general: misfortune usually lays bare his talent, good fortune usually conceals it."

'To this Nasidienus replied, "May the gods reward you with every 75 prayer you make! You are so kind a man, so civil a guest," and he called for his slippers. That was when on every couch you would have seen the buzz of whispers exchanged in confidential ears.' I'd have preferred to watch no other shows than these; but come on, tell me the things you found to laugh at after these. 'While Vibidius is asking the 80 slaves whether the flagon has also been broken, as he's not being given any cups when he asks for them, and while we laugh at pretended jokes, egged on by Jester, back you come, Nasidienus, with altered looks, like a man intending to mend bad luck by means of skill: then 85 follow slaves, carrying on a huge trencher the disjointed limbs of a crane sprinkled generously with salt, and with meal, and the liver of a white goose, fattened on rich figs, and the forelegs of hares torn off, to make more agreeable eating than if someone ate them with the 90 loins; then we saw blackbirds served up with their breasts burnt, and wood-pigeons without the rumps, real delicacies, if only the master of the house had not given us an account of their origins and properties; off we ran, taking our revenge on him by tasting nothing whatever, as though Canidia, worse than African snakes, had breathed her poison 95 on them.'

EPISTLES

BOOK 1

EPISTLE 1

Maecenas, celebrated by my earliest Muse and intended theme of my last, you seek to shut me up again in my old school, though sufficiently proven and presented with the wooden baton. My age and desires are not the same. Veianius lies hidden in the country, having hung up his weapons on the door of Hercules' temple, so that he 5 doesn't have to beg the crowd again and again at the end of the match to be discharged. I have someone who constantly makes my well-rinsed ear ring with his advice: 'Turn loose the ageing horse if you are sensible in time, in case he stumbles at the last, broken-winded, and invites mockery.'

So now I lay aside both verses and all other trifles; what is right 10 and fitting, that's my interest and pursuit, and in this I'm wholly absorbed; I store up and organize material so that I may be able to draw upon it before long. And should you happen to ask who is my leader and whose house offers me shelter, there's no master I'm bound to swear loyalty to, and wherever the weather drives me is where I seek 15 a roof. Sometimes I become active and take the plunge into civic life, an unwavering guardian and attendant of true virtue; sometimes unconsciously I slip back into the rules of Aristippus and I try to place circumstances under my control, not vice versa.

As the night seems long to those whose mistress proves false, as 20 the day protracted to those who work for hire, as the year tedious to a minor hemmed in by his mother's strict supervision, so thankless and slow flow for me the hours that put off my hope and intention of applying myself with vigour to doing a thing that benefits alike the 25 poor, alike the rich, but, if neglected, will harm alike young and old. It remains that I should seek guidance and consolation for myself from these simple lessons.

You may not be able to strain your gaze as far as Lynceus could, but that wouldn't be a reason to turn up your nose at having your eyes anointed if blear-eyed; and, because you despair of matching 30 unbeaten Glycon's physique, you wouldn't say no to keeping your

body free from the knots of gout. It's possible to take some steps
forward, even if we're not allowed to go any further.

Let's say your heart is in a fever of greed and miserable longing for
what you lack: well, there are spells and sayings to enable you to soothe
35 the pain and dispel a great part of the malady. Ambition makes you
swollen: specific remedies exist that will be able to restore your health
if with due purification you read the booklet three times. Whether
you're the slave of envy, anger, sloth, wine, or lust, no one is so savage
40 that he cannot be tamed, if only he lends a patient ear to treatment.

The beginning of virtue is the avoidance of vice, and the begin-
ning of wisdom to have got rid of folly. You see how anxiously, how
energetically, you seek to avoid those dangers you believe to be most
serious, a handful of cash in the bank and ignominious rejection at the
45 polls. Tireless trader that you are, you rush to furthest India, braving
sea, rocks, fire to keep poverty at bay: are you not prepared to learn
and listen and trust one who is wiser, in order to avoid caring about
50 the things you foolishly admire and crave? What brawler who goes
the round of the villages and crossways would turn up his nose at
being crowned with an Olympic wreath, if he had the hope or option
of winning the much-prized palm without a struggle? Silver is less
valuable than gold and gold than virtue.

'O citizens, citizens, first you must seek money; virtue after cash':
55 this is the rule proclaimed by Janus from top to bottom, this the
instruction that young and old alike chant back, dangling satchels
and slate from left arm. You have sense, you have morals, you have
eloquence and honesty, but you are a few thousands short of the four
hundred; you will prove to be a nonentity. Yet boys at play cry, 'Play
60 by the rules and you'll be ruler!' Let this be our wall of bronze, to
have no guilty secrets, no crime to turn us pale. Tell me, please, is
Roscius' law better or the jingle of schoolboys that offers a kingdom
to those who do right, a chant repeated by men like the manly Curius
65 and Camillus? Is it better advice you get from the man who tells
you to get wealth, wealth by honest means if you can, if not, however
you can, wealth, so you can have a closer view of Pupius' lamentable
plays, or the man who helpfully encourages and makes you fit to defy
capricious Fortune, standing free and straight-backed?

70   But if by chance the Roman people should ask me why I make use
of the same colonnades as they, but don't have the same opinions, why
I don't follow what they themselves like or shun what they dislike,

I would give them the reply that once upon a time the cunning fox
gave the sick lion: 'Because I'm frightened by these tracks that all lead 75
towards your den and none away from it.' You are a beast with many
heads. For what and whom should I follow? Some men get pleasure
from taking state-contracts, others with cakes and fruit hunt miserly
widows, and catch old men to send to their game reserves; many have 80
their wealth increase by means of interest no one notices. But granted
that men are swayed by different aims and different interests, can the
same people persist for an hour in approving of the same things? 'No
bay in the world outshines lovely Baiae's.' If this is said by a rich man,
lake and sea feel to their cost the hasty master's amorous gaze; but if 85
his morbid fancy grants authorization, tomorrow it's tools up for you
workmen and off to Teanum. If the marriage bed in honour of his
house's attendant spirit stands in his hall, nothing, he says, is finer,
nothing better than the life of a bachelor; if it doesn't, he swears that
only married men have a comfortable life. What knot am I to use to 90
hold fast this face-changing Proteus? What of the poor man? Have a
laugh: he changes garret, bed, baths, and barber, he hires a boat and
gets just as sick as the rich man transported in his yacht.

If I come your way with my hair cut unevenly by some barber, you 95
laugh; if by chance my brand-new tunic conceals a tattered shirt, or
my toga hangs awkwardly and askew, you laugh: how do you take it
when my judgement is at odds with itself, disowning what it desired,
eager to reclaim what it lately rejected, ebbing and flowing and clash-
ing with the whole system of life, knocking down, building up, and 100
changing square to round? You think my unreasonableness is the
usual thing and neither laugh nor believe I need a doctor or a guard-
ian appointed by the praetor, though you are the one who keeps my
fortunes safe and gets angry at a badly cut fingernail of the friend who 105
hangs upon and is centred on you.

To sum up, the wise man is inferior to Jupiter alone, being rich,
free, honoured, beautiful, in short a king of kings: above all he is
sound, unless troubled by a cold.

EPISTLE 2

Lollius Maximus, while you have been declaiming at Rome, Praeneste
has found me rereading the poet of the Trojan War; he states what is

morally beautiful, what is morally shameful, what is expedient, and
what is not, more plainly and better than Chrysippus and Crantor.
5 Let me tell you why this is the opinion I have formed, if you don't
have something to occupy your attention.

The tale in which Greece clashed in protracted war with a barbar-
ian land because of Paris' love embraces the fiery passions of foolish
kings and peoples. Antenor recommends cutting off the cause of the
10 war: what of Paris? He says nothing can compel him to reign in safety
and to live in happiness. Nestor is eager to conclude the dispute
between the son of Peleus and the sons of Atreus; the first is fired by
love, but both in common by anger. Whatever folly the kings commit,
15 the Greeks count the cost. By means of faction, trickery, crime, lust,
and anger wrong is done inside and outside the walls of Troy.

On the other hand, in Ulysses he has set before us an instructive
model of the power of wisdom and virtue; he subdued Troy and, exer-
20 cising forethought, observed the cities and manners of many men; he
endured many hardships while he strove to win for himself and his
men a return home across the broad seas but could never be drowned
in the waves of adversity. You know the Sirens' songs and Circe's
cups; had he drunk these in foolish greed along with his comrades,
25 he would have become the ugly and brutish slave of a harlot mis-
tress and lived as an unclean dog or a sow that loves the mire. We are
simply ciphers, born to consume the fruits of earth, Penelope's good-
for-nothing suitors, young courtiers of Alcinous excessively busied in
30 looking after their physical needs, who thought it splendid to sleep till
midday and to induce anxiety to rest to the sound of the lyre.

To cut a man's throat, robbers stir themselves before night is gone;
to save your own life, won't you wake up? And yet if you won't do this
when you're in health, you'll be running when suffering from dropsy;
35 and if you don't call for a book and lamp before daylight, if you don't
direct your attention to honourable studies and pursuits, envy or love
will keep you awake in torment. For why is it you are in a hurry to
remove things that hurt the eye but, if anything eats into your soul,
40 you put off the time for effecting a cure for a year? A task begun is
half done: dare to be wise: begin! The man who postpones the hour
for right living is like the countryman waiting for the river to stop
flowing: but on it glides and shall glide, rolling its waters for all time.

45 We are on the lookout for money and for a rich wife to bear us chil-
dren, and wild woodland is brought into subjection by the plough.

But the man whose lot it is to have what is sufficient should pray for nothing more. No house or estate, no pile of bronze or gold has ever relieved the sick body of an owner of its fevers, or his mind of its worries. The possessor must have good health if he means to enjoy 50 the stores he has gathered. If a man is subject to fears and cravings, he gets as much pleasure from his house and fortune as a man with eye-trouble does from paintings, or that a gout-sufferer from foot-warmers, or that someone whose ears are painfully blocked gets from the playing of the lyre. Unless the receptacle is clean, whatever you pour into it turns sour.

Scorn pleasures: pleasure does harm when the cost is pain. The 55 greedy man is always in need: look for a fixed limit in your heart. The envious man grows thin when his neighbour's fortunes grow fat: Sicily's tyrants never thought up a torture greater than envy. The man who will not check his anger will wish undone what his indig- 60 nant mood prompted, when he was quick to seek retribution by force for his unappeased hatred. Anger is short-lived madness: rule your passion, for if it does not obey you, it gives you commands; restrain it with a bridle, restrain it, I tell you, with chains.

A horse of pliant neck is guided by its trainer, and readily learns to 65 go the way its rider indicates; the young hound marked out for hunting does service in the woods from the time it first barked at a stag's hide in the yard. Now, while still in your youth, drink in my words with a clean heart, now trust yourself to your betters. The wine-jar will long keep the fragrance of what tinged it for the first time. But 70 whether you lag behind or vigorously press ahead, I neither wait for the slowcoach nor tread on the pace-setter's heels.

EPISTLE 3

Julius Florus, I'm eager to know in what region of the world Claudius, stepson of Augustus, does service abroad. Is it Thrace that detains you, and the Hebrus, bound in snowy fetters, or the straits that run between the neighbouring towers, or Asia's fertile plains and hills? 5

What is the learned suite composing by way of literary work? This too I wish to know. Who takes it upon himself to write of Augustus' exploits? Who extends the fame of his years of peace and years of war to distant ages? What is being produced by Titius, soon sure to

10   win renown among Romans? He had no fear of drinking deep from
     Pindar's spring, and dared to scorn open pools and streams. How is
     his health? Does he think of me? Does he attempt with the Muse's
     favour to fit Theban metres to the Latin lyre, or does he swell and
15   work out his rage in the art of tragedy? Tell me, what keeps Celsus
     busy? I've warned him and must warn him many times more to look
     for stores of his own, and to avoid touching whatever writings Palatine
     Apollo has taken under his charge, or else some day perhaps the flock
     of birds will come to reclaim the plumage that is theirs, and the poor
20   crow, stripped of the bright feathers he stole, becomes a laughing
     stock. What are you venturing on yourself? What beds of thyme are
     you busily flitting round? You have a considerable talent, one that
     has been well tilled and not left to become overgrown and unsightly.
     Whether you sharpen your tongue for pleading cases or practise to
25   give an opinion on civil law or fashion charming verse, you will win
     the first prize of the victor's ivy. But if you could lay aside your cares,
     those cold compresses on your mind, you would rise to where heav-
     enly wisdom would lead you. This task, this pursuit let us pursue
     with eagerness, small and great alike, if we would live in our country's
     esteem as well as our own.
30   This too you must write in your reply, whether you have as much
     regard for Munatius as you ought. Or does your goodwill, like a wound
     not quite stitched, fail to close properly and tear open once more? Is it
     hot-bloodedness that drives the pair of you on, wild horses with necks
35   untamed, or a general ignorance of life? Wherever on earth you are,
     too good a pair to break the bond of brotherhood, a heifer vowed for
     the altar is being fattened for your return.

                                EPISTLE 4

     Albius, genial critic of my satires, what should I say you are up to
     these days in the country round Pedum? Writing something to sur-
     pass the work of Cassius of Parma's pen, or strolling peacefully among
5   the healthy woods, your mind fixed on all that befits one who is wise
     and good? You didn't used to be someone without intelligence. The
     gods gave you beauty, the gods gave you wealth and the art of enjoy-
     ment. What more would a fond nurse pray for her beloved charge if
     he can think rightly and express his feelings, if Fortune gives him in

abundance popularity, renown, good health, and a stylish way of life 10
thanks to a purse that is always full? In the course of hopes and anx-
ieties, of fears and fits of anger, believe that every day that dawns is
the last for you. The hour you don't hope to see will come as a bonus,
and make you glad, too.

As for me, whenever you want a laugh at a porker from Epicurus'
herd, make sure you come and see me, plump and sleek from looking 15
after my body's needs.

EPISTLE 5

If you can bring yourself to recline at my table on couches made by
Archias, and aren't afraid to dine from a modest dish on all sorts of
vegetables, then, Torquatus, I shall expect you at my house at the end
of the day. You will drink wine that was bottled in Taurus' second
consulship racked off between marshy Minturnae and Petrinum near 5
Sinuessa. But if you have anything better, have it sent, or else put
up with my regime. My hearth has long been spotless and the furni-
ture polished for you. Have done with airy hopes and the struggle for
wealth, and Moschus' case: tomorrow by reason of Caesar's birth it is
a holiday that gives permission to lie in; you shall have leave without 10
penalty to prolong the summer night in friendly conversation.

What's the good of wealth to me, if I'm not allowed to profit from
it? The man who refrains from spending money and is too tight
with his purse-strings through worrying about his heir resembles a
madman. I shall begin the drinking and scattering of flowers, and 15
I shall allow myself to be thought of as reckless, if you wish. What
cannot be managed by drunkenness? It lays bare the heart's secrets,
bids hopes to be fulfilled, thrusts the coward onto the battlefield; it
relieves the troubled mind of its burden and teaches new skills. What
man has not been made eloquent by a brimming wine-cup, or free 20
when poverty seeks to imprison him?

Here is what I am under orders to provide, and willing and com-
petent for the task I am, that no faded coverlet or dirty napkin cause
you to wrinkle up your nose, that no tankard or plate should fail to
show you your reflection, that there should be no one to broadcast
beyond my doors what is said among trusting friends, that like may 25
meet and share a place with like. I will arrange for you to enjoy Butra's

company, and Septicius', and Sabinus' too, unless an earlier engage-
ment, or a girl he prefers, keeps him from attending: there's room as
well for several guests you may bring along, but dinner-parties that
are too crowded suffer from the smell of rank armpits.

30   Do write back, letting me know how large a gathering you would
like us to be, and, dropping all other business, use the back-door to
give that client who occupies your hall the slip.

EPISTLE 6

'Make an idol of nothing' is perhaps the one and only thing, Numicius,
that can make a man happy and keep him so. Yonder sun and stars and
seasons that pass in fixed degrees can be contemplated by some with-
5   out a trace of dread: what do you think of the earth's gifts, what of the
sea's, showering wealth on the distant Arabs and Indians, what of the
shows, the applause and favours of the friendly Roman people, in what
manner do you suppose they should be viewed, with what feelings and
eyes? He who fears their opposites is idolizing these things in much
10 the same way as he who desires them; in either case it is the thrill that
causes trouble, the moment either one of them is startled by some
unexpected appearance. Whether a man feels happiness or grief, desire
or fear, what does it matter, if, when he has seen something better or
worse than he expected, he stares at it with riveted eyes, paralysed in
15 body and mind? Let the wise man be called madman and the just man
unjust, should he pursue justice itself beyond due bounds.

       Off you go now, gaze admiringly on silver plate and antique marble,
bronzes and artworks, idolize gems and Tyrian dyes; take delight in
20 being stared at by countless eyes when you are chatting, make your
busy way to the forum early and to your home late, in case Mutus
reaps off more grain from the land his wife's dowry brought him, or
(how scandalous, considering he sprang from meaner stock!) he wins
your admiration rather than you his. All that lies beneath the earth,
25 time will bring into the light of day; what now shines bright, it will
bury deep in obscurity. When Agrippa's colonnade and Appius' high-
way have looked on your well-known form, it still remains for you to
go where Numa and Ancus have passed down before.

       If your chest or kidneys are afflicted by a sharp disease, seek a cure
for the disease. If you want to live in a desirable manner, well, who

doesn't? If virtue alone can provide this, be bold, drop trifles and get 30
on with it.

If, just as you think a sacred grove is mere firewood, so you regard
virtue as only words, then watch out that a rival doesn't make harbour
ahead of you and you lose your ventures from Cibyra and Bithynia;
let a thousand talents round off the sum and as many again, let a third 35
thousand be added and then enough to square the pile. Obviously
a wife and dowry, credit and friends, birth and looks are the gift of
queen Cash, while Persuasion and Venus lend beauty to the well-
to-do man. The Cappadocian king is rich in slaves but short of cash:
don't be like him. Lucullus, as the story goes, when asked if he could 40
lend a large number of cloaks for the theatre, said, 'How can I provide
so many? Still, I'll have a look and I'll send along what I find that I
have.' A short time later he wrote that he had five thousand cloaks
available; the man giving the show should take some or all of them.
It's an impoverished house where there isn't much to spare, much 45
that escapes the owner's eye and benefits pilferers. So, if money alone
can make and keep a man happy, you should be first to return each
new day to this task and last to abandon it.

If it is pomp and popularity that confer happiness on a man, let 50
us buy a slave to call off names in our ear, to nudge us in the left side
and press us to stretch out our hand across the stepping stones: 'This
one has influence in the Fabian tribe, that one in the Veline; this other
will give the bundle of rods to whomever he pleases, and will snatch
the curule ivory from whoever he wants without giving it a second
thought.' Throw in 'Brother!' 'Father!' and deftly adopt each man 55
according to his age.

If the man who dines well lives well, then, the moment day breaks,
let's be off to where our appetite leads, let's go to get fish or game, just
like Gargilius in the story: at first light he would tell his slaves to pack
up hunting nets and spears and make their way through the forum
crammed with people, so that, with the same crowd looking on, one mule 60
of all the train might return carrying on its back a boar he had bought.
Let's bathe when our stomachs are full, their contents not yet digested,
forgetting what is proper and what not, deserving to be recorded on
the wax of Caere, like the wicked crew of Ithacan Ulysses who valued
forbidden pleasure more highly than the land of their birth.

If, as Mimnermus thinks, there is no joy without love and merriment, 65
in love and merriment spend your days.

Live long and fare you well. If you know anything better than the
things I've just been discussing, be a good fellow and pass it on: if not,
join me in following these.

EPISTLE 7

Though I promised to be in the country for just a few days, I am false
to my word and have been missed for the whole of August. And yet,
5 if you want me to live sound and in good health, then, Maecenas,
the indulgence you grant me when ill you will grant me when fear-
ing for my health, while the first figs and the heat make the funeral
marshal a conspicuous figure with his lictors' dingy togas, while every
father and fond mother is pale with fear for the children, while atten-
tiveness in carrying out duties and the petty business of the forum
10 bring on fevers and unseal wills. But if winter powders the Alban hills
with snow, your own bard will go down to the seacoast and take care
of himself, huddled up with his books: he will visit you once more,
dear friend, if you permit, together with the west winds and the first
swallow.

15   Not in the way a Calabrian invited his guest to eat his pears have
you made me rich in land. 'Do eat some, please.' 'I've done well, thank
you.' 'Oh, you must take away as many as you like.' 'No, thank you.'
'Your little ones will be delighted to see you bring them these little
presents.' 'I'm just as obliged to you for your gift as if I were being
sent on my way loaded down.' 'Just as you like; you'll be leaving them
20 for the pigs to eat up today.' The foolish spendthrift makes a present
of what he despises and has no use for: a field sown like this yields
and every year will yield only ingratitude. The good and wise man
says he is ready to help the deserving and knows besides the differ-
ence between coins and lupine seeds. I shall continue to show myself
25 deserving, considering as well my benefactor's great name. But if you
will never allow me to leave you, you must give me back strong lungs,
black hair well forward on the brow, you must give back sweet talk,
give back graceful laughter, and the shedding of tears in the midst of
drinking for wanton Cinara going off with another lover.

30   It happened once that a lean little vixen had crept through a narrow
chink into a bin of grain and, having fed herself, was striving with
swollen stomach to get out again but without success. A weasel hard

by remarked to her, 'If you want to escape from there, be sure to
return to the narrow hole as thin as you were when you entered it.' If
I am taken to task by this parable, then I hand over everything I have
had from you; I neither praise the sleep of humble folk when I'm full 35
of fattened fowls nor exchange my ease and freedom for the wealth of
Arabia. Many a time you have commended me for being modest and
have heard yourself called to your face 'patron' and 'father', nor have
I been a word less appreciative in your absence: examine whether I
can restore your gifts cheerfully.

It was a good answer given by Telemachus, son of the long-suffering 40
Ulysses, 'Ithaca is not a place suited to horses, as it does not extend
over level ground for racing or abound in rich grass: son of Atreus,
I shall leave you your gifts as being more suited to you.' Humble
things are appropriate for one who is humble: what pleases me now is 45
not queenly Rome, but quiet Tibur or peaceful Tarentum.

Philippus, the famous pleader of cases, a man of vigour and cour-
age, was once returning home from work in the early afternoon. As
he was now advanced in years, he was complaining that the Carinae
were too far from the Forum, when, so the story goes, he caught sight
of a close-shaven man in the shade of a barber's empty shop who was 50
quietly cleaning his own fingernails with a pocket knife. 'Demetrius,'
he said (this lad was not backward in catching his master's orders),
'off you go, find out and bring me word: where he comes from, who
he is, of what status, who his father is and who his patron.' He goes, 55
comes back, gives his report, that the man is called Vulteius Mena
and is an auctioneer, of modest means and blameless record, known
to work hard and to take it easy on the right occasion, to make money
and to spend it, to take pleasure in his humble friends and a home
of his own, and, after business is concluded, in the games and the
Campus. 'I'd like to hear all you tell me from the man's own lips; 60
invite him to come to dinner.' Mena can't really believe it, and turns
it over in his mind in silent amazement. In short, he replies: 'No,
thank you.' 'Can *he* decline *my* invitation?' 'He does, the insensitive
fellow, and either shows you no respect or is afraid of you.' The next
morning Philippus surprised Vulteius as he was selling cheap odds 65
and ends to the common folk in their working clothes and was first
to make his greeting. Vulteius put forward his work and the ties of
his job as his excuse for not having visited Philippus that morning,
in short for not having seen him first. 'On this one condition you

70 may assume I have forgiven you, that you have dinner with me today.'
'As you please.' 'Well, then, come mid-afternoon; for the moment,
carry on, work hard and add to your wealth!' When he arrived for
dinner, he chatted about anything that came into his head and then at
last was sent off to his bed.

Once he had been seen to run regularly like a fish to the concealed
75 hook, in the morning a client and by now a constant guest at table, he
was invited to accompany Philippus to his estates near Rome when
the Latin Festival had been appointed. From his seat in the carriage
drawn by ponies he poured endless praise on the Sabine country and
air. Philippus noted this and smiled, and while he sought to give him-
80 self relief and amusement from any source, by giving Vulteius seven
thousand sesterces and offering him a loan of a further seven, he per-
suaded him to buy a small farm. Not to detain you too long with a
rambling tale, our stylish friend changes into a country fellow and
prattles away about nothing but furrows and vineyards; he makes
85 ready his elms, almost kills himself in his pursuits, and ages through
his passion for gain. But when he had lost his sheep to theft and his
nanny-goats to disease, when the harvest had fooled his hopes and
ploughing had worn out his ox, troubled by his losses he grabbed his
riding horse at dead of night and set off in a temper for Philippus'
90 house. As soon as Philippus saw him, covered in scurf and unshaven,
he said, 'Vulteius, you seem hard-worked and over frugal to me.'
'Believe me, patron, you'd call me wretched, if you meant to give me
95 my true name! And so I beg and implore you in the name of your
Attendant Spirit, of your right hand, of the gods of your hearth and
home, restore me to my former way of life.'

Let the man who has once seen how much what he has given up
outdoes what he has sought return speedily and claim once more what
he has abandoned. It is right that each man should measure himself
by his own foot-rule and standard.

EPISTLE 8

Muse, at my request duly convey greetings and good wishes to Celsus
Albinovanus, friend and secretary of Nero.

If he asks how I am, tell him I may be promising many fine things,
but the life I'm leading is neither morally proper nor agreeable; not

because hail has beaten down my vines or the heat has nipped my olives, 5
and not because my cattle sicken in the distant pastures, but because,
less sound in mind than in all my body, I wish to hear nothing, to
learn nothing, that may alleviate my illness; I quarrel with doctors who
care about my health, get angry with friends, because they are eager to 10
rescue me from my life-threatening coma; I pursue what has done me
harm and shun what I believe will do me good, and, inconstant as the
wind, I love Tibur when in Rome and Rome when in Tibur.

After this ask him how his own health is, what luck he's having
in his duties and his own life, what impression he's making on the
young man and his suite. If he says, 'Things are fine,' be sure first 15
of all to show your pleasure, then to drop this warning in the dear
fellow's ears: 'As you put up with your fortune, Celsus, so we shall put
up with you.'

EPISTLE 9

Septimius apparently understands better than anyone else what value
you attach to me, Claudius. For when he asks, and by entreaty actu-
ally compels me to try to commend him and present him to you, as
one who is worthy of the character and family of Nero, whose choice
falls only on what is honourable, when he judges that I perform the 5
function of a closer friend, he sees what I am capable of and knows it
better than I do myself.

It's true, I gave him many reasons why I should be excused from
the duty and allowed to go; but I was afraid I might be thought to
have portrayed my influence as less than it is, concealing my own
capacities and obliging only myself. In this way, in my eagerness not 10
to be accused of a greater fault, I have stooped to the privileges of a
confidence bred by the city. But if you approve of this laying aside
of modesty at a friend's request, enrol him as one of your group and
regard him as a fine, brave fellow.

EPISTLE 10

To Fuscus, lover of the city, I, lover of the country, send my greet-
ings. In this one point, it's true, we differ considerably but in all else

we're practically twins, with the feelings of brothers—whatever one
5   says 'no' to, the other does too—we nod our assent together, a couple
of old familiar doves. You occupy the nest; I praise the brooks of the
lovely countryside, its woodland and rocks overgrown with moss. In
short, I know life and am a king the moment I leave behind those
10 things you extol to the heavens with loud applause, and, like the slave
who refuses the sacrificial cakes and runs away from his master the
priest, it is bread I want and now prefer to honeyed cakes.

If it is our duty to spend our life agreeably to nature, and our first
task is to find a site for building our house, do you know a place pref-
15 erable to the blissful countryside? Is there a place where the winters
are more mild, where a more welcome breeze tempers both the Dog-
star's fury and the Lion's motions, when once he has caught the sharp
rays of the sun and been roused to frenzy? Is there a place where
mean anxiety is less prone to distract our slumber? Is grass inferior in
20 fragrance or beauty to mosaics of African stone? Is it purer, the water
that strives to burst its leaden pipes in our streets, than that which
purls murmuring down a sloping brook? Clearly it is, for trees are
nursed amid the mottled columns, and praise is showered on houses
that have a view on to distant fields. Drive out nature though you will
25 with a pitchfork, yet she will always hurry back, and, before you know
it, will break through your perverse disdain in triumph.

The man who lacks the skill to compare with Sidonian purple
fleeces that drink up Aquinum's dye, will not suffer a loss more sure
or one closer to his heart than he who shall prove unable to distinguish
30 false from true. If a man has taken too much delight in Fortune's
smiles, he will reel under the shock when she changes. If something
wins your admiration, you will be loath to give it up. Avoid anything
grand: though your home be humble you may outrun in life's race
grandees and the friends of grandees.

35 The stag was a better fighter than the horse and used to drive him
from the pasture they shared, until the loser in this lengthy con-
test begged the assistance of man and accepted the bit; but after he
parted from his enemy in haughty triumph, he did not get rid of the
rider from his back or the bit from his mouth. In this way the man
40 whose fear of poverty makes him forfeit freedom, that surpasses the
wealth of mines, will in his greed carry a master and be a slave for
ever, because he does not know how to live on a little. If a man is not
content with his fortune, it will be like what happens sometimes with

a shoe, tripping him up if it is too big for his foot, and chafing him if it is too small. If your lot makes you happy, Aristius, you will live wisely, and you won't let me go on my way without a telling off, when I shall 45 be seen to be gathering more than enough and not calling a halt. Once a man has amassed money it gives him orders or does his bidding, though it deserves to follow rather than lead the twisted rope.

I am dictating these lines to you behind Vacuna's crumbling shrine, happy in everything else apart from not having your company to 50 share.

EPISTLE 11

What did you think of Chios, Bullatius, or of famous Lesbos, how did elegant Samos strike you, or Sardis, royal seat of Croesus, or Smyrna and Colophon, are they superior or inferior to their reputation? Do they all pale in significance compared to Mars' Field and the river Tiber? Or are you setting your heart on one of Attalus' cities, or does 5 Lebedus win your praise, wearied as you are by travel on sea and land? 'You know what Lebedus is like; a town more desolate than Gabii and Fidenae; but there I'd have been prepared to live, and, forgetting my friends and by them forgotten, to gaze out from the land at the sea's distant rage.' 10

But the man who makes his way to Rome from Capua will not be willing to stay in an inn just because he is spattered with mud and rain; and the man who has grown stiff with cold does not praise bakehouses and baths as furnishing in full a happy life. Again, if a stiff south wind 15 should have tossed you on the deep, that's no reason for selling your ship on the other side of the Aegean sea. For a man secure in health and position Rhodes and Mytilene in their beauty do just as much as a travelling cloak in summer, a training vest when snowy winds blow, the Tiber in winter, a stove in the month of August. While you may, 20 and while Fortune keeps a kind look on her face, at Rome you may politely reject Samos and Chios and Rhodes in their remoteness. And you, my friend, accept with grateful hand whatever hour the god has blessed you with, and do not put off pleasures to some unknown time, so that you may say, in whatever place you have been, you have lived happily; for if it is reason and forethought that take away our cares, 25 not a site that commands a wide sweep of ocean, it is their climate,

not their mind, that men change when they rush across the sea.
A busy idleness harasses us: with ships and four-horse chariots we
30 seek to live well. What you seek is here, it is at Ulubrae, if you don't
lack a well-balanced mind.

EPISTLE 12

If, Iccius, you are enjoying as you should the Sicilian produce you
collect for Agrippa, it is impossible that a greater abundance could
be bestowed on you by Jupiter. Have done with complaining: a man
is not poor if he possesses in full the right to enjoy things. If your
5 stomach, lungs, and feet are in good condition, the wealth of kings
will not be able to add anything greater to your store. But if, as may be
the case, you shun what is available to all and live on nettles and other
greens, you will go on living in such a way, even if Fortune's clear
10 stream suddenly floods you with gold, either because money cannot
change your nature or because in your eyes all else is inferior to virtue
alone.

We marvel that the cattle of Democritus ate up his farmland and
cornfields while his swift mind, separated from his body, roamed
abroad, whereas you, surrounded by the contagious itch for profit,
15 possess a far from trivial knowledge and still set your thoughts on
elevated things; what causes keep the sea from rising, what regulates
the year, whether the planets wander at large of their own accord or
at the bidding of some power, what hides the moon's orb in darkness,
what brings it into light, what is the meaning and what the effect of
20 the world's discordant harmony, whether it is Empedocles who is mad
or the brilliant Stertinius.

But whether it is fish, or leeks and onions that you butcher at
dinner, treat as a friend Pompeius Grosphus, and if he asks you for
anything, grant it freely; Grosphus will ask for nothing that is not
right and fair. The current price for friends is low, when good men
are in need of anything.
25 But so you may not be in ignorance of how the Roman state is
faring, the Cantabrian has been humbled by Agrippa's valour, the
Armenian by Claudius Nero's. Phraates on bent knee has accepted
the imperial sway of Caesar; golden Plenty pours forth her fruits on
Italy from brimming horn.

EPISTLE 13

As I instructed you many times and at length, Vinius, when you began your journey, you are to deliver these volumes duly under seal to Augustus if he is well, if he is in good humour, and, finally, if he asks for them; this is so that you should not blunder in your eagerness to please me and through officiousness bring resentment on my poor 5 writings by serving me with excessive zeal. If the weight of shouldering my books happens to gall you, fling them away rather than wildly throwing down your pack where you are told to deliver it, turning your father's name of Asina into a joke and becoming the talk of the town. Be sure to use your strength in traversing hills, streams, and 10 bogs. As soon as you arrive there, having achieved your purpose, be sure to keep your burden so placed that you don't happen to be carrying your little pack of books under an armpit, as a country fellow might carry a lamb, or tipsy Pyrria a ball of wool she has stolen, or a fellow tribesman his felt cap and slippers when asked out to dinner. 15

And see you don't tell all and sundry you have sweated in carrying verses that could hold the eyes and ears of Caesar, but press on though many beg you with their entreaties. On your way and farewell; take care you don't trip up and smash what has been put in your care.

EPISTLE 14

Bailiff of my woods and of the little estate that allows me to be myself, which you disdain because it provides a home to five families and is accustomed to send five good heads of house to Varia, let's have a contest to see if I more vigorously root out thorns from the mind or you from the land, and whether Horace or his property is in better 5 shape. Although I am held back here by my loving concern for Lamia, who is mourning for a brother, grieving inconsolably for the loss of a brother, yet my mind and heart incline to this place and would gladly shatter the bolts that deny them access to the racetrack.

I call one who lives in the country happy, you so name one who lives 10 in the city. The man who finds another's lot attractive of course finds his own disagreeable. Both are foolish and unjustly find fault with the innocent place: it's the mind that's at fault, which never escapes from itself.

You, as a factotum, used to yearn for the country, offering up silent
15 prayers, but now as a bailiff you long for the city and its games and
baths: you know that I am consistent with myself and take my leave sor-
rowfully whenever hateful matters of business drag me back to Rome.

Our ideals are not the same; this is where the difference between
you and me lies: for what you hold to be wilds and inhospitable heath,
20 the man who shares my sentiments calls lovely, and hates what you call
beautiful. It's the brothel, I see, and the greasy cook-shop that inspire
in you a longing for the city, and the way that place in the back of
beyond will grow pepper and incense sooner than grapes, while there
is no tavern close at hand that can supply you with wine, no castanet-
25 playing hostess to whose clatter you can make the ground shake with
dancing: and yet you exert yourself on fields long since untouched
by the hoe and look after the ox's needs once he's unyoked, filling his
belly with the leaves you have stripped from branches; when you are
unoccupied there is the stream to bring fresh work, if there has been
30 a shower of rain, for your heavy toil is required to teach it to spare the
sunny meadow.

Come now, let me tell you what it is that breaks up our harmony.
The man who cut a figure in togas of fine wool and hair shining with
perfumed oils, who, as you know, needed no gifts to please greedy
Cinara, who would drink the clear Falernian from midday, is now
35 satisfied with a short meal and a nap on the grass beside the stream.

I feel no shame at having indulged myself in pleasures; the shame
would come from not having cut them short. Where you live, no one
disparages my blessings with sidelong looks, or poisons them with the
bite of secret hatred; my neighbours laugh at the sight of me shift-
40 ing clods and stones. You would rather be eating your rations with
slaves in the city; you long to rush to join their number: a shrewd
slave envies you the use of firewood, livestock, and garden. The ox
longs for a saddlecloth when weary of work, the horse for the plough:
let each be content to practise the trade he knows, that's my advice.

EPISTLE 15

What kind of winter has Velia, my friend Vala, what's the climate at
Salernum, what sort of people live there, what's the road like (for
Antonius Musa makes Baiae surplus to my needs, and yet he puts

me in bad odour there, since I am soaking myself in cold water in the
depths of winter. Of course the town complains that its myrtle groves 5
are avoided and its sulphur baths despised, despite their reputation
for driving the chronic ailment out of the muscles, and it takes a dim
view of patients who presume to plunge head and stomach under
the showers from Clusium's springs or head for the chilly country-
side of Gabii. I have to change my resort and steer my horse past 10
the familiar places to stop. 'Where are you heading for? My journey
doesn't take me to Cumae or Baiae,' the rider will say, pulling on the
left rein in his anger; but a horse hears through its bridled mouth);
which townsfolk are fed by a greater supply of corn, whether they
drink rainwater gathered in tanks or have constant spring water in 15
wells the year round (for I have no time for the wines of that region;
at my place in the country I can put up with and tolerate anything;
whenever I come to the seaside, I look for something mellow and of
noble spirit, to banish troubled thoughts, to flow with rich hope into
my veins and heart, to supply words, to lend me the grace of youth 20
in the eyes of a Lucanian mistress); which stretch of country rears
more hares and which more boars; which part of the sea gives greater
hiding to fish and urchins, so that I can return home from there fat
and Phaeacian: all this you must write to me and I must believe your 25
every word.

Maenius, after stoutly using up all his mother and father had left
him, began to get a reputation for wit, a clever parasite at large, not
the sort to keep to a regular manger, or to know friend from foe if
he had not had a meal, merciless at thinking up any kind of insult 30
against anyone you like, the ruin and tempest and abyss of the market,
he would present everything he had gained to his greedy stomach.
Whenever he had got little or nothing from those who praised or
feared his wicked tongue, he would dine on plates of tripe and cheap 35
lamb, enough to satisfy three bears, so that he actually said that
spendthrifts should have their bellies branded with white-hot iron,
like a reformed Bestius. But this same fellow, if ever he got hold of
some larger booty, would turn it all into smoke and ashes and say, 'It
really doesn't surprise me that some men eat up their property, since 40
there's nothing better than a plump thrush, nothing more beautiful
than a large sow's womb.'

I, of course, am a man like this: for I praise a safe and humble lot,
brave enough when means fail; but when something better and richer

45 comes my way, I, the selfsame fellow, say that only men such as you
have sense, whose wealth is there to see, based on handsome country
homes.

EPISTLE 16

To save you asking, my dear Quinctius, whether my farm supports
its master with ploughland or enriches him with berries of olive, or
whether it is with apples or meadows or elms clothed with vines, the
character and lie of the land shall be described to you in full detail.
5 There is an unbroken line of hills, except for a shady valley that separ-
ates them, yet such that the sun looks upon its right side when rising
and warms its left when departing in flying chariot. The climate would
win your approval. What if you knew that the bushes yield a rich crop
of ruddy cornel-cherries and plums, that oak and ilex delight the
10 cattle with their abundant acorns and their master with their abun-
dant shade? You'd say that Tarentum with all its leafage had come
nearer home. A spring also, fit to give its name to a river (and such
that Hebrus is not so cool or pure when it winds through Thrace),
flows with healing powers for a sickly head and a sickly stomach. This
15 retreat, so charming, yes, if you believe me, so beautiful, keeps me
safe and sound, you'll be pleased to know, in September's season.

Now you, my friend, live your life in a desirable way if you are
concerned to be in reality what people say you are. For a long time
now every Roman among us has confidently asserted that you are a
happy man: but I fear that, regarding yourself, you may give more
20 credit to others than to your own opinion, or that you may consider
someone other than a good and wise man to be happy, or that, if the
people keep saying you are a man in sound and good health, you may
try to conceal your secret fever as the dinner hour approaches, until
trembling descends on those greasy hands. It is the fool who seeks to
hide an untreated sore with false shame.

25 If someone were to speak of wars fought by you on land and sea,
flattering your receptive ears with these words, 'May Jupiter, whose
thoughts are kind both to you and to Rome, keep safe the secret
whether the people pray more for your well-being than you for
theirs', you could recognize in them the praises of Augustus: in
30 allowing yourself to be called wise and free from vice, aren't you

replying, do tell me, with your own name? 'Well, of course I enjoy being called a good and wise man as much as you do.' But those who gave you this title today will, if they want, take it away tomorrow, just as, if they confer the fasces on someone unworthy, they will snatch them away from the very same man. 'Lay them down, they're ours,' they say: 35 I lay them down and sadly withdraw. If the selfsame people should shout after me, 'Thief!' and call me a pervert, or allege that I had strangled my father, am I to be upset by their lying accusations and change colour? Who takes pleasure in false honour or is alarmed by slanderous ill-repute except a man who is full of flaws or in need of a doctor? 40

Who is the good man? 'He who observes the decrees of the senate, the laws and privileges, whose verdict resolves many weighty legal disputes, whose surety ensures that property is retained, whose testimony that cases are won.' But this man is seen by everyone under his roof and all his neighbours to be ugly inside, though a creature 45 fair to the eye with his attractive hide. Should a slave say to me, 'I am no thief or runaway', my reply would be, 'You have your reward, you escape a flogging.' 'I haven't killed a person.' 'You won't feed the crows on a cross.' 'I'm honest and serve you well.' His Sabine owner throws back his head and says, 'No, no!' For the wary wolf fears the 50 pitfall, the hawk the suspected snare, and the pike the hidden hook. Good men are loath to do wrong because they love virtue: *you* won't be likely to commit a crime because you fear punishment: let there be any hope of escaping detection and you'll make no difference between holy and unholy. For when you steal one bushel of beans from a thou- 55 sand, it's the loss, in my eyes, not the crime that's more tolerable on that account.

The 'good man', who attracts the eyes of all the forum and every public platform, whenever he seeks to appease the gods, be it with a pig or an ox , cries out in a loud voice 'Father Jupiter!', in a loud voice 'Apollo!', but moves his lips, fearing to be heard: 'Fair Laverna, grant 60 that I escape detection, grant that I appear to be just and upright, veil my sins in darkness, my deceptions in clouds.'

In what respect the miser is better or more free than a slave when he stoops to pick up a coin fixed to the pavement at crossroads, I do not see; for the one who harbours desires will also harbour fears; 65 besides, the man who lives in fear will never be free in my eyes. A man loses his weapons and quits the post of bravery if he never ceases to rush around and is overwhelmed in making his money greater.

70 Since you can sell a prisoner of war, don't kill him; he will make a
useful slave: let him be a shepherd or plough the fields, the sturdy
fellow, let him take to the sea and spend the winter as a merchant in
the midst of the waves, let him benefit the price of corn, bringing in
food and fodder.

The man who *is* good and wise will dare to say, 'Pentheus, ruler of
75 Thebes, what shameful punishment will you force me to stand and
suffer?' 'I will deprive you of your possessions.' 'You mean, I take it,
my cattle, my money, my couches, my silver plate: you may take them.'
'I will keep you in handcuffs and fetters under a cruel jailer.' 'The god
himself will set me free, whenever I wish.' I take it his meaning is this:
'I shall die.' Death is the final finishing-line in life's race.

EPISTLE 17

Although you look after your own interests quite well enough, Scaeva,
and know how on earth it is proper to associate with the great, learn
the view of your humble friend, who has yet some learning to do, as if
a blind man were wanting to point out the way; yet consider whether
5 even I have something to say that you may wish to make your own
property.

If what delights you is pleasant rest and sleeping till the sun has
risen, if what offends is the dust and noise of wheels, or the tavern,
my advice will be to go to Ferentinum. For it is not only the rich who
10 experience joys in life, and the man who has passed unnoticed from
birth to death has not lived badly. If you want to benefit your friends
and to treat yourself a little more generously, be sure to approach a
rich table when hungry.

'If Aristippus was content to dine on greens, he would not want
to associate with kings.' 'If he knew how to associate with kings, my
15 critic would turn his nose up at vegetables.' Tell me which of these
two men's words and behaviour wins your approval, or rather, as the
younger man, listen to why the view of Aristippus is preferable; for
the story goes that he used to baffle the snapping jaws of the Cynic in
this way: 'I play the hanger-on for my own profit, you for the people's;
20 my way of behaving is much better, much more honourable. I act
as a friend is required to do, so that I may have a horse to ride and
a king to maintain me: you ask for inexpensive things but you are

inferior to the provider, though you boast of needing no man's char-
ity.' Every lifestyle, every social position, every degree of prosperity
suited Aristippus, and, while he would set his sights on greater things,
he was generally content with what he had: on the other hand, I'd   25
be amazed if a change of lifestyle suited the man whose endurance
clothed him in double rags. The one will not wait for purple cloth-
ing and will proceed through the busiest of streets wearing whatever
he has put on, and he will play either part with perfect elegance; the   30
other will shun a cloak woven from Milesian wool worse than a dog or
a snake, and will die of cold if you don't give him back his rags. Give
them back and let him live his ill-mannered life.

To achieve great deeds in war and to display the captured enemy
to one's fellow citizens is to touch the throne of Jupiter and to scale
the heavens: but to have found favour with leaders in society is not   35
the lowest form of renown. It isn't every man who has the luck to visit
Corinth. The man who was afraid of not winning did nothing. Fair
enough, but what of the man who reached his goal, did he act like
a man? Well, here if anywhere is the object of our enquiry. The one
shudders at the burden as being too great for his little spirit and little   40
frame: the other shoulders it and carries it to the end. Either man-
hood is an empty name or the man of enterprise is right in seeking
honour and its reward.

Those who say nothing about their poverty in the presence of
their king will get more than the one who asks; it makes a difference
whether you take gifts in moderation or grab them. And yet this was   45
the central point, the source of your behaviour all along. 'My sister
lacks a dowry, my mother is a poor old soul, my farm can't be sold
or trusted to keep us alive.' The man who says this is shouting out,
'Give us food!' His neighbour chimes in with 'And me!' The morsel
will be split as a divided present. But if the crow could eat in silence,   50
he would have more of the feast and far less quarrelsome envy. If a
man is taken as a companion to Brundisium or lovely Surrentum, and
he complains about bad roads and the bitter cold and rain, or weeps
and wails over his forced money-box and stolen money for travel, he
is reproducing the tricks of the mistress who often laments the theft   55
of a favourite chain or an anklet, so that soon her real grief at a real
loss is believed by no one. The man who has once been fooled can't
be bothered to lift up an impostor with a broken leg at the crossroads,
though the tears course down his cheeks and he swears by holy Osiris,   60

'Believe me, I'm not trying to trick you; have a heart and lift up a cripple!' 'Look for a stranger to these parts,' his neighbours shout back noisily.

EPISTLE 18

Lollius, frankest of men, knowing you as I do, you will shrink from wearing the guise of a hanger-on when you have claimed to be a friend. As a married woman will differ from a prostitute and have a different way of life, so a friend will be distinct from an untrustworthy
5 hanger-on. The vice that is opposite to this one is almost greater, a boorish moroseness, jarring and offensive, that seeks to recommend itself with hair clipped to the skin and black teeth, while wishing to pass for undiluted candour and true virtue. Virtue is a mean between vices, remote from both extremes. The one man inclines more than is
10 appropriate towards compliance, and, a mocker on the lowest couch, so reveres the rich man's nod, so repeats his words and picks up his remarks as they fall unnoticed, that you'd believe it was a schoolboy repeating the lessons dictated by a severe teacher, or someone performing the second part of a mime. The other comes to blows often
15 over goat's wool, and fights his corner armed with trifles: 'To think, if you please, that I shouldn't be believed before anyone else, that I shouldn't bark out fiercely what I really think! A second life isn't reward enough.' Well, what's the point at issue? Whether Castor or
20 Dolichos has more skill; whether the Minucian or the Appian Way is the better road to Brundisium.

  If a man is stripped bare by ruinous passion or fatal gambling, if vanity both clothes and perfumes him beyond his means, if unremitting hunger and thirst for money hold him fast, or the shame and dread of
25 poverty, he is hated and treated like a pariah by his rich patron, though that man is often better equipped by some ten vices, or, if not hated, he is put on the right track, for, like a loving mother, the patron wants him to be wiser and more virtuous than himself. He says to him what is pretty nearly true: 'My wealth (don't argue against me) allows for a lack
30 of prudence; your means are paltry: a narrow toga is right for a client who has sense; stop competing with me.' Whenever Eutrapelus wanted to cause anyone harm he used to give him expensive clothing: 'For soon enough the lucky fellow will adopt along with his fine tunics new plans

and hopes, he'll sleep till daybreak, he'll put off honourable duties for
the sake of a whore, he'll feed his debts, and finally become a Thracian in   35
the arena, or drive for pay some greengrocer's clapped-out old horse.'

Just as you'll be sure never to pry into your patron's secrets, be sure
to keep one safe if entrusted to you, even though both wine and anger
put you on the rack.

Be sure not to praise your own favourite pursuits or to criticize
those of others, and when he wishes to hunt, be sure not to be penning   40
verse. This was how the goodwill between the two brothers Amphion
and Zethus was severed, until the lyre that had earned the one's stern
look of distrust fell silent. It's thought that Amphion yielded to his
brother's mood: you, too, must yield to a powerful patron's gentle   45
commands, and whenever he takes out into the country his hounds
and his mules, weighed down with Aetolian nets, up you get and cast
aside the glum spirit of your unsociable Muse, so that you may share
his dinner, eating food bought with effort; this is the customary task
of Roman men, of benefit to reputation, life, and limb alike, especially   50
when you are in good health and able to outstrip the hound in run-
ning or the boar in strength. Add that there is no one who can handle
manly weapons more gracefully: you know how loud the onlookers
shout when you take part in contests in Mars' Field; finally, when
only a youth you saw stern service in the Cantabrian wars under a   55
leader who even now is taking down our standards from the Parthians'
temples, and is assigning anything that is wanting to Italian arms.

And in case you draw back and absent yourself without excuse, make
sure that, however much you take care to do nothing out of time and
tune, you do on occasion amuse yourself at your family's home in the   60
country; your forces divide up the boats, under your leadership the
battle of Actium is reproduced by your slaves in true hostile fashion,
your brother is your adversary, the lake is the Adriatic, until swift Victory
crowns with her leafy garland one or the other of the commanders. The   65
man who believes that you comply with his own favourite pursuits will
enthusiastically commend your own sport with both thumbs.

To continue with my advice, if *you* need an adviser in any respect,
take care many a time what you say and about what man and to whom
you say it. Avoid the man who asks questions, for he is also a gossip;
open ears do not keep secrets faithfully, and a word once let slip flies   70
on its way beyond recall. Don't let a maidservant or young slave who
works inside the marble threshold of your estimable patron make your

heart ache with desire, in case the master of the beautiful, dear boy
75 or girl enriches you with a gift of such little worth or torments you by
withholding the favour.

Time and again give thought to what kind of a person you are rec-
ommending, in case before long another's shortcomings bring shame
on your head. We are deceived from time to time and introduce some-
one unworthy: therefore, if taken in, make no effort to protect one
80 crushed by his own failing, so that you may keep safe from harm a
man you know thoroughly, should he be the victim of accusations,
and safeguard one who puts his trust in your protection: when he
feels the bite of Theon's malicious teeth, don't you feel at all that in a
short time the danger will pass to you? For it's your own safety that's
85 threatened when your neighbour's wall is in flames, and fires that are
ignored usually gain in strength.

Those who have never tried it think it a pleasant occupation to
cultivate the acquaintance of a powerful patron: the man who has
tried regards it with dread. While your ship is on the ocean wave,
give all your attention to it, in case a change of wind carries you back.
Melancholy types have no use for a cheerful soul, or merry ones for
90 a melancholy, or the quick for the staid, or the idle for the active and
energetic; drinkers who down the Falernian in the midnight hours
have no time for you if you refuse proffered cups, however much you
swear you dread fevers at night. Banish the cloud from your brow: a
95 reserved person generally assumes the look of secrecy, and one who
keeps his counsel that of surliness.

In the course of all this be sure to read and to question learned men
as to how you can pass your days tranquilly; are you to be tormented
and harassed by greed that forever makes you penniless, by anxiety
100 and the hope for things indifferent? Is virtue acquired through train-
ing or is it a gift of nature? What reduces cares, what makes you a
friend to yourself? What creates a calm mind absolutely, public office
or the delights of profit or a secluded journey along the side-path of
a life unnoticed?

105 As for myself, whenever Digentia refreshes me, whose chilly brook
Mandela drinks, that village whose folk are wrinkled with the cold,
what do you suppose my feelings are? What do you believe, my friend,
are my prayers? May I have what I now possess, or even less, and for
the span of years remaining to me, if the gods wish any to remain,
may I live for myself; may I have a good supply of books and of food

provided in advance to see me through the year, and may I not waver   110
in suspense with the hope of each uncertain hour. No, it is enough to
pray to Jupiter who provides and takes away, to give me life and give
me means: a well-balanced mind I will furnish for myself.

EPISTLE 19

If you put your trust in Cratinus of old, learned Maecenas, no
poems written by drinkers of water can live or give pleasure for long.
Ever since Liber enlisted barely sane poets among his satyrs and
fauns, the sweet Muses as a rule have smelled of wine in the morning.   5
Homer's praises of wine convict him of being a wine-lover; father
Ennius himself never sprang forth to tell of wars without several
drinks in him. 'I shall assign the forum and Libo's well to the sober,
I shall debar the joyless from singing': as soon as I published this   10
edict, poets were not slow to compete in drinking wine by night or to
stink of it by day.

What if someone were to imitate Cato with his grim and savage
expression, with his bare feet and with the assistance of a weaver of a
toga that is too short, would he put before our eyes Cato's virtue and
character? His tongue that tried to rival Timagenes was the undoing   15
of Iarbitas, as he aimed and strived to be regarded as witty and elo-
quent. A model whose defects lend it to imitation leads people astray;
so if through accident I went pale, they would drink cumin to drain
the colour from their faces. O you imitators, servile herd, how often
have your antics stirred me to anger, how often to laughter!   20

I was first to plant footsteps that were free on virgin soil, treading
for myself where no others had set foot. The bee that trusts in itself
will rule the swarm as its leader. I first introduced to Latium the iam-
bics of Paros, following the rhythms and spirit of Archilochus but not   25
his subject matter and words that hounded Lycambes. And in case
on this account you should crown me with scantier leaves, for being
afraid to change the rhythms and form of his verse, masterly Sappho
fashions her verse in the metre of Archilochus, and so does Alcaeus,
though he differs in themes and arrangement, and doesn't seek out a   30
father-in-law to smear with spiteful verses, or weave a noose for his
bride with libellous poems. This man I have brought to the public's
ears, I, Latium's lyric bard, when no other lips had sung his verse

before. It is a joy to bring things untold, and to be read by the eyes and
held in the hands of gentlemen.

35   Would you like to know why the ungrateful reader in private praises
and loves my modest efforts at writing but in public unfairly disparages
them? Well, it's not *my* way to hunt for the votes of the fickle populace
by spending money on dinners and making gifts of worn-out clothes,
not *my* way, as one who listens to great writers and avenges them, to
40 bring myself to seek the approval of the tribes of teachers who lecture
on literature from their platforms: 'That's the reason for those tears.'
If ever I say, 'I'm ashamed to give a reading of my unworthy writings
in packed halls and to give these trifles any claim to attention,' one
of them says: 'You're laughing at us and keeping these verses for the
ears of Jupiter: for you are confident that you alone among poets drip
45 honey drops, and you think yourself quite splendid.' In response to
this I am reluctant to look down my nose at him, and, in case, if it
comes to a wrestling match, he tears me with his sharp nails, I cry
out, 'I'm not happy with the place you've chosen,' and demand an
intermission. For sport of that kind gives rise to an excited contest
and anger, and anger in turn to fierce disputes and deadly war.

EPISTLE 20

You seem, my book, to have your eyes on Vertumnus and Janus, no
doubt to offer yourself for sale, well scrubbed with the pumice of the
Sosii. You have no time for the keys and seals so dear to the modest; it
grieves you to be shown to a few and public places win your approval,
5 though this was not the way you were raised under my roof. Avoid the
place you are so eager to go down to. Once I've let you into the world
there will be no coming back. 'For pity's sake, what have I done? What
was in my mind?' you will say, when any harm comes to you, and yet
you know you'll be packed away into a corner when your admirer has
had his fill and becomes bored.

But if the prophet does not lose his wisdom through annoyance
10 with the offender, you will win hearts in Rome until your youth de-
serts you; when the public's fondling hands have begun to make you
shed your bloom, either in silence you will provide food for philistine
lice or you will run away to Utica or be bound up and sent to Ilerda.
The one who warned you, to whom you turned such deaf ears, will

have the laugh, like the fellow who in anger pushed his disobedient   15
ass over the cliff: for who would strive to keep the creature safe against
its will? This end also lies in wait for you, that stammering old age will
come upon you teaching schoolboys their ABC at the ends of streets.

When the sun's less fiery heat attracts a greater audience to you, be
sure to say that I was a freedman's son and, in humble circumstances,   20
spread wings too large for my nest, so adding to my virtues whatever
you subtract from my birth; say that I found favour with the foremost
men of Rome in war and peace and was a fellow of small stature, grey
before my time, fond of the sun's rays, quick to anger but not hard to   25
win round again. If anyone happens to ask you my age, let him know
I saw out my forty-fourth December in the year that Lollius escorted
Lepidus as his elected colleague.

BOOK 2

EPISTLE 1: TO AUGUSTUS

Since you alone support on your shoulders so many heavy burdens
of office, protecting our Italian state with arms, furnishing her with
morals, and improving her with laws, I would be offending against the
public interest should I waste your time, Caesar, with protracted dis-
5 course. Romulus, father Liber, Castor and Pollux, though welcomed
into the temples of the gods after their mighty deeds, while they
inhabited the earth and cared for the human race, ending fierce wars,
distributing land and founding towns, they complained bitterly that
10 their services were not met with the goodwill they expected. He who
crushed the terrible Hydra and laid low the well-known monsters by
his Labours determined by fate, discovered that envy is only at last
undone by death. For when a man oppresses by his weight talents
inferior to his own, he scorches them with his fiery brilliance: but
once his light is quenched in death, he, too, will inspire love.
15 Yet upon you, while you are still among us, we happily bestow hon-
ours in good time, and raise altars to swear by in the name of your
divinity, acknowledging that nothing like you has arisen or will ever
arise in ages to come. But this people of yours, wise and just in prefer-
ring you alone to our own leaders and to those of the Greeks, values
20 all else by a wholly different rule and method, scorning and having no
time for anything except what it sees has lived out its days and passed
from the earth; such enthusiasm does it show for things of the past
that it insists that the Tables forbidding criminal acts, enacted by the
25 ten men, the treaties of our kings made on equal terms with Gabii or
the stern Sabines, the books of the Pontiffs and the time-worn scrolls
of prophets were spoken by the Muses on the Alban Mount.

If, because all the earliest writings of the Greeks are quite the best,
30 Roman writers are weighed in the same balance, there is no reason
why we should say much: the olive has nothing hard inside, the nut
nothing hard outside; we have come to the peak of success; we paint,
play music, and wrestle with more skill than the well-oiled Achaeans.

If poems, like wines, are improved by the passage of time, I would 35
like to know which year bestows value on our pen's scribblings? Say an
author has passed away a hundred years ago, must he be judged one of
the perfect ancients or one of the worthless moderns? Let some limit
banish quarrelling. 'The old and respectable writer is the one a hun-
dred years dead.' What of the one who died a single month or even 40
one year before that—which category are we to put him in? The poets
of old or those this generation or the next should reject?

'Well, he will surely find a proper place among early writers
whose age falls short by a brief month or even by a whole year.'
I accept your concession, and as with the hairs in a horse's tail I pluck 45
out and remove one year and then likewise another, little by little,
until the man who refers to historical records and who values worth
by years collapses, baffled by the argument of the dwindling heap, and
is impressed by nothing unless Libitina has hallowed it.

Ennius, the wise and brave, that second Homer, as the critics 50
describe him, seems to be indifferent to how the promises of his
Pythagorean dream turn out. As to Naevius, is he not in our hands
and fixed in our minds almost as if he was writing yesterday? Such
sanctity inhabits every ancient poem. Whenever opinions differ as 55
to which is the better of the two, among the writers of old Pacuvius
carries off the name of the learned one, Accius the elevated, while it's
said that Afranius' toga was the same size as Menander's, that Plautus
moves rapidly following the model of Epicharmus, that Caecilius
wins the prize for dignity and Terence for artistry. These are the 60
writers that mighty Rome learns by heart, these those she watches,
packed into the narrow space of the theatre; these she reckons and
counts as poets from the days of Livius the writer to our own time.

Sometimes the public see straight, sometimes they go wrong.
If they so admire and praise early poets that they prefer nothing else 65
and put nothing else on an equal footing, they are in error: if they
believe that their diction is sometimes too dated, and often too harsh,
if they acknowledge that much of it lacks force, they are showing
sense, they agree with me, and make their judgement with Jupiter's
favour. For myself, I'm not attacking Livius' poems and don't think
destruction should fall on his lines recited to me as a boy by Orbilius 70
the Caner; but that they should be thought faultless and beautiful,
and all but perfect, I find astonishing; if among them a perfectly

75 chosen word happens to dart out, and if one or two verses are a little
better turned, then these unfairly carry and sell the whole poem.

It annoys me that anything is criticized, not because people think
it is coarse or inelegant in style but because it is modern, and that,
instead of indulgence, honour and prizes are claimed for early writers.
80 Should I question whether a play of Atta's stays on its feet as it walks
through the saffron and flowers, almost to a man our elders would cry
out that a sense of propriety was dead, since I would be trying to find
fault with what stately Aesopus and skilful Roscius once acted: it's
either that they think nothing right which doesn't meet their approval
or else they consider it shameful to heed the younger generation and
85 to acknowledge that what they learned when their chins lacked beards
should be destroyed now they're old men. Besides, anyone who praises
Numa's Salian hymn, wishing to be thought the only person to know
what he knows as little of as I do, does not support and applaud genius
dead and buried but attacks our own today, in his spite having no time
for us and what we write.

90 But if the Greeks had found novelty as offensive as we do, what
would nowadays be old? Or what would the public have as its prop-
erty to read and thumb, each man to suit himself? From the time
that Greece abandoned her wars and began to engage in idle amuse-
ments, drifting into frivolous habits as Fortune showed her favour,
95 she burned with enthusiasm, now for athletes, now for horses, and
fell in love with sculptors who worked in marble, ivory, or bronze,
she stared with enraptured eyes and soul at painters' panels and took
delight now in flute-players, now in tragic actors. Like a baby girl
100 playing under her nurse's watchful eye, what she eagerly desired to
have she soon abandoned when bored with it. What likes and dislikes
are there that you wouldn't suppose could be easily changed? This
was the effect of happy days of peace and prosperous winds.

At Rome it was for a long time agreeable and an honoured custom to
be awake early with doors open, to furnish clients with legal advice, to
105 pay out secured money to honest debtors, to listen to one's elders, to
tell a younger man by what means his property could be increased and
his ruinous self-indulgence curbed. The fickle people have changed
their minds and are on fire with a single passion—writing; sons and
110 strict fathers take dinner with their hair wreathed in leaves, dictating
lines of verse. I myself, who profess to write no verses, am discov-
ered to be as great a liar as the Parthians, waking before sunrise and

calling for pen, writing paper, and book-holders. A man who doesn't
know how to handle a ship is afraid of ships; no man dares adminis-   115
ter southernwood to someone ill unless he has learned its use; doc-
tors undertake the work of doctors; carpenters handle the tools of
carpenters: we write poems indiscriminately, whether we have poetic
training or not.

And yet this aberration, this mild lunacy, has its merits; consider
how great these are: a bard is rarely tainted with avarice; verses are   120
what he loves, this his one passion; financial loss, slaves running away,
fires, he laughs at; he doesn't plan to practise any fraud against a part-
ner in business or a young ward; he lives on pulses and inferior bread;
although a poor soldier and an idle one, he does his city service, if you   125
allow this point, that even small things can assist great enterprises.
The poet moulds the soft, lisping mouth of a child, even then turn-
ing the ear away from vulgar expressions, and in a short while shaping
the heart by precepts for friendship, correcting harshness and envy
and anger; he tells of noble deeds, equips the rising generation with   130
famous examples, consoles the helpless and sick at heart. From what
source would the unmarried girl in concert with chaste boys learn
prayers, if the Muse had not given them a bard? Their chorus asks
for help and feels the gods' kindly presence, it begs for showers from   135
heaven, winning favour by the prayer he has taught them, it turns
away disease, drives away fearful dangers, gains divine blessing and a
season rich in fruits. By poetry the gods above are won over, by poetry
the gods below.

The farmers of old, stout fellows blessed with little wealth, after
gathering in the harvest sought to bring relief to their bodies at holi-   140
day time, yes, and to their minds that used to endure hardship in the
hope of an end. Together with their children and faithful wife who
had shared their tasks they would propitiate Earth with a pig, Silvanus
with milk, and with flowers and wine their Genius who never forgot
life's shortness. This custom gave rise to the Fescennine licence that   145
poured forth country insults in alternate verse, and the freedom,
received as the years came round, sported in friendly fashion, until
the jesting, now turned savage, began to change into open madness,
and to range through the homes of decent folk, fearing no punish-   150
ment for its threats. Those who were harried by its bloody teeth felt
the pain keenly; even those who had escaped its bite felt concern
about the state of the community; in the end a law and penalty were

brought in, forbidding the portrayal of anyone in abusive song: fear
155 of the cudgel made these fellows change their tune and revert to
entertainment without unpleasant language.

Conquered Greece took prisoner her rough conqueror and intro-
duced the arts to rustic Latium. So it was that the stream of that
turbulent Saturnian metre ran dry, and cleanness drove out the foul-
160 smelling liquid; but for many a long year traces of the country lived
on and even yet remain. For it was at a late stage that he applied his
shrewd mind to the writings of the Greeks, indeed it was when he
found peace after the Punic wars that he began to ask what benefit
Sophocles brought, and Thespis and Aeschylus. He also attempted to
165 try his hand at adapting the plays in a worthy fashion, and took satis-
faction in the exercise, as he naturally possessed vigour and grandeur;
for he has enough of the tragic spirit and his boldness of expression
is successful, but his want of skill makes him ashamed and fearful of
erasing a line.

It's thought that comedy, as deriving its subject matter from every-
day life, involves very little effort, but it imposes a heavier burden, as
170 the indulgence it can expect is less. See how Plautus sustains the role
of the helpless young lover, of the close father, of the deceitful pimp,
what a great Dossenus he is in handling his greedy parasites, how
175 loosely his comic sock fits as he careers over the stage; for he can't
wait to put the coins in his cash-box, not worried after that whether
his play falls flat or stands on a firm footing.

The man whom Fame carries to the stage in her windy chariot is
deflated by the indifferent spectator and puffed up by the apprecia-
180 tive one: so trivial, so small a thing it is that undermines or builds up
again a soul that craves praise. Goodbye to a theatrical career, if deny-
ing the prize sends me home deflated, and awarding it, triumphant.

Often even the bold poet is terrified and put to flight when men
superior in number but inferior in worth and status, stupid fellows,
185 lacking in refinement, and ready to fight it out if the knights do not
share their judgement, clamour in the middle of a play for a bear or
boxers; for these are what the rabble enjoy. Why, these days all the
pleasure taken even by the knights has passed from their ears to the
empty delights of the wandering eye. For four hours or more the cur-
190 tain is kept down, while squadrons of cavalry and troops of infantry
fly over the stage in rout; eventually kings deserted by fortune are
dragged on, hands bound behind their backs, war-chariots dash past,

together with wagons, carriages, ships, and carried along as spoils of
war come statues of ivory and Corinthian bronze.

If he were on earth, Democritus would laugh, whether the mob's 195
eyes were drawn to some hybrid cross between a panther and a camel
or to a white elephant; he would observe the people more intently
than the actual plays, as giving him far more opportunities for enter-
tainment; as for the playwrights, he'd consider they were telling their
tale to a deaf ass. For what voices have ever succeeded in drowning 200
out the noise that echoes round our theatres? You would think it was
the roaring of Garganus' woods or the Tuscan sea, so great is the din
that accompanies the viewing of entertainment, of works of art and
foreign wealth, and when some actor stands on stage, tricked out in 205
this gear, right hand clashes with left. 'Has he said anything yet?'
Nothing at all. 'Then why is he going down so well?' It's his woollen
cloak with its Tarentine dye resembling violet.

And in case you think I am being ungenerous in my praise of others
when they handle well what I myself would refuse to try if asked, I
think that poet is able to walk a tightrope, who with his illusions makes 210
my heart ache, stirs it up, soothes it, fills it with groundless fears, and,
like a magician, sets me down, now in Thebes, now in Athens.

But come now, give some brief attention, as is due, to those as well
who prefer to entrust themselves to a reader than endure the disdain 215
of a contemptuous spectator, if you wish to fill with books that gift so
worthy of Apollo and to spur on bards to seek out more eagerly the
green slopes of Helicon.

There's no doubt we poets often do much harm to our own cause
(to hack at my own vines here), in offering you our book when you are 220
anxious or weary; when we take offence at a friend having the nerve to
criticize one of our verses; when we prepare to read out passages again
though the encore did not come; when we complain that the effort spent
on our poems and the fine thread with which they are spun pass unno- 225
ticed; when we hope that the result will be that, the moment you learn
we are composing poetry, you will oblige us by summoning us without
our asking and put an end to our poverty and compel us to write.

Just the same, it is worth while finding out what kind of servants 230
care for the shrine of Virtue, conspicuous in war and peace and not to
be entrusted to an unworthy poet. A favourite of Alexander the Great
was the notorious Choerilus, who in exchange for his rough and mis-
begotten verses entered as received his Philips, coins issued by a king.

235 But just as ink when handled produces a mark that stains, so writers often defile glorious actions with their ugly verse. That same king who extravagantly purchased such absurd poetry at so great a price ordered by edict that no one except Apelles should paint his portrait, 240 and no one other than Lysippus should make bronze that sought to capture the features of brave Alexander. But if you called upon the owner of that judgement so exact in viewing works of art to consider books and these gifts of the Muses, you'd swear he had been born in the heavy atmosphere of Boeotia.

245 But no discredit is brought on your judgement of them or on the gifts they have received, to the great credit of the giver, those poets loved by you, Virgil and Varius; and the features of famous men are not more clearly visible reproduced in bronze statues than are their 250 character and minds portrayed in the work of a bard. And as for me, I should not prefer my 'talks' that crawl along the ground to a celebration in verse of great exploits, to a tale of far-flung lands and rivers, of fortresses on mountain-tops and barbaric kingdoms, of wars ended 255 all the world over under your auspices, of bars that enclose Janus the guardian of peace, and of Rome striking fear into the Parthians with you as our emperor, if only my abilities were equal to my desires; but neither does your majesty admit of humble verse nor does my sense of shame dare to attempt a task beyond my strength to bear.

260 No, excessive attentiveness proves irritating to one we love, especially when it seeks to recommend itself through the art of poetry: for a man is quicker to learn and happier to remember what he finds laughable than what he approves of and esteems. I can't be bothered 265 with annoying attentiveness, and I have no desire to be displayed anywhere in wax, with features moulded for the worse, or to have my praises sung in badly fashioned verses, in case I should blush to be presented with so crass a gift, and together with my poet, outstretched in a closed box, I should be carried into the street that sells incense 270 and aromatic herbs and pepper and anything else that gets wrapped in fatuous sheets of paper.

EPISTLE 2: TO FLORUS

Florus, faithful friend of the distinguished and good Nero, suppose someone by chance should want to sell you a slave born at Tibur or

Gabii, and should deal with you as follows: 'Here's a lad with a fair
complexion, handsome from top to toe, who's yours to have and hold
for eight thousand sesterces, house-bred, ready for service at his mas-   5
ter's bidding and with some knowledge of elementary Greek, capable
of turning his hand to any skill; the clay is moist and you'll be able
to fashion it into whatever shape you like; not only this, he'll sing for
you in a voice untrained but agreeable, as you enjoy your wine: now
many assurances make a salesman less easy to trust, when he praises   10
beyond due measure the wares he wants to get rid of: I'm not in any
financial difficulty; though not well off, I'm no debtor: not one of the
slave-dealers would make you this offer; not every man would get the
same bargain readily from me. One time he shirked his work and, as
slaves do, he hid under the stairs, fearful of the whip hanging on the   15
wall. Let me have your cash, if you have duly noted his running away
and aren't put off in any way.' The seller, I take it, would get his price
without any fear of a penalty. You bought him with your eyes open, his
fault accepted; the condition of sale was stated to you: do you just the
same take the fellow to court and put him to the trouble of a lawsuit
that's unjust? I told you when you were leaving Rome that I was idle,   20
I told you I was practically disabled when it came to such obligations,
so that you wouldn't lose your temper and take me to task that no
letter of mine was coming back to you. What good did I do then, if,
when right is on my side, you still contest it? Moreover, you also com-
plain that I don't send you the lyrics you expected, false to my word.   25

A soldier of Lucullus, while he snored away at night, exhausted,
had lost to a penny the savings he had gathered through many trials
and tribulations: after this, furious as a wolf, just as angry with himself
as with the enemy, and savagely baring hungry teeth, he dislodged,
they say, from its very strongly fortified position a garrison belonging   30
to the king, that was rich in considerable treasure. Winning fame for
this feat, he was decorated with gifts of honour and received in addi-
tion twenty thousand sesterces in cash. It happened that shortly after
this his commander, eager to storm some fortress or other, started to   35
exhort the same man with words that would put fire even into a cow-
ard's belly: 'Onward, my fine fellow, to where your own courage calls
you, and good luck be yours, to win great rewards for your service!
Why do you stand there?' At this the soldier, a sharp fellow for all his
country ways, said, 'Onward, onward will he go to the place you wish,   40
the man who has lost his money-belt.'

I had the luck to be educated in Rome and there to be taught how greatly Achilles' anger harmed the Greeks. Kindly Athens added a little more training, in the sense that I was eager to distinguish
45 between the straight and the crooked, and to search for truth amid the groves of Academus. But the harshness of the times evicted me from that pleasing spot, and the tide of civil war carried me, a novice in war, into an army that was to prove no match for the strong arms of Caesar Augustus. As soon as Philippi discharged me from there,
50 brought down to earth with clipped wings and stripped of my father's home and estate, poverty made me bold and drove me to write verse: but now that my means are sufficient, what doses of hemlock will ever be able to cleanse my system of bile, if I didn't think it better to sleep than to write verses?

55 The years as they pass rob us of all pleasures, one by one; they snatch away humour, love, feasting, play; they strive to wrest my poems from me; what would you have me do?

Moreover not all men have the same tastes, the same likes: you
60 delight in lyric verse, this man in iambic, that in Bion's talks with their pungent wit. I might almost say it is like having three dinner-guests who disagree and call for completely different food to be served because their tastes vary. What should I put before them? What should I not? You refuse what your neighbour orders; what you ask for disgusts the other two, you may be sure, who think it sour to the taste.

65 Apart from everything else, do you suppose I can write poetry at Rome in the midst of so much anxiety and effort? One man calls on me to act as a guarantor, another to drop all business duties and listen to his writings; a third is lying ill on the Quirinal hill, a fourth on the far side of the Aventine, both in need of a visit; the distances to
70 walk, you see, are reasonably convenient. But the streets are clear, so that nothing gets in the way of your thinking up verses. In hot haste comes a contractor with mules and porters, and a huge contraption heaves now a block of stone, now a wooden beam; mournful funeral processions struggle to pass massive wagons, this way runs a
75 mad dog, that way a sow spattered with mud: now go and turn over in your mind melodious verse! The whole chorus of poets loves the woodland and flees from the city, duly following the god who is their patron, Bacchus, who delights in sleep and shade: do you wish me to
80 utter verse and follow in the bards' narrow tracks when surrounded with din by night and day? A man of talent who chooses the quiet

of Athens as his home and devotes seven years to his work, growing
old over his bookish pursuits, generally emerges with less voice than
a statue and makes the people shake with laughter; here, amid the
waves of life, amid the storms of the city, am I to think it worthwhile 85
to weave together words that can awaken the music of the lyre?

Two brothers at Rome, an orator and a lawyer, existed on such
terms that the one would hear from the other's mouth nothing but
compliments, so that the one was to his brother a Gracchus, the
other to his brother a Mucius. And are our melodious poets any less 90
troubled by madness like this? I am a writer of lyric verse, this man
of elegies. Ah, what a wonderful work to see! It is something the nine
Muses have adorned! Consider first with what pride, with what an air
of huge importance we let our eyes wander over the temple open to
Roman bards! And before long, if you happen to have the time, follow 95
as well and hear at a distance what each has to offer and how he weaves
a garland for his brows. We strike each other, trading blows one for
another and wearing our opponent down, like Samnites in a lengthy
bout that lasts till daylight fails. I come off by his vote an Alcaeus;
who do I judge him to be? Who if not a Callimachus? If he appears to 100
claim more, he becomes a Mimnermus and grows in esteem through
his adopted title. Much do I put up with in order to pacify the easily
provoked tribe of bards when I am writing and humbly suing to win
the people's votes; but once my ambition has ended and I return to
my senses, I would block my ears that were open to their reading and 105
fear no reprisal.

Those who compose bad verses are mocked; but they are delighted
when they are writing and they are their own admirers, happy souls,
of their own accord praising whatever they have written, should no
comment come from you. But the man who desires to write a poem
that conforms to the rules of art will take up, along with his writing 110
tablets, the spirit of a conscientious censor; he will have the cour-
age, if any words have too little lustre or are lacking in weight or are
thought unworthy of honour, to remove them from their place, how-
ever reluctant they are to make way, still lingering inside Vesta's pre-
cincts: words long unknown to the people he will kindly unearth and 115
restore to the daylight, striking terms which were once uttered by
men like Cato and Cethegus but now are weighed down by unsightly
neglect and lonely old age; he will add to the register new words, sired
by father Need: forceful and clear and truly like an unsullied stream, 120

he will pour forth his resources and make Latium blessed with wealth of speech; he will cut back overgrown foliage, smooth excessive roughness with salutary attention, and remove what lacks vigour; he will give the impression of one amusing himself but at the same time he will strain himself to the utmost, like a dancer who at one moment
125 dances the part of a Satyr, at another that of a clumsy Cyclops.

I should prefer to be thought a deluded and incompetent writer, provided my defects please or at least escape me, rather than to have my wits and bare my teeth in frustration. There was once at Argos a man of respected family, who used to believe he was listening to
130 some wonderful tragic actors, as he sat happily giving his applause in a theatre that was empty; all other civic duties he would perform in the correct fashion, showing himself certainly as a good neighbour, a genial host, agreeable to his wife, capable of showing mercy to his slaves and not becoming frantic if the seal on a flagon of wine was
135 broken, capable of avoiding a precipice or uncovered well. When this man had been restored, thanks to the regular assistance and care of his relatives, driving out his illness and bile with undiluted hellebore, and had returned to his senses, he said, 'I tell you, friends, you have
140 killed me, not saved me, in robbing me of my pleasure and taking away by force my mind's fondest illusion.'

Of course, it is expedient to cast childish pastimes aside and to be wise, leaving to children the sport that suits their age, and, instead of searching for words to fit the music of the Latin lyre, to learn by heart
145 the rhythms and measures of true life. Therefore I talk to myself and silently call to mind this advice: if no amount of water could quench your thirst, you would describe your condition to doctors: what of the fact that the more you acquire, the more you desire to have, aren't you brave enough to confess this to anyone? If a wound was not healing
150 by means of the root or herb prescribed to you, you would give up the treatment, since no benefit was coming from root or herb. People had told you that perverse stupidity departed from the man gifted with prosperity by the gods; and although you are in no way wiser since becoming richer, do you make use of the same advisers? But if wealth
155 could make you sensible, if it could make you less subject to desire and fear, why, you would blush, if a greater miser than you alone was living on the earth.

While it is true that what a man has purchased with balance and bronze belongs to him, ownership in some cases, if you take the word

of legal experts, is conferred by possession; the farm that provides 160
your food belongs to you, and the bailiff of Orbius, when he harrows
the cornfields to present you soon with grain, is aware that you are
their owner. You part with cash and receive grapes, chickens, eggs,
a jar of strong drink: why, in this way you are gradually buying the
farm that had cost perhaps three hundred thousand sesterces, or even 165
more, to buy. What difference does it make whether what you live on
was paid for recently or some time ago? The man who once bought
a farm at Aricia or Veii bought the vegetables he dines on, though
he thinks otherwise; he bought the firewood with which he heats the
bronze pot as night's chill draws on; but he calls it all his own up to 170
the point where the poplar planted along the fixed boundaries keeps the
quarrelling of neighbours at bay; as if anything was for ever one's own
that in a moment of flitting time, now as a result of a request, now for
a price, now through force, now through death that ends all, changes
owners and passes into another's control. In this way, since no man is 175
given permanent use of something, and heir succeeds another's heir
as wave does wave, what is the benefit of estates or granaries? Or what
good are woodland pastures in Lucania joined to pastures in Calabria,
if Death, not to be won over by gold, reaps great and small?

Gems, marble, ivory, Tuscan figurines, paintings, silver plate, 180
clothes dyed with Gaetulian purple—there are men who do not have
these, there is one who does not care to have them. Of two broth-
ers one prefers to Herod's rich palm-groves being idle and having
fun and enjoying an oil massage, the other, wealthy and unflagging, 185
from sunrise to evening's shadow tames his wooded estate with fire
and steel. Why this is so, the Genius knows, that companion who con-
trols our birth-star, the god whose concern is human nature, mortal
throughout each man's life, varying in features, bright and gloomy.
I shall enjoy what I have, taking from my modest heap as much as 190
occasion demands, and I shall not fear an heir's judgement of me, for
finding no more than I have given him: and yet I shall also wish to
know how much the open and genial giver is distinct from the spend-
thrift and how much the man of thrift is at odds with the miser. For it 195
makes a difference whether you scatter your money indiscriminately
or whether, neither reluctant to incur expense nor eager to make more
money, but rather as you used to do as a lad when Minerva's holiday
came round, you snatch enjoyment of the brief but welcome time.
Let us not reckon with filthy poverty ever entering our home: for my

200 own part, whether I sail as a passenger on big ship or small, that passenger will be one and the same man. I am not driven along by swelling sails or a favourable wind from the north, but nonetheless my life's course is not in the teeth of southerly gales, and in strength, talent, looks, character, situation, and means I am last of the foremost, always ahead of the last.

205 You are not a miser: fine. What then? Have all other faults now deserted you together with this one? Is your heart free from pointless ambition? Is it free from the fear and resentment of death? Dreams, magic's terrors, marvels, witches, ghosts of the night, Thessalian

210 miracles—are these things you laugh at? Do you number your birthdays with gratitude? Do you forgive your friends? Are you becoming more forbearing and a better person as old age approaches? What's the good of taking out one thorn when you have several in you? If you don't know how to live as you should, make way for those who know the art. You have had fun enough, eaten enough, and drunk enough:

215 it's time for you to leave, or else a generation that can be frivolous more stylishly will mock you for drinking too freely and roughly show you the door.

EPISTLE TO THE PISOS: THE ART OF POETRY

Should a painter choose to join on to the neck of a horse the head of a human, and to put feathers of different colour on bodies brought together from all animals, so that what above was a beautiful woman

5 ended horribly with an unsightly fish, would you contain your laughter, my friends, if allowed a personal viewing? Believe me, my dear Pisos, a book will be just like such a painting if, like the dreams of a sick man, its features are imagined fantastically, in such a way that neither foot nor head is given to a shape to make it achieve unity. 'But

10 poets and painters have always enjoyed an equal licence to dare anything they wish.' We know this, and we both request and grant this indulgence in turn; but not so as to show the savage mating with the tame, snakes pairing with birds, lambs with tigers.

Works with stately beginnings and grand promises often have sewn

15 into their fabric one or two purple patches to shine out far and wide, as when we have a description of Diana's grove and altar, or a winding stream that rushes on its way through lovely fields, or the river Rhine

or a rainbow. These have their place but it is not for the present time.
And perhaps you know how to portray a cypress: what is the good of   20
this, if you were given money to paint a man swimming for his life
from a wrecked ship? That was a wine-jar when the potter began his
moulding; why, as his wheel runs round, does it come out as a vase?
In short, let the work be anything you like, but at least let it constitute
a single whole that is homogeneous.

The majority of us bards, you father and you young men worthy
of your father, deceive ourselves by our notion of what is right: in   25
striving to be concise I become difficult to understand; when I aim
at smoothness, I lack sinews and vigour; one who promises grandeur,
falls into bombast; another, over cautious and fearful of squalls, crawls
along the ground; another, eager to bring variety to a unified piece by
introducing marvels, depicts a dolphin in woods and a boar in waves.   30
The desire to avoid a fault can lead to error, if it lacks art.

In the area near the school of Aemilius there is a craftsman, the
lowest in reputation, who will represent you nails and copy wavy hair
in bronze but who lacks success in his work as a whole because he
doesn't know how to portray an entire figure. Now, should I want to   35
write something, I should no more wish to be like him than to live
with a crooked nose, while drawing admiring looks for my black eyes
and black hair.

Choose a theme that is equal to your powers, you writers, and reflect
a long while on what your shoulders refuse, and have the strength, to   40
carry. The man who selects a subject that suits his abilities will find
that eloquence and clarity of order do not desert him. The merit and
charm of order, if I am not mistaken, will be this, that the author of
the promised poem will say at the moment what should be said at
that moment, and will defer and leave out much for the present time,   45
showing fondness for one phrase and contempt for another.

You will succeed in expressing yourself admirably, with nice judge-
ment and care in linking words together, if a clever combination brings
novelty to a familiar word. If, perhaps, you are obliged to indicate
obscure notions by new terms, you will have the chance to form words   50
unknown to the ears of men like the kilted Cethegus, and freedom to
experiment will be yours to have, so long as you exercise it moder-
ately; and words that are new and recently formed will win accept-
ance if they flow from a Greek source and the channels are opened
frugally. Why indeed shall Romans grant this licence to Caecilius and

55 Plautus but refuse it to Virgil and Varius? In my own case, why am
I grudged the right to increase our account modestly, when the tongues
of Cato and of Ennius have enriched our native speech and brought
to light new vocabulary? It has always been allowed, and always will
be, to issue words that carry the mint-mark of the day.

60   As woods change their leaves when each year declines, and the earli-
est fall: so with words the old generation perishes, and, like our own
young, the newborn flourish and grow strong. We are owed to death,
we and what is ours; whether Neptune, welcomed on shore, defends
65 our fleets from northern gales, a king's work, or a marsh, long a waste
for the sluggish oar, feeds neighbouring towns and feels the plough's
heavy weight, or a river has changed its course, so ruinous to corn-
land, and has learned a better path, the works of man will perish,
and so much the less shall the glory and charm of language remain
70 and live on. Many terms that have now fallen into disuse shall be
born again, and these that enjoy honour today shall fall away, if usage
wishes, with whom resides the judgement, the authority, and the rule
of speech.

       Homer showed in what metre the achievements of kings and lead-
75 ers and the grim tale of war could be written. Verses unequally joined
together framed first of all lament, later also the grateful response to
answered prayer: but as to who was the first writer to produce tiny
elegies, scholars do not agree, and the case is still to be decided. Rage
armed Archilochus with the iambus, her own weapon; this foot was
80 adopted by the comic sock and stately buskin, as it suited alternate
speech, was able to rise above the noise of the pit and was naturally
appropriate for action. To the lyre the Muse granted power to tell of
gods and children of gods, the victorious boxer, the horse that comes
85 first in the race, the heartaches of young men, and the freedom of
wine. If I lack the ability or knowledge to keep to the various forms
and styles of poetic works, why do people hail me as a poet? Why out
of a perverse modesty do I prefer ignorance to learning my art?

90   A comic theme has no wish to be handled in tragic verse; likewise
Thyestes' banquet disdains to have its story told in poetry that is
informal and almost worthy of the comic sock. Let each thing occupy
the place assigned as proper for it. Yet sometimes even comedy raises
the tone of her voice, and an angry Chremes storms with swelling
95 utterance; and Telephus and Peleus in a tragedy often express their
grief in the language of prose, when the pair of them, impoverished

and banished, abandon their grandeur of speech and words a foot
and a half in length, if they want their lament to touch the spectator's
heart.

It is not enough for poems to be beautiful; they must be affect-
ing, and lead the listener's soul wherever they wish. As people's faces 100
smile on those who smile, so they respond to those who shed tears: if
you want me to weep, you must first feel grief yourself: that is when
your misfortunes hurt me, Telephus or Peleus; if the words you speak
are assigned to you ineptly, I'll either fall asleep or burst out laughing. 105
Melancholy words suit a sorrowful countenance, words full of threat-
ening an angry one; merry words suit a man who jokes, solemn words
a man of stern demeanour. For nature first moulds us internally to
suit every manner of experience; it makes us happy or drives us to
anger or brings us down to the ground and wrings our hearts with 110
the burden of grief; then, with the tongue as medium, it proclaims
the feelings of the heart. If the speaker's words do not chime with his
experiences, the Romans will raise a guffaw, horse and foot both.

It will make a great difference whether a god is speaking or a hero,
an old man advanced in years or one whose blood is hot, still in the 115
vigour of his youth, a married woman of rank or a bustling nurse, a
wandering merchant or one who tills some verdant acres, a Colchian
or an Assyrian, a man bred in Thebes or in Argos.

Either follow tradition or invent what is consistent. If, when you 120
write, you happen to take as your subject the admired Achilles, let
him be energetic, moody, ruthless, fierce, let him say that laws are not
for him and claim all things at the point of his sword. Let Medea be
proud of spirit and indomitable, Ino tearful, Ixion treacherous, Io a
wanderer, Orestes melancholic. If you entrust to the stage a theme not 125
tried before and dare to form a new character, let it stay to the end as
it was when first it appeared on stage, and let it be consistent. It is dif-
ficult to treat themes common to all in an individual way; and so you
are more correct in spinning a poem about Troy into acts than if, for 130
the first time, you give the public something unknown and unsung.
A body of material that is open to all will become your own legal prop-
erty if you do not repeatedly circle around the wide pathway all may
tread or make it your business as a faithful translator to render word
for word or to jump slavishly into a tight spot from which shame or 135
the laws of your chosen work forbid you to set foot: and be sure not to
start as the cyclic poet of old: 'Of Priam's fortune shall I sing, and war

renowned.' What will this boaster produce that justifies such bom-
bast? Mountains will heave in labour and born shall be a ludicrous
140 mouse! How much better the poet who makes no embarrassing effort:
'Tell me, Muse, of the man who after Troy's capture saw the ways
of many men and their cities.' His aim is to supply, not smoke after
flame, but light after smoke, that then he may go on to describe strik-
145 ing wonders, Antiphates, Scylla, Charybdis, and the Cyclops, too. He
neither begins Diomedes' return from the death of Meleager nor the
Trojan War from the twin egg: always he hurries on to the outcome
and whirls the listener into the middle of his tale, as if it was known
150 to him, leaving out what he fears his treatment cannot make striking,
and in such a way resorting to fiction, so mixing the true with the
false, that the middle of his tale does not clash with the start, nor the
end with the middle.

    Let me tell you what I, together with the public, look to find: if you
want an enthusiastic audience that waits for the curtain and remains
155 seated right to the moment when the singer says, 'Now give your
applause', you must take note of the behaviour of every age-group
and allow their characters an appropriate tone as they alter with the
years. The child who now knows how to reply in words and treads the
ground with steady feet, delights in playing with his mates, flies into
160 a rage and ceases to be angry without thought and changes from one
hour to another. The youth who still lacks a beard, freed at last from
his tutor, is delighted by horses and hounds and the grassy space of the
sunny Campus, like wax in his capacity for being moulded, stubborn
towards advisers, slow to make sensible provision for the future, lavish
165 with money, idealistic, with strong desires but swift to alter his fan-
cies. Changing his interests, one whose age and outlook has brought
him to manhood seeks wealth and friendships, makes himself a slave
to status in the city, and is fearful of having taken an action he would
find it hard to change later. Many troubles encompass an old man,
170 both because he seeks to acquire things and, finding them, wretch-
edly abstains, afraid to use them, and because he manages everything
fearfully and with coldness, putting things off, far-reaching in hope,
sluggish, greedy for a longer life, difficult, complaining, praising time
gone by when he was a lad, reproving and condemning the younger
175 generation. Many are the blessings the years bring with them as they
come towards us, many the blessings they take away as they withdraw
behind us. So, in case we assign to a youth the part of old age, and to

a lad that of a man, be sure that we always dwell carefully on traits
associated with, and appropriate to, time of life.

Either an event is acted out on stage or the action is in the form of
narrative. Minds are stirred less vividly by what is conveyed through   180
the ear than what is brought before their trusty eyes, and what the
spectator presents to his own sight: but be sure not to bring on stage
what should be enacted behind the scenes, and to remove from sight
much that an actor's eloquent tongue may report in due course before
our eyes. Let us not have Medea butchering her sons in front of the   185
people, or wicked Atreus cooking human innards on stage, or Procne
turning into a bird, or Cadmus into a snake. Anything you show me in
this fashion, I disbelieve and find disgusting.

A play should not be smaller or longer than five acts, if, once seen,
it wants to be demanded and staged again. No god should intervene,   190
unless a knot occurs that needs such a deliverer, and there should be
no fourth actor anxious to speak his lines. The chorus should bravely
sustain the role of an actor and do the duty of a man, and not sing any-
thing between acts that is irrelevant to, or not closely connected with,   195
the plot. It should support good men and offer them friendly coun-
sel, control the angry and love those who fear to do wrong; it should
praise the food of a modest table, praise the blessings of justice, the
laws, and peace with her open gates; it should keep secrets and pray   200
and entreat the gods that fortune might return to the wretched and
leave the arrogant.

The double-pipe, not, as now, bound with brass and rivalling the
trumpet, but thin and simple, with few stops, was sufficient for accom-
panying and helping the chorus and filling with its breath seats that   205
were not yet too crowded; there, of course, the people would assemble,
easily counted since few in number, honest folk, true to their partners
and god-fearing. After a conquering race began to widen its terri-
tory and a more spacious wall encircled its city, and on holidays the   210
Genius was appeased with daylight drinking that brought no penalty,
a greater freedom was given to both rhythms and tunes; for what taste
would an uneducated crowd have, released from their toils, country-
man mixing with townsman, low fellows with well-born? As a result
the piper added to his early art physical movement and provocative   215
gesture, trailing a long robe as he lounged over the stage; as a result,
the notes of the austere lyre increased in number, and a briskly paced
fluency brought with it an unfamiliar delivery, while the thought, full

of practical wisdom and prophetic of the future, was not at variance
with that of lot-drawing Delphi.

220   The poet who competed in tragic song for a cheap goat soon also
presented woodland satyrs in skins, and in a rough way that main-
tained his dignity attempted to raise laughter, for this reason that
novelty's attractive charm was needed to hold the spectator, now that
he had performed the sacrifices and, well drunk, had won freedom
225   from the law's restraints. But it will be appropriate to win the audi-
ence's goodwill towards the laughing, bantering satyrs and to make
the change from serious to humorous in such a way that no god, no
hero, is brought on, lately seen in royal purple and gold, and moves,
230   by his vulgar style of talk, into a badly lit hovel, or, while shunning the
earth, catches at clouds and empty air. Tragedy, disdaining to babble
frivolous verses, will take her place among the naughty satyrs like a
married woman invited to dance on holidays, a little ashamed of her
actions. It won't be my way, my dear Pisos, if writing satyr plays, to
235   favour only nouns and verbs that are plain and authorized by use; nor
shall I strive so to depart from the tragic tone that it makes no differ-
ence whether Davus is talking with the shameless Pythias, who has
just won a talent by bamboozling Simo, or Silenus, who guards and
240   serves the god in his charge. I shall aim to produce poetry so newly
formed from the familiar that anyone at all may hope for the same
result but sweat much and toil in vain as he attempts the same: such
is the power of connection and combination, such the distinction that
attaches to common or garden words. When fauns are brought on
stage from the woodland, they should be careful, in my view, never
245   to play the silly youngster with wanton language, as though they were
born at the crossroads or almost dwell in the forum, or to crack their
dirty jokes that bring shame on their heads: for offence is taken by
250   those who have a horse, a father, or wealth, who do not receive with
favour or reward with a crown whatever goes down well with one who
buys roasted chickpeas and nuts.

A long syllable immediately followed by a short is called Iambus, a
swift foot; and so he ordered the name 'trimeters' to be applied to his
lines, though he delivered six beats that were the same throughout,
255   from first to last. But not so long ago, in order to reach the ears a
little more slowly and with more weight, he admitted steady spon-
dees into his hereditary rights, being an obliging and accommodat-
ing soul, without, however, taking friendliness so far as to vacate his

established position in the second and fourth feet. He makes only an infrequent appearance in the 'noble' trimeters of Accius, and as for Ennius' verses, launched onto the stage with their ponderous weight, 260 he pursues them with the shameful charge of too hasty and thoughtless workmanship and ignorance of poetic art.

Not any old critic notices verses that lack rhythm, and Roman poets have been granted indulgence they do not deserve. Should I, for this reason, leave the tracks and write with no regard for discipline? Or 265 am I to suppose that *everyone* will notice my faults, avoiding risk and taking care not to stray beyond the hope of being pardoned? This way in the end I have avoided blame and earned no praise. Gentlemen, day and night turn in your hands and think on Greek models. Yet your ancestors, you say, praised Plautus for his metrical skill and 270 wit. Too tolerant, not to say stupid, was their admiration of both, if only you and I know how to distinguish between vulgarity and elegance, and have the nous to recognize the correct rhythm with fingers and ear.

Thespis, they say, discovered the unknown genre of the tragic 275 Muse, transporting his pieces on wagons, to be sung and performed by players whose faces were smeared with wine-lees. After him Aeschylus, inventor of the mask and the lordly robe, both laid a platform of low planks and gave instruction in the use of grand language 280 and the buskin's stately gait. These were succeeded by Old Comedy, that won considerable praise; but its freedom fell into excess and an outrageous edge that deserved to be controlled by law; the law was obeyed, and to its shame the chorus fell silent, once its right to cause offence was removed.

Our own poets have left no style untried, and not the least honour 285 did they win when they had the courage to leave the footsteps of the Greeks and to celebrate deeds at home, whether they presented tragedies or comedies with Roman themes. And Latium would not be more supreme in her courage and glory in war than in her literature, 290 were it not that her poets, each and every one of them, cannot endure the tedium and effort of revising their work. Make it your aim, you who have the blood of Pompilius in your veins, to censure any poem that has not been pruned by many a day and many an erasure, and not polished ten times over to satisfy the test of the close-cut nail.

Because Democritus believes that natural talent is a greater bless- 295 ing than miserable craftsmanship, and debars from Helicon poets

who have their sanity, a sizeable number of them don't bother to have
their nails or beards trimmed, and choose lonely places to frequent,
300 giving the baths a wide berth. For one who has never entrusted to the
barber Licinus a head that three Anticyras cannot cure will certainly
win the esteem and name of a poet. Ah, what an idiot I am, to cleanse
myself of bile as springtime's season draws near! No other man would
compose better poems. But it's just not worth it. So I'll perform the
305 role of a knife-sharpener, that has the power to make iron sharp but of
itself has no share in cutting; despite not writing anything myself, I'll
give instruction in the poet's function and duty, what sources should
supply his stores, what nurtures and shapes a poet, what is appropri-
ate for him and what is not, where the right path leads and where the
wrong.

Both the source and first principle of good writing is moral sense:
310 the Socratic corpus will be able to show you the subject matter, and,
once they see this set before them, words will readily follow. He who
has learned his duty to his country and to his friends, what love is due
a parent, a brother and a guest, the obligations that fall on a senator
315 and a juryman, the tasks a leader must perform when sent to war,
without question knows how to assign the requisite qualities to each
of his characters. My advice to one who is trained in representation
is to look to life and manners for his model and to draw from there
language that possesses life. Sometimes a play that has well-drawn
characters and an attractiveness based on its ethical passages, but at
320 the same time is lacking in charm, force, and art, gives an audience
greater delight and holds its attention better than verses devoid of
substance and tuneful bagatelles.

To the Greeks the Muse gave native talent, to the Greeks speech in
well-rounded utterance; they craved nothing except glory. Romans,
325 by contrast, learn in school by means of lengthy calculations how
to divide the *as* into a hundred parts. 'Let's hear the answer from
Albanus' son: if one ounce is taken from five-twelfths, what is left?
You could have told us by now.' 'A third.' 'Bravo! You'll be able
to look after your funds. Add an ounce and what does *that* make?'
330 'A half.' When once this canker, this thirst for petty cash, has blighted
their souls, do we expect that poems can be fashioned worthy of being
smeared with cedar-oil and kept in a polished cypress chest?

Poets aim either to confer benefit or to give pleasure, or to
say things which are at once both pleasing and helpful to life.

Whatever instruction you pass on, be sure to be brief, so that with speed 335
the mind may grasp it receptively and retain it faithfully. Everything
superfluous flows away from a mind that is full to the brim. Fictions
intended to give pleasure should approximate to the truth, so that a
play should not ask for credence in whatever it wants, or a living child 340
be pulled out of Lamia's belly, after she has had dinner. The centur-
ies of elders chase off the stage all that is not of solid worth, while
the haughty Ramnes have no time for poems lacking in charm: the
writer who blends the profitable with the agreeable wins every vote,
by charming and instructing the reader at the same time. This is the 345
book that makes money for the Sosii; this the one that both crosses the
sea and extends a writer's life to a distant day, making him famous.

There are, however, faults which we may wish to countenance; for
the string does not always produce the sound which hand and heart
intend, and often returns a sharp when a flat is called for; the bow will 350
not always strike whatever target it threatens. But when the beaut-
ies in a poem are more numerous, I, for one, shall not be offended
by a few blemishes, which either carelessness has let fall on the page
or human nature has taken insufficient care to avoid. What, then,
do we conclude? As a copying clerk is not forgiven if he persists in
making the same mistake, however many warnings he receives, as a 355
lyre-player invites mockery if he constantly gets it wrong with the
same string, so, I think, the poet who often shirks his work becomes
another Choerilus, whose two or three good lines make me laugh with
surprise; yet I also take it amiss whenever the excellent Homer dozes
off; but it is permissible that sleep should steal up on a work of such 360
length.

Poetry is like painting: one picture attracts you more, the nearer
you stand, another, the farther away. One favours shade, another
will wish to be seen in the light, showing no fear of the critic's sharp
insight; one gave you pleasure on a single occasion, another will 365
continue doing so, though you turn back to it ten times.

Young sir whose age is greater, although you have judgement in
your own right and have a father's words to train you in the right
thoughts, take up and keep in your heart what I say to you now, that
only certain pursuits are, by rights, permitted to be average and of
middling quality. The expert in points of law or pleader of cases who 370
does not possess the excellence of the eloquent Messalla or know
as much as Aulus Cascellius yet has his value: but that poets should

be middle of the road, is something not permitted by gods, men or billboards. As at agreeable dinner-parties, music played out of tune, 375 scented ointment that is thick and poppy-seeds coated with Sardinian honey give offence, since the meal could proceed without these things, so a poem whose birth and devising are for the pleasure of the soul, if it falls short of the highest standard, even by a little, sinks to the bottom.

Someone who cannot play games keeps away from the weapons 380 of the Campus, and having no skill with ball, discus, or hoop, he keeps himself to himself, in case the thickly packed ring of spectators breaks into unrestrained laughter: but someone who doesn't know how dares to fashion verse. Why not? He's free, indeed freeborn, and what's more, he's assessed at the property qualification of a knight, and there's no misdemeanour on his record to detract from his respectability.

385 You, I'm sure, will say nothing and do nothing without Minerva's approval: such is your judgement, such your intelligence. Yet if you do write anything in the future, let it come to the ears of the critical Maecius, or your father's, or my own, and let it be kept back for nine years, keeping your parchment sheets inside the house. You will be at 390 liberty to destroy what you have not published; a word, once uttered, does not know how to return.

As long as mankind dwelled in the woods, Orpheus, the priest and spokesman of the gods, kept them from bloodshed and a disgusting diet, so giving rise to the tale that he tamed the hearts of ravening tigers and lions; the tale also runs that Amphion, who founded the 395 city of Thebes, made stones move at the sound of his lyre and led them wherever he wanted by the alluring spell of his appeals. In early times what counted for wisdom was separating the public from the private, the sacred from the mundane, preventing people from indulging in indiscriminate intercourse, establishing laws for wedded life, building towns, and engraving laws on tablets of wood. It followed 400 that honour and renown fell to bards and poetry, as coming from the gods. Winning fame after these, Homer and Tyrtaeus by their verses whetted the spirits of men for the battles of Mars: by means of verse oracles were delivered, and the way to lead one's life was shown, by 405 Pierian strains the favour of kings was courted and entertainment found that marked an end to lengthy toils, in case you should perhaps blush for the Muse skilled in the lyre and Apollo, lord of song.

It is often asked whether nature or art makes a poem praiseworthy: my own view is there is no good in study unaccompanied by a rich vein of natural ability or in talent that is untrained; so true is it that the one demands the help of the other and forms with it a friendly pact. The athlete who is eager to reach the longed-for finishing-post has endured and done a great deal in his young days, sweating and shivering, denying himself wine and women: the piper who plays the Pythian piece has first of all learned his skill and been in dread of a teacher. These days it's enough for someone to say, 'I compose wonderful poems: devil take the hindmost: what brings me disgrace is being left behind and admitting that I simply don't know what I never learned.' 410 415

Like the auctioneer, who gathers a crowd to buy his wares, the poet invites yes-men to answer the call of profit, if he is rich in land and rich in money put out at interest. But if he is one who can properly serve up a fine dinner, and stand surety for an impoverished client not to be trusted, and rescue another caught up in the toils of a murky lawsuit, I'll be surprised if the lucky fellow will know how to tell a false and a true friend apart. Now, in your case, whether you have given someone a gift or wish to give one, be sure not to bring him in the fullness of his joy to listen to verses you have written: for he will exclaim 'Beautiful! Good! Perfect!' His cheeks will lose their colour over these pieces, he will even distil teardrops from his sympathetic eyes, he will dance and thump the ground with his foot. 420 425 430

As the words and actions of hired mourners at a funeral express almost more than those whose tears come from the heart, so your servile mocker shows more emotion than the one who is genuine in his praise. They say that kings, if anxious to see into a man's heart to judge if he deserves their friendship, ply him with many cups of wine, putting him to that ordeal: if you mean to compose poetry, be sure that you are never taken in by the intent that lies concealed inside the fox. 435

If ever anyone read any of his work to Quintilius, he would say, 'Put this right, please, and this': if you said, after trying two or three times without success, that you couldn't do any better, he would tell you to blot them out and to return the badly turned verses to the anvil. If you preferred to defend the fault instead of altering it, he would expend not one word more, not a single effort, to stop you loving yourself and your work alone without a rival. A man of honesty and good sense will 440 445 criticize verses that lack energy, he will find fault with those that are harsh, he will make a horizontal stroke with his pen and smear a black sign opposite those that lack refinement, he will prune back pretentious ornamentation and force you to admit light to what is not clear enough, he will show up what has been expressed ambiguously, he will alter what requires to be changed, he will become an Aristarchus: he will not say, 'Why should I give offence to a friend when it is a matter of trifles?' These trifles will bring a friend into serious difficulties when once he has been mocked and received unfavourably.

As when a man is plagued by the accursed scab or the king's ailment or a fit of madness caused by Diana's anger, so men of sense are afraid of coming into contact with a crazy poet and take to their heels: children tease and chase him, knowing no better. He with head in the air spouts verses and wanders on his way, but if, like some fowler intent on catching blackbirds, he falls into a well or pit, then, however long he cries out, 'Hey, fellow citizens, come and help!', there wouldn't be anyone to show interest in pulling him up. Should anyone be concerned to bring help and lower a rope, my comment would be, 'How do you know he didn't throw himself in deliberately and has no wish to be saved?' and I'd tell the story of the Sicilian poet's death. Empedocles, in his eagerness to be regarded as an immortal god, leapt in cold blood into the hot glow of Etna. Let poets have the right and power to die in this manner. He who saves a man's life when he wants to die is doing the same as a murderer. It isn't the first time that he has acted like this, and, if he is pulled out, he won't immediately become a human being and abandon his desire for a famous death. It isn't very clear either what has caused his persistence in composing verses: did he commit sacrilege by pissing on top of his father's ashes or by disturbing some consecrated piece of ground? He has certainly lost his wits, and like a bear that has succeeded in breaking the bars set across its cage, he puts the lot of them to flight, learned and unlearned alike, with his remorseless recitations; indeed the man he catches he holds fast in a great hug and reads him to death, a leech that will not leave the skin alone until it has gorged itself on blood.

EXPLANATORY NOTES

ABBREVIATIONS

AP   *Ars Poetica* (the *Epistle to the Pisos: The Art of Poetry*)

DRN   Lucretius, *De rerum natura* (*On the Nature of the Universe*)

H.   Horace

Porph.   Porphyrio (ancient commentator on Horace)

Ps.-Acro   Pseudo-Acro (ancient commentator on Horace)

ROL   E. H. Warmington (ed.), *Remains of Old Latin*, Loeb Classical Library, 4 vols. (Cambridge, Mass., 1936–40)

SATIRES, BOOK 1

SATIRE 1.1

The satirist begins by expressing amazement that different people always envy the lot of others though they would not swap places given the chance, but he proceeds (after briefly noting satire's ability to convey serious truths through humour) to focus on the pointlessness of amassing wealth, since one can only use or enjoy a small amount at a time. He concludes by rejecting the other extreme of profligacy, advocating the path of moderation in all things.

14   *Fabius*: like many of the names in the *Satires*, we are dependent on the ancient commentators (such as Porphyrio and Pseudo-Acro) for the identity of Fabius, and it is at least probable that they are guessing or deducing from the context of the *Satires* themselves. Indeed, the point of virtually all H.'s named examples is clear, even if not how precisely they make that point. Porph. here proposes Fabius Maximus Narbonensis as author of several books relating to Stoicism.

25–6 *just as teachers . . . to learn their ABC*: probably an allusion to Lucretius' Epicurean poem *On the Nature of the Universe* (*De rerum natura*, DRN) and the image of his poetry as like honey smeared on a cup of bitter medicine, helping readers take in his philosophical message. Allusions to Lucretius and an affinity with Epicureanism are common in H., especially in the *Satires*.

33   *tiny ant*: the first of many uses of beast fables in the *Satires* (and *Epistles*) reflecting their (partly disingenuous) claim to homespun wisdom.

57   *the fierce Aufidus*: the modern Ofanto, a river in southern Italy. The image of the swollen, muddy river links with that of Lucilius' copious but unrefined composition of poetry at 1.4.11 and 1.10.50–1, and behind it of Callimachus' description of bad poetry as like the muddy Euphrates (*Hymn to Apollo* 108–9) to connect the ethical moderation advocated here to the poetic moderation of H.'s refined satire.

65 *the wealthy Athenian*: Ps.-Acro identifies him as Timon, but this miser indifferent to popular disapproval seems rather different from an active misanthrope, especially one like Timon, made so by ingratitude to his generosity shown in times of hardship, as depicted in Plutarch, Lucian, and eventually Shakespeare.

68 *Tantalus*: in mythology, he was punished for serving his son Pelops' flesh to the gods (or disclosing secrets or stealing nectar and ambrosia) by being 'tantalized' in the Underworld by fruit which always retreated when he reached for it and by water up to his neck which drained away when he tried to drink.

91 *Mars' Field*: the Campus Martius, just outside the walls of Rome, contained the Circus Flaminius, where chariot races were held. The Latin does not specify 'at the races' and H. may also be referring to training horses for military service.

95 *Ummidius*: otherwise unknown, to H.'s contemporaries as to us, as 'a certain' indicates. Some see a play on the cash (*nummi*) he weighs or on his being 'immoderate' and chopped 'in the middle' (*in medio*).

100 *Tyndareus' daughters*: an allusion to Clytemnestra who, in many versions, used an axe to kill her husband, Agamemnon.

101 *Naevius or Nomentanus*: Nomentanus is an exemplary spendthrift and mentioned in similar terms at 1.8.11, 2.1.22, 2.3.175, 2.3.224; it is unclear whether the parasite who plays a substantial role in 2.8 is meant to be the same figure. The ancient commentators speculate on his identity, but it is notable that Seneca pairs the name with that of Apicius as gourmands at *On the blessed life* 11.4. It is unclear whether Naevius is a miser in polar opposition to Nomentanus (Porph.) or whether they are both spendthrifts in contrast to the misers criticized earlier.

105 *Tanais and Visellius' father-in-law*: clearly extremes of some kind, but unclear what. Porph. identifies the former as a eunuch freedman of either Maecenas or Plancus, and the latter as a man with a hernia from too much sex. Tanais is also the river Don and usually represents the far north in Latin poetry (e.g. H., *Odes* 3.10.1); the antithesis may relate to this.

119 *like a guest who has dined well*: another allusion to Lucretius, here his argument against the fear of death at *DRN* 3.938–9, in keeping with the broadly Epicurean tone of much of the *Satires*.

120 *Crispinus*: Porph. claims Plotius Crispinus was a Stoic philosopher, and he is mentioned in similar terms at 1.3.139, 1.4.14, and 2.7.45. His myopia (or possibly conjunctivitis) is caused by excessive study but also symbolizes his limited perception.

SATIRE 1.2

The theme of moderation continues, focusing now on those who rush to one extreme to avoid the other, before settling specifically on the question of sex, where the extremes of adultery with respectable *matronae* and obsession with courtesans are equally rejected. The emphasis shifts slightly onto sexual desire as a bodily appetite to be satisfied in any way one can, which renders the dangers incurred by adultery pointless.

1 *Honourable Companies*: the Latin word *collegia* covers various types of clubs and associations, but here ironically evokes the trade guilds of more respectable professions than those listed.

2 *'actresses'*: specifically, actresses in mime, the least respectable dramatic genre (closer to farce than its silent modern namesake, and including dialogue), though all actors at Rome were considered disreputable and denied citizen rights. They recur as potential mistresses at line 58.

3 *the singer Tigellius*: a Sardinian singer, mentioned in several of the *Satires*.

4 *'What a generous soul he was!'*: the context and the identity of the mourners makes it clear that this is an ironic criticism of his extravagance.

12 *Fufidius*: a usurer of this name is mentioned several times by Cicero, but it may by now represent a typical miser.

16 *toga of manhood*: the all-white *toga pura* replaced the purple-fringed *toga praetexta* when elite boys entered manhood at about 16, but they were not entitled to enter into such financial arrangements until the age of 25.

20–1 *the father in Terence's play*: Menedemus, eponymous character of the Roman comedy, *Heauton Timorumenos* or *The Self-Tormentor* (163 BC).

25 *Maltinus*: the grammarian Nonius Marcellus claims that *malta* means an effeminate man, citing a line of Lucilius (fr. 744 *ROL*), and this name was probably coined accordingly.

27 *Rufillus . . . Gargonius of a billy-goat*: this line is 'quoted' at 1.4.92 as one which could be taken as indicating H.'s malice, but we might be sceptical about deducing from this that these are real people. The diminutive Rufillus might suggest affectation, and it is notable that, in Catullus 69, it is a Rufus who smells of goat.

28–9 *women . . . a low-hanging flounce*: respectable *matronae*, whose long robes (*stolae*) had a flounce (*instita*) for added concealment.

32 *Cato*: M. Porcius Cato 'the Elder' or 'the Censor' (234–149 BC), a byword for stern, old-fashioned morality, hence the unexpectedness of his reaction here. H. omits the second part of the anecdote, in which Cato sees the youth leaving the brothel frequently and tells him that he praised him for going there from time to time, not for living there (Ps.-Acro).

36 *Cupiennius*: the name suggests the Latin *cupido*, 'erotic desire'.

cunts wearing white: the Latin *cunnus* has a comparable level of obscenity and shock value, whether taken literally or as synecdoche for aristocratic women wearing white *stolae*.

37   *It's worth your while to lend an ear*: reproduces a phrase from Ennius'
     Annales (fr. 494 Skutsch = 471 *ROL*), a typical satiric debasement of lofty
     epic language in a low context.

44   *irrigated*: literally 'pissed through', the urinary metaphor making even
     more degrading the reference to anal rape, a common (in threats, at
     least) assertion of dominance or method of unofficial punishment in the
     Graeco-Roman world.

45   *what the law prescribes*: the Latin *iure* could also mean 'and quite right
     too', but Roman law did permit the wronged family to enact severe retri-
     bution, even before Augustus' later legislation 'for restraining adultery'
     in 18 BC.

     Galba: presumably an adulterer from the aristocratic Sulpician family,
     who either fears or has suffered the punishments described.

48   *freedwomen*: former slaves formed part of a *demi-monde* in which Roman
     men could indulge their sexual and perhaps even romantic urges, and
     it has been speculated that some of the 'mistresses' of Latin love elegy
     are of this status. Certainly, H. argues against the all-consuming passion
     which is characteristic of the elegists and their precursor Catullus.

     Sallust: possibly the historian, though his most famous sexual exploit
     was precisely the opposite, adultery with a *matrona*, no less than Fausta,
     daughter of Sulla and wife of Milo.

55   *Marsaeus . . . Origo*: even Porph. and Ps.-Acro only paraphrase what H.
     himself says here. Marsaeus' name may suggest a connection with the
     Marsi of central Italy, and more tenuously with the flayed satyr Marsyas.
     Origo's ('origin, birth, lineage') may play on the fact that Marsaeus precisely
     is not a 'lover of lineage'.

63   *maid dressed in a toga*: the standard dress of a male Roman citizen was not
     worn by respectable women, but was the costume of the courtesan. See
     also line 82.

64   *Villius . . . Fausta*: probably the Sextus Villius mentioned as a friend of
     Fausta's husband Milo (see second note on line 48 above) by Cicero
     (*Ad familiares* 2.6.1). 'Son-in-law' is, of course, an ironic designation
     for 'daughter's lover'. Fausta's name means 'Lucky', misleadingly for
     Villius.

67   *the door was shut against him*: Villius plays the role of the locked-out lover
     (*exclusus amator*), a stock figure of love elegy, often performing a song-by-
     the-closed-door (*paraklausithyron*).

     Longarenus: unknown, but evidently another of Fausta's lovers.

68-72 *Suppose . . . What would his reply be?*: personifications are a feature of
     diatribe, but close verbal echoes signal that this talking penis is a hilari-
     ously obscene parody of Nature's reprimand of those fearing death in
     DRN 3.929–65. Indeed H. goes on to align the penis's sentiments with
     'what nature advises'.

72–6 *But how much better . . . what should be avoided*: Epicurean language in keeping with the message of sexual desire's being a bodily need, whose pleasure lies in having been satisfied rather than in the process, in Epicurean terms a *katastematic* pleasure. Much of the second half of the satire recalls Lucretius' 'diatribe' against passionate love at *DRN* 4.1030–287.

80 *Cerinthus*: following the reading of the manuscripts and the Oxford Classical Text, he must be a jeweller. Bentley's conjecture *tuo* for *tuum* would make the comparison between the lady's leg and that of Cerinthus, who would then be a beautiful boy, as his name ('bees' bread') might suggest. It is also the name of the beloved of the (later) female elegist Sulpicia.

86 *Kings*: the significance of this is not entirely clear, but it might play on the further meaning of *reges* as 'patrons'.

90 *Lynceus*: in myth, the preternaturally keen-sighted watchman of the *Argo*.

91 *Hypsaea*: Porph. identifies her as Plotia Hypsaea, but as usual we might suspect an invented type of blindness either literally (a better antithesis to Lynceus) or to a lover's flaws.

92 *'What a leg! What arms!'*: an ironic allusion to an epigram (*Palatine Anthology*, 5.132) of H.'s contemporary Philodemus, who was both an Epicurean and a writer of erotic epigrams. The epigram contains no fewer than thirteen exclamations 'Oh', evoked by H.'s restrained pair.

95 *Catia*: Porph. claims she wore a short skirt to show off the beauty of her legs (clearly based on this line) and that she committed adultery in the temple of Venus.

96–8 *hedged by a rampart . . . hangers-on*: the emphasis on obstacles and especially the language of love as war (*militia amoris*) evokes the world of love elegy.

101 *Coan silk*: the famed (and famously transparent) product of the island of Cos, associated with courtesans and, in the following decades, particularly linked by Propertius with his beloved Cynthia.

105–8 *Our friend sings . . . what runs away*: a close imitation of Callimachus, *Epigram* 31 (*Palatine Anthology*, 12.102.)

113 *to separate void from substance*: the return of an Epicurean approach to the question of sex is marked by an allusion (with Lucretian echoes) to its materialist view of the universe as consisting of vacuum and matter.

114–16 *When your throat is parched . . . peacock and turbot*: the parallel of hunger and thirst reinforces the Epicurean depiction of sex as an emotionless bodily need.

117 *maid or slave-boy*: the absolute power held by masters over the bodies of their slaves included the right to exact sexual favours, or to rape them (from the modern, but not the ancient point of view).

121   *Galli*: eunuch priests of the Eastern goddess Cybele, and hence able to endure the endless postponements of sexual gratification.

   Philodemus: see note on line 92 above. The epigram alluded to does not survive, though it is interesting that another (*Palatine Anthology*, 5.126) depicts a very similar scenario to that of the caught-out lover at the end of the satire. There is also a pun on his name meaning 'lover of the common people'.

126   *Ilia and Egeria*: respectively the mother of Romulus and Remus by the god Mars, and the nymph who advised and married Rome's second king, Numa, hence the highest of Roman aristocracy. This is a Romanization of the sentiments of the third-century BC Cynic poet Cercidas, who recommends using the 'Aphrodite of the marketplace' and imagining yourself 'Tyndareus' son-in-law' (i.e. having sex with Helen).

131   *fearing for . . . her dowry*: a husband could divorce his adulterous wife and, unlike in divorce under other circumstances, keep part of her dowry.

   and me for myself: the surprising climax of this breathless sentence *could* be part of the counterfactual scenario which 'I don't worry about' but surely hints that the satirist does not practise what he preaches and speaks from bitter experience. The whole scene may evoke the typical scenario enacted in the low comic drama known as the 'adultery mime'.

133   *bank-balance*: an adulterer might be compelled to make financial restitution to the wronged husband.

   backside: see note on line 44 above, though the punitive insertion of radishes, spiky fish, and other painful objects may also be alluded to.

134   *Fabius*: if this is the Stoic of 1.1.14, he might argue that the wise man should be indifferent to suffering and not feel 'misery'.

SATIRE 1.3

A generalized attack on inconsistency focuses on why people ignore their own faults while criticizing those of their friends, when they ought to palliate or even put a positive 'spin' on the latter. Criticism of this general failing is linked to ridicule of its philosophical equivalent, the Stoic doctrine that all crimes are equal.

4   *Tigellius*: see note on *Sat.* 1.2.3.

   Caesar: presumably Octavian, the only reference to him in *Satires* 1, and the father invoked is Julius.

7   *Bacchus*: suggests a wild hymn to Dionysus, possibly a dithyramb.

8   *treble . . . lowest*: even Tigellius' vocal range goes to extremes.

9–11 *often he would tear along . . . Juno's sacred baskets*: this draws on Cicero's condemnation of extreme speed or slowness in walking in *De officiis* 1.131. The precise ritual in which Juno's sacred objects are being carried in procession is uncertain, but the image is clear.

15 *a million sesterces*: equivalences with modern currency are notoriously difficult, but when Augustus a little later imposed a property qualification (or census) for senators, this was the figure, a very large sum.

21 *Maenius*: mentioned by Lucilius, and Porph. has an anecdote about his proclaiming that he wished he had 400,000 sesterces-worth of debt, replying when asked why, that he owed 800,000, marking him as a spendthrift and a wit.

Novius: barely characterized here and unidentified by the commentators, but his name may suggest that he is a 'new man' (*novus homo*).

27 *an Epidaurian snake's*: a snake sacred to the god of healing, Aesculapius, who had a temple at Epidaurus, near Argos, or perhaps one brought from there to his temple in Rome. The healthy eyesight of such snakes provides additional contrast to the diseased eyes of self-examination.

29–30 *the fastidious standards*: lit. 'keen noses', continuing the sensory metaphor.

38–9 *a lover in his blindness . . . charmed by them*: as in the last satire, an allusion to Lucretius' diatribe against passionate love, and specifically the pet-names with which lovers delude themselves about the beloved's flaws, but H. goes on to invert the picture and use it as a *positive* model for how friends should treat each other's flaws.

40 *Balbinus . . . Hagna's polyp*: unknown, unless the connection with the Balbinus who joined Sextus Pompeius is correct, but the names could suggest that he 'stammers' (*balbus*) and that her 'chaste' Greek name is as much of a euphemism as any in Lucretius.

47 *Sisyphus*: Porph. claims this was a favourite dwarf of Mark Antony.

76 *Again*: marks the transition into the attack on the Stoic doctrine that all crimes are equal, using a word (*denique*) typical of Lucretius.

77 *the other faults that attach themselves to fools*: Stoics also believed that everyone except the Stoic 'wise man' (*sapiens*) was mad or foolish; H. appropriates the notion ironically.

82 *crucified*: considered a degrading punishment, particularly associated with slaves.

82–3 *men of sanity . . . Labeo*: H. brands the Stoic doctrine on crime with the insanity they impute to all non-Stoics; the Labeo whom Porph. suggests would be too young when the poem was written, so many identify this as C. Atinius Labeo, who, as tribune in 131 BC, tried to have the censor thrown from the Tarpeian Rock on the Capitoline Hill (from which traitors, beginning with the Vestal Virgin Tarpeia, were thrown).

86 *Ruso*: not known beyond the context of this passage, but evidently enforced listening to his histories at a recitation is the price of failing to pay interest on a debt.

87 *gloomy Kalends*: the first of the month, when interest on loans was due.

91 *by Evander's hands*: legendary Arcadian king who first settled the site where Rome later stood; H., or perhaps the host in free indirect discourse, massively exaggerates the antiquity of the cup.

92 *my side of the dish*: Roman diners shared couches, tables, and dishes.

94–5 *What . . . a legal agreement?*: the standard practical (as opposed to philosophical) objection to the Stoic position, that harsh punishment of trivial offences leaves no room for a proportionate response to more serious crimes.

97–8 *instinct . . . expediency itself*: H. opposes the Stoic position partly by referring to their own adherence to the laws of nature, partly by developing an Epicurean view of how human society develops through expediency and convention, holding much in common with Lucretius' description of this in *DRN* 5.

100 *acorns and lairs*: the basics of human existence; acorns are a conventionally primitive food in Roman thought, but the low detail is a satiric touch.

103–4 *verbs and nouns*: the development of language was an important issue in ancient philosophical (as in modern anthropological) thought on early humans.

107–8 *Helen . . . cause of war*: the archetypal cause of the archetypal war, that of the Greeks against Troy, is shown to be far from the first caused by sexual desire. The obscene word *cunnus* (see second note on 1.2.36 above) both emphasizes the low, physical nature of the desire (equivalent to that for acorns!) and injects a satiric note into the lofty ascent of man.

108 *an unrecorded death*: memorialization of the dead is a key motif in Homer and his reception; those dying before the Trojan War lack this consolation.

116–17 *young cabbages . . . the gods' holy emblems*: the harsh law-code of Draco in archaic Athens prescribed equal punishment for these crimes.

123 *the power of a king*: as holding absolute and arbitrary power to punish; the Roman aversion to the term has been exaggerated but is still considerable.

124–5 *If the wise man . . . a king*: Stoic doctrine; the inclusion of the cobbler, though not inconsistent with the doctrine, inevitably ridicules it.

127 *father Chrysippus' meaning*: Greek philosopher, *c.*280–207 BC, and head of the Stoa following its founder Zeno and his successor, Cleanthes, but often seen as the key formulator of Stoic doctrine. The interlocutor is clearly a Stoic.

129 *Hermogenes*: clearly a singer, frequently mentioned later in *Satires* 1 with the additional name Tigellius. Scholars disagree whether this is meant to be the same Tigellius mentioned at 1.2.3 and 1.3.4, but it feels awkward to have a different singer of the same name in the same satire.

130 *Alfenus*: despite attempts to link him with contemporary figures, clearly a retired barber for the nonce.

133–6 *Naughty boys . . . most mighty of mighty kings*: the beard and stick are emblems of the philosopher, here distorted into the object of and ineffectual defence against derisory attack. The humour and naughtiness of the boys surely represents the comic satirist's irreverent attack on the lofty philosopher-king.

137–40 *while you, a king . . . my genial friends will pardon me*: ironically, despite being a 'king', the Stoic wise man lacks a retinue even of friends because of his harshly judgmental attitude, while H., despite his 'folly' by Stoic standards, has the pleasure of (Epicurean) friends who show the leniency advocated throughout the satire.

139 *Crispinus*: see note on *Sat.* 1.1.120.

142 *in my private station shall live a happier man than Your Majesty*: asserting the joys of Epicurean quietism, with an additional, if specious, contrast between non-involvement in politics and the 'kingship' of the Stoic wise man.

SATIRE 1.4

After the three 'diatribes', H. reflects on the nature of satire. He traces its antecedents in Greek Old Comedy before criticizing the careless poetic technique of the father of satire, Lucilius. He then defends his own satires, both on aesthetic grounds and against charges of abusive slander. He traces his own moral training (and his practice as a satirist) to his father's pointing out of good and bad exemplars.

1 *Eupolis . . . Old Comedy*: Eupolis (*fl.* 429–412 BC), Cratinus (*fl.* 450–423), and Aristophanes (*c.*455–386) were the three most celebrated authors of so-called 'Old Comedy' in fifth- and fourth-century Athens, engaging with contemporary political issues and often attacking political figures (*komoidoumenoi*, or 'objects of comic attack'). Although the Romans considered satire a native form without specific Greek antecedents, the earthy tone and abusive, political subject matter made Old Comedy a privileged forebear.

5 *Lucilius*: see Introduction. The extent of his debt to Old Comedy is wildly exaggerated, in keeping both with H.'s archaeology of satire and his polemic against Lucilius.

7–8 *witty . . . but unpolished*: the contrast between the content produced by talent (*ingenium*) and the style produced by skill (*ars*) is central to H.'s attack on Lucilius and more generally to 'Callimachean' poets' attitude to 'archaic' authors.

8 *with a sensitive nose*: lit. 'well-blown', and hence able to detect the stench of vice and folly.

10 *on one leg*: proverbially 'very easily'.

11 *muddy river*: see note on *Sat.* 1.1.57.

14 *Crispinus*: see note on *Sat.* 1.1.120. The context might suggest that he also writes poetry, but the challenge might equally be between H.'s speed in composing satire and Crispinus' in writing philosophical prose.

17–18 *I thank the gods . . . in very few words*: the self-deprecation is clearly
     ironic, since his brevity fits the ideals of both aesthetic and ethical mod-
     eration espoused throughout *Satires* 1.

21   *Fannius*: clearly a self-promoting but unadmired poet. Regardless of his
     quality, as a living poet his work would not have been allowed in Pollio's
     library, Rome's first public library, established in the early 30s BC, which
     housed only the works of dead writers. Other interpretations of the Latin
     are possible, but the general sense is clear.

23   *to read it in public*: recitations were an important part of the dissemination
     of poetry in Rome.

24–5 *for the reason . . . most of them deserve censure*: the satirist's concern that
     the objects of his attack will be hostile, and the attendant threats to his
     freedom of speech, are recurrent motifs from H. onwards, notably in
     Sat. 2.1, Persius 1, and Juvenal 1.

26–7 *either greed or wretched ambition . . . crazy with love*: the targets of the
     first two satires of this book.

28   *Albius*: the name recurs at line 109 among the negative exempla pointed
     out by H.'s father. Strict chronology tells against them being the same
     person, but H. proleptically shows himself putting his father's teaching
     into practice.

34   *hay tied to his horns*: used to mark out aggressive bulls.

37   *bakehouse or water-tank*: public facilities for the poor respectively to bake
     their bread and fetch water, hence the low readership—slaves and old
     women—alleged for H.'s poetry.

42   *conversational prose*: evokes H.'s own title for the collection, *Sermones* or
     Conversations. The question of whether everything in verse was 'poetry'
     was a vexed one in antiquity (for instance, Aristotle denies the philosoph-
     ical verse of Empedocles that title) but satire's rejection of the status of
     poetry is part of its self-representation as low, realistic, and generally the
     opposite of the loftier poetic genres, especially epic.

45   *whether comedy is poetry or not*: links back to the opening lines of this
     satire; note that the ostensibly negative qualities ascribed to comedy (as to
     satire) are also its strengths in relating to (a construction of) real life.

48–52 *'But the father . . . torches'*: the interlocutor's examples are actually stock
     characters and situations from the more domestic, social, and romantic
     'New Comedy' associated with Menander and the Romans Plautus and
     Terence, than the political Old Comedy of Aristophanes. As H.'s response
     shows, the subject matter of this genre too can be paralleled in satire.

52   *Pomponius*: clearly a 'real-life' equivalent of the disobedient, courtesan-
     loving son of New Comedy.

60–1 *'When once . . . asunder'*: a quotation from Ennius' *Annales* (fr. 225–6
     Skutsch), the canonical Roman epic before the composition of Virgil's
     Aeneid, and the specific object of parody by Lucilius. The gates of the
     temple of Janus were opened when Rome was at war.

62 *even when he was dismembered . . . the limbs of a poet*: a famous line playing on the established parallel between a body (*corpus*) of work and that of the poet himself. Even if Ennius' words did not scan as hexameters, H. claims, they would still be recognizable as poetry.

65–6 *Sulcius and Caprius*: it is just possible that these are other, more aggressive satirists, but far more probably they are informers, feared by robbers but not by the innocent. The Latin for 'indictments' (*libelli*) can also mean 'poetry books' (and H. so designates *this* book at line 71 below and at the very end of *Sat.* 1.10), which reinforces the parallel between informers and satirists.

69 *Caelius and Birrius*: in terms of the analogy, these must be robbers living in fear of Sulcius and Caprius, so that the addressee is an equivalently vicious or foolish target for satire.

71 *dangling from a pillar*: outside a bookshop, where books would be tied as an advertisement and for browsers to sample.

72 *those of Hermogenes Tigellius*: see note on *Sat.* 1.3.129. Some see this as a gibe at his meanness in browsing not buying, but the point is surely that his lack of taste is as marked as that of the mob; this specific flaw of this comprehensively flawed character is particularly stressed in *Sat.* 1.10.

73 *except my friends*: central to Epicureanism and to H.'s broader view of life. The emphasis on a select readership is foreshadowed in Lucilius, but is especially characteristic of Horatian satire.

85 *has a black heart*: lit. 'is black', with no ethnic connotations, but the ethical imagery of black and white is pervasive in the *Satires*.

86 *four persons . . . three couches*: three per couch was the norm, marking the *scurra* as an extra.

87–9 *one of whom is in the habit . . . secrets of the heart*: the *scurra* was a sort of jester, a social inferior invited to dinner to entertain with his witty and often abusive banter. H. draws a parallel between this and his own brand of gently amusing satire.

89 *god who makes men free*: a play on one of the Latin names for the wine-god Dionysus, *Liber*, since wine makes tongues as well as men 'free'. Again, the issue of freedom of speech is subtly introduced.

92 *Rufillus . . . Gargonius of a billy-goat*: an exact quotation of 1.2.27, though the previous line replaces the ironic *facetus* ('the height of fashion') with the blunt *ineptus* ('silly'). H. thus dramatizes the reception of his own earlier satires, but we should still be sceptical about whether any of this refers to real events.

94 *Petillius Capitolinus*: despite Porph.'s fantasies of Jupiter Capitolinus' crown being stolen, nothing is known beyond what can be deduced from this passage and even the common conjecture that the 'theft' is in the form of embezzlement cannot be certain, though the interlocutor's tone and the noble name do suggest 'white-collar crime'.

100–1 *ink . . . venom*: continuing the colour imagery; *aerugo* is metaphorically 'venom' or 'malice' but literally the rust on bronze.

103   *outspoken*: lit. 'free', a play both on the satirist's freedom of speech and the
      origins of the outspokenness in H.'s freedman father.

105   *my excellent father*: H. roots his satire in the common-sense teaching
      of his father, based not on (Greek) philosophical doctrines but on the
      very Roman tradition of exemplarity, imitating positive examples and
      shunning the negative. The passage is overtly autobiographical, though
      caution must always be used in taking such passages literally. It has
      something in common with Demea's instructions to his son in Terence's
      Adelphoe 413–20, though the negative portrayal of that character makes
      the parallel problematic. On the surface, Lucilius' literary dependence on
      Old Comedy is contrasted with H.'s 'real-life' dependence on his father,
      though characteristic Horatian irony would suggest there is more to this
      passage than that.

109–10 *Albius' son . . . Baius*: that these are spendthrifts (or victims of spend-
      thrift fathers) can only be deduced from the context, a further parallel
      with H.'s own practice in the *Satires*. The context would most naturally
      imply that Albius' *son* is the spendthrift, but the father's appearance as an
      extravagant collector at line 28 above might put the blame on him.

111–12 *prostitute . . . Scetanus*: a high-class courtesan (*meretrix*) rather than
      streetwalker. This is part of the advice H. gives in *Sat.* 1.2. Scetanus is
      unknown.

113–14 *adulterous wives . . . Trebonius*: a further allusion to *Sat.* 1.2, this time
      the central argument. Trebonius is unknown.

115–20 *A philosopher . . . you won't need cork to swim*: the contrast between
      Roman exemplarity and Greek philosophizing is made explicit. Cork was
      used as a flotation aid for the young learning to swim.

130–1 *those . . . to earn pardon*: emphasis again on moderation, even in virtue,
      and on the differing severity of vices, as stressed in *Sat.* 1.3.

143   *the Jews*: in Roman times, Judaism was famous for its proselytizing zeal.

SATIRE 1.5

A description of a journey to Brundisium (or possibly Tarentum) with Maecenas
and others. H. engages closely with Lucilius' satire on a journey to Sicily, but
applies the principles of refinement and concision set out in the previous poem
in such a way that the journey itself embodies them. H.'s brevity, unexpected
emphases, and omission of many details are also related to the fact that the
journey was a politically charged one, either that to Brundisium in 38 BC or to
Tarentum in 37 for a meeting between Mark Antony and Octavian. H., the suf-
ferer from conjunctivitis, only sees and the Callimachean poet only describes
what it is safe to see and describe.

1   *Aricia*: modern Ariccia, 15 miles south-east of Rome on the Appian Way.
    The contrast between 'great Rome' and the 'modest inn' is suggestive of
    H.'s poetics.

2 *Heliodorus*: usually taken to be Apollodorus of Pergamum, whose name does not scan in hexameters, using a play on Apollo as Helios, the sun god; Caesar chose him in 45 BC to tutor his adopted son, Octavian. Gowers' suggestion that it refers to the author of the poem *Sights of Italy*, and that H. took not the poet but the book itself as a guide (like taking Baedeker on holiday) is attractive (E. Gowers, 'Horace' *Satires* 1.5: An Inconsequential Journey', *Proceedings of the Cambridge Philological Society*, 39 (1993), 48–66).

3 *Forum Appii*: another town on the Appian Way, 42 miles south-east of Rome, on the edge of the Pomptine marshes, and north-western end of a canal across them, on which H. continues his journey.

5–6 *Being lazy . . . in a single stretch*: probably a self-conscious contrast with Lucilius' *Journey to Sicily*, a fragment of which (fr. 102–5 *ROL*) suggests that he did get to Forum Appii in one stretch.

7–8 *declared war on my stomach*: i.e. by fasting.

9–10 *Now night . . . stars*: amusingly incongruous epic language.

24 *Feronia*: an Italian goddess, who had a shrine near Tarracina (Anxur), at the south-eastern end of the canal. The address (apostrophe) to her is an epic touch.

28 *Cocceius*: L. Cocceius Nerva, who was sent to Antony by Octavian in 41 BC and helped to forge the pact of Brundisium the following year, as alluded to in the following line.

30–1 *I apply . . . trouble*: both H.'s conjunctivitis and his smearing of ointment to treat it can be read symbolically in relation to his tactful refusal to see (or report) political matters which he is not supposed to see, and which are therefore unexpectedly and tantalizingly absent from this satire.

32 *Fonteius Capito*: praenomen Gaius, suffect consul in 33 BC, and, according to Plutarch, sent by Antony to bring Cleopatra to Syria in 36.

32–3 *flawless nature*: lit. 'made to the fingernail', i.e. like a sculpture so smooth that a fingernail cannot detect flaws.

34 *Fundi*: another town on the Appian Way, in the land of the Volsci.

with Aufidius Luscus as its praetor: the phrase (in the ablative absolute) evokes the similar use of Roman consuls' names to designate a year, a typical satiric debasement of lofty language but also suggesting Luscus' self-importance; his names evoke the muddy Apulian river Aufidus of *Sat.* 1.1 and, being 'one-eyed', the problems with vision which pervade this satire.

35–6 *regalia . . . charcoal*: despite being only a municipal official, Luscus wears the *toga praetexta* of consuls and other high magistrates, and the *latus clavus* of senators. The significance of the charcoal is less clear, and the notion that he is preparing to burn incense does not seem sufficiently absurd, even if it is to his guests rather than to the gods.

37 *the city of the Mamurrae*: Formiae, another name which does not fit hexameters, and home to Mamurra, Caesar's chief engineer and object of some of Catullus' most vicious poems.

38 *Murena*: presumably Aulus Terentius Varro Murena, Maecenas' brother-in-law, later executed in 22 BC for a conspiracy against Augustus.

40 *Sinuessa*: near modern Mondragone, and the southernmost point at which the Appian Way touched the coast of the Tyrrhenian sea.

    Plotius: Plotius Tucca, part of the so-called circle of Maecenas and later, with Varius, editor of the *Aeneid* following Virgil's death. All three friends also had connections with Philodemus and the Epicurean circle on the Bay of Naples, and H.'s paean to friendship here has an Epicurean ring. All three are also among H.'s ideal readers at 1.10.81, which is identical to this line but with *Maecenas* in place of *Sinuessae*.

    Varius: L. Varius Rufus, a great poet, whose works are almost entirely lost, perhaps best known for his *De morte*, probably an Epicurean attack on the fear of death, and the tragedy *Thyestes*, performed at Augustus' Actian games in 29 BC.

    Virgil: P. Vergilius Maro, author of *Eclogues*, *Georgics*, and *Aeneid*, probably the greatest of Rome's and perhaps of all poets.

45 *Campanian bridge*: taking the Appian Way over the river Savo, 3 miles from Sinuessa.

46 *state suppliers*: under Caesar's *lex Iulia de repetundis* of 59 BC, these *parochi* were obliged to supply the provisions listed to those on public business.

47 *Capua*: the main city of Campania, a byword for luxury.

49 *ball games . . . digestion*: H.'s ailments again prevent him from being involved with (and reporting) Maecenas' activities, though the ball games sound innocuous enough. Gowers suggests that *pila lippis*, juxtaposed with *inimicum* (lit. 'hostile'), encrypts an allusion to the battle of Philippi, where H. fought on the 'wrong' side (E. Gowers, 'Blind Eyes and Cut Throats: Amnesia and Silence in Horace *Satires* 1.7', *Classical Philology*, 97 (2002), 145–61).

51 *Caudium*: town in Samnium and site of a notorious Roman defeat in 321 BC. There is a double wordplay whereby Cocceius' (see note on line 28 above) villa not only overlooks, but is superior to and hence looks contemptuously down on the inns.

51–3 *Now, Muse*: a mock-epic invocation introducing the mock-epic 'battle' of insults between the low-life 'heroes' Sarmentus and Messius. Warriors' (infinitely more noble) lineage is also a staple of descriptions of epic duels. Lucilius also seems to have included a mock-epic 'battle' in his *Journey to Sicily*.

52 *Sarmentus*: according to a scholiast on Juvenal, a freedman and clerk of Maecenas; on *scurrae* ('jesters'), see note on *Sat.* 1.4.87–9; *sarmenta* means 'twigs' or 'kindling', appropriate to his 'scrawny' build and his ability to provoke fiery arguments.

Messius Cicirrus: his name means 'cockerel' and some speculate that this was a stock figure in the local comedy known as Atellane farce, but it more probably alludes to his strutting, combative nature.

54 *Oscans*: a people of south-western Italy; the generalized, ethnic nature of Messius' lineage is a bathetic deflation of the expected list of noble names.

55 *the mistress is still living*: in the sense of his former owner when a slave, rather than his lover; mentioning her instead of a father or grand-father emphasizes Sarmentus' servile origins.

56–7 *wild horse*: the precise point of the insult is unclear, but it must relate to the equivalent scene in Lucilius where one 'combatant' calls his opponent a rhinoceros.

62 *Campanian disease*: unknown and much speculated about.

63 *the shepherd Cyclops' dance*: the one-eyed giant Polyphemus, famous from the *Odyssey*, but also as a pastoral lover in Theocritus 6, evidently as a character in a dramatic dance, perhaps a pantomime.

64 *a mask or tragic buskins*: the latter are high boots, which are the generic marker for tragedy. There may be a specific gibe about Messius' ugliness and height, or the point may be more broadly that he is like a Cyclops even without a costume.

65–6 *fulfilled his vow ... gods*: a parody of the retiring professional's dedication of his tools, applied to the servile Sarmentus.

66–7 *clerk ... any the less*: Messius implies that Sarmentus is a runaway slave, still under the jurisdiction of his original owner, rather than one legitimately freed by Maecenas.

71 *Beneventum*: an old Samnite city, under Roman rule since the early third century.

73–4 *Vulcan's blaze*: a lofty, epic-sounding metonymy for a humble kitchen fire.

77–8 *Apulia ... Atabulus*: H.'s native region, as emphasized by his use of the local name for the sirocco.

79 *Trivicum*: unknown, but almost certainly the modern Trevico.

82–5 *Here ... stomach*: H.'s sexual disappointment and resulting wet dream fit with his self-deprecating persona, but might also symbolize fears that the diplomatic mission might prove an empty hope (K. J. Reckford, 'Only a Wet Dream? Hope and Skepticism in Horace, *Satire* 1.5', *American Journal of Philology*, 120 (1999), 525–54) or more broadly the satire's own refusal to provide the political 'money shot' with which it teases the reader.

87 *little town whose name can't be fitted into verse*: an allusion to a similarly self-conscious periphrasis in Lucilius. Many have attempted to identify the town, but Gowers ('Horace, *Satires* 1.5') suggests that it may be a deliberate red herring.

91–2 *Canusium . . . Diomedes*: modern Canosa, main city of Daunia in northern Apulia. The Greek hero settled in this region on finding his wife unfaithful when he returned from the Trojan War.

94 *Rubi*: another Apulian town, modern Ruvo, 29 miles beyond Canusium.

96 *Barium*: modern Bari, famous for its fishing industry.

97–8 *Gnatia . . . angry*: usually called Egnatia. H. probably means simply that the town had a poor water supply, rather than any more elaborate charter myth.

99–100 *tried . . . melts without fire*: evidently a local *thauma* or natural wonder.

Apella the Jew: the name may play on *a* (without) *pellis* (skin) to allude to circumcision. Jews are often cited in Roman literature as notoriously superstitious.

101–3 *I've learnt . . . mood*: Epicurean sentiments, with clear Lucretian echoes. The tranquillity and separateness of the gods, and hence their lack of positive or negative intervention in earthly affairs, was a central tenet of the philosophy, and Lucretius in *DRN* 6 devoted much space to explaining the natural causes of apparent wonders.

104 *Brundisium . . . journey*: a very abrupt ending, especially if the ultimate goal of the journey was not Brundisium but Tarentum. The semi-apologetic claim to length is clearly ironic, since this is the shortest satire in the collection so far, considerably shorter than Lucilius' must have been, and marked throughout by brevity and omissions. The parallelism of story and journey in this line reflects their wider parallelism, notably as both reflect the principles of satiric composition expounded in the previous poem.

SATIRE 1.6

A discussion of the importance of birth and ancestry in contemporary society, especially as it relates to an obsession with political ambition, leads into two parallel descriptions of H.'s relationships with his two 'fathers': his adoption and rebirth into the circle of Maecenas, and his upbringing and education overseen by his freedman father. The satire closes with a sketch of the simple, unambitious life which H. leads as a result.

1 *Lydians who inhabit Etruria's lands*: according to tradition, Etruria was colonized by settlers from Lydia in north-west Asia Minor.

3–4 *ancestors . . . legions*: an odd claim, not paralleled elsewhere, and the explanation that these are *Etruscan* legions seems a little forced.

6 *a freedman's son*: a much-debated autobiographical claim. Unlike freedmen themselves, their children had full citizen rights.

8 *gentleman*: nicely captures the double sense of *ingenuus*, literally 'free-born' but also metaphorically 'noble'.

9 *Tullius*: Servius Tullius, sixth king of Rome, traditionally the son of a slave-woman, and a classic example of the overcoming of humble origins.

12–13 *Laevinus . . . into banishment*: an unknown, but evidently decadent, member of the *gens Valeria* and hence a descendant of P. Valerius Poplicola, involved with Brutus, Collatinus, and others in the expulsion of Rome's last king, Tarquinius Superbus.

14–15 *black mark*: usually assigned by the censors to strip senators of their rank for conduct unbecoming, but here the people pre-emptively and metaphorically assign it by refusing to elect Laevinus.

17 *ancestral busts*: busts or masks of distinguished ancestors (*imagines*), displayed in aristocratic homes and at funerals as reminders of the family's glorious past. Such ancestry carried much weight in elections.

20 *Decius*: P. Decius Mus, a *novus homo* or first senator in his family, became consul in 340 BC and traditionally died while 'devoting' himself and the enemy to the gods below.

20–1 *Appius the censor*: Appius Claudius Pulcher, censor in 50 BC with L. Calpurnius Piso, and severe in his examination of the senatorial roll.

22 *my own hide*: probably an allusion to the fable of the ass in the lion's skin.

23–4 *Glory . . . high-born*: the personified Glory, like a Roman general in a triumphal procession, leads those she has conquered, who ironically are precisely those who aspire to be at the head of such a triumph.

24–5 *Tillius . . . tribune*: evidently a man of low birth who has lost his status as a senator (and hence the right to wear the 'stripe' or *latus clavus*), perhaps through expulsion by the censors, but who has regained it by being elected tribune of the plebs. L. Tillius Cimber was one of Caesar's assassins, but the identification with this figure is uncertain.

26–7 *binds the black leather thongs . . . chest*: distinctive senatorial dress: the four leather thongs attaching the shoe to the leg and, once more, the *latus clavus*.

30 *Barrus*: his disease *is* the desire to be thought a beauty, but his name ('Elephant') might suggest that his desire is unattainable as well as excessive.

38 *Syrus . . . Dionysius*: typical slave-names, often appearing in Roman comedy.

39 *the rock*: see note to *Sat.* 1.3.82–3.

Cadmus: a contemporary executioner, according to Porph., which suits the context.

40 *Novius*: also mentioned at 1.3.21, but here his name's implication of 'new man' is central.

sits . . . he's what my father was: the imagery is from the theatre, where the *lex Roscia* assigned different seats for senators, knights, and lower orders, but should not be taken too literally and refers more generally to social rank. The implication that Novius is a freedman (like the speaker's father) is probably an exaggeration, since they could not hold office at this time.

41–2 *a Paulus or a Messalla*: paradigmatically noble families, with perhaps a specific nod at the contemporary Paullus Aemilius Lepidus and Messalla Corvinus.

47–8 *but in earlier days . . . as tribune*: H. was a military tribune in Brutus' army at Philippi.

55 *Virgil . . . Varius*: see note on *Sat.* 1.5.40.

59 *a Tarentine nag*: Tarentum, in southern Italy, was a byword for wealth and luxury.

61 *nine months later*: H.'s initiation into the circle of Maecenas is depicted as a sort of rebirth after nine months' gestation, with Maecenas as a surrogate father.

72 *Flavius' school*: presumably the local school in H.'s home-town of Venusia.

75 *Ides*: the 13th or 15th, depending on the month.

76–8 *as any knight or senator would teach offspring of his own*: there were three stages to a typical Roman elite education: an elementary grounding with a *ludi magister*, literary and linguistic study with a *grammaticus*, then the art of rhetoric with a *rhetor*.

97 *rods and chairs*: the *fasces* and the curule chair are symbols of the higher magistracies.

101 *morning calls*: elite Romans received regular morning visits (*salutationes*) from their clients and their peers as a means of asserting their status.

107–9 *Tillius . . . wine-container*: the earlier tribune is now a praetor, the second highest magistracy, and expected to have an impressive entourage carrying satirically mundane objects on a very short journey.

113–14 *Circus . . . Forum*: the Circus Maximus and the Forum Romanum.

114–18 *a dish of leeks . . . Campanian ware*: simple food, simply served, is a typical way to symbolize and exemplify a simple life; this motif recurs throughout *Satires* 2. The Campanian bronze- or earthenware contrasts with luxurious gold and silver tableware.

120 *Marsyas*: a satyr, whose statue was in the Forum, near the praetor's tribunal, where legal cases were heard. The statue is imagined as having to hear endless cases argued by Novius.

124 *Natta*: an unknown miser. H.'s insistence on good oil shows moderation in the simplicity of his lifestyle.

126 *the Field*: the Campus Martius, Rome's exercise and military training area.

the game of ball: *trigon* seems to have been a three-player catching game. For H.'s aversion to ball games, see note on *Sat.* 1.5.49.

129 *prisoners of . . . ambition*: avoiding the evils of ambition by staying out of politics is another Epicurean doctrine, frequently asserted by Lucretius.

131 *quaestor*: the lowest of the three magistracies on the *cursus honorum*, which made the holder a senator. The reference to this, rather than the praetorship or consulate, emphasizes the futility of ambition, since so many fail to progress beyond the first step.

SATIRE 1.7

The first of the three anecdotal satires describes, in mock-epic terms, a legal dispute between a Roman exile and a half-Greek businessman held before Brutus, when he was proconsul of the province of Asia in 43–42 BC. Its pervasive imagery of sharp blades, cut throats, and curtailed freedom of speech culminates in a pun on the Roman's name *Rex* and Brutus' assassination of the would-be 'King' Julius Caesar.

1–2 *Rupilius Rex*: apparently a former praetor from Praeneste, possibly mentioned in one of Cicero's letters. He was 'outlawed' (*proscriptus*) in 43 BC by the triumvirate of Antony, Octavian, and Lepidus, and seems to be in Asia as part of Brutus' entourage. That his name *Rex* also means 'king' will provide the satire's punch-line. Persius is otherwise unknown, but his Roman name and business activities in Greek-speaking Asia suggest parentage drawn from both areas, hence 'cross-breed'.

3 *suffering . . . barber*: barber-shops, often doubling as the pharmacists where ointment for conjunctivitis could be bought, were places of gossip and joke-telling. As ever in the *Satires*, mention of poor vision suggests a refusal to 'see' political realities, while the barbers' razors are the first of many sharp blades in this poem.

5 *Clazomenae*: city on the south coast of the gulf of Smyrna, on the west coast of Asia Minor (modern Turkey).

8 *a Sisenna or a Barrus*: probably ad hoc types of practitioners of bitter invective. L. Cornelius Sisenna was a historian of the Social War and Sulla's dictatorship.

11 *great warriors*: as in 1.5.51–4, the slanging match is incongruously depicted in terms of an epic battle.

12 *Hector . . . Achilles*: Homer's *Iliad* describes Achilles' killing of Hector to avenge his friend Patroclus.

16–17 *Diomedes and Lydian Glaucus*: in *Iliad* 6, these warriors, a Greek and a Trojan ally, meet but do not fight because of the guest-friendship between their families. Famously and puzzlingly, Glaucus exchanges his gold armour, worth eleven times as much, for Diomedes' bronze; H. cynically interprets this as a bribe from the cowardly Glaucus to save his life.

18–19 *when Brutus . . . Asia*: in 43 and 42, though his control of the province was the result of conquest rather than constitutional procedure.

20 *Bacchius and Bitho*: gladiators; *par* ('pair') is a technical term for two matched gladiators.

25–6 *Dog-star*: Sirius, whose rising coincided with the blasting heat of late summer, is common in similes and in its own right as a symbol of destruction, but Persius wittily gives special point to likening Rupilius to it in the context of praising Brutus and the rest of the staff as beneficent astral bodies.

26–7 *like a winter torrent . . . axe*: river imagery is common for speech (cf. note
on *Sat.* 1.1.57) but this simile has a (mock-) epic feel. The point of the axe
is a little obscure, but Gowers ('Blind Eyes and Cut Throats') suggests an
allusion to the executioner's axe which cut off the power of Republican
free speech.

28 *scion of Praeneste*: Rupilius, stressing his Italian identity in contrast to
Persius' florid Greek rhetoric.

29–31 *hurled back insults . . . heels*: H. neatly links the imagery of Rupilius' insults
as being like Italian vinegar with that of the man himself as being the vine-
dresser. The Elder Pliny notes that the cuckoo's call was used to criticize those
who had not finished pruning their vines before the bird itself arrived.

32 *Greek . . . Italian vinegar*: the placing of the national terms in the same line
points the ethnic dimension of the dispute. Vinegar is often used of sour
wit or abuse.

34 *regicide*: the untranslatable Latin pun, lit. 'killing kings/people called Rex
(*reges*)', makes the punch-line clearer than is possible in English.

SATIRE 1.8

The speaker is a statue of Priapus in the gardens of Maecenas on the Esquiline
Hill, which has been civilized and transformed from its grisly past as a mass
cemetery. Two witches, representing the dark forces of disorder and unreason,
threaten this stability, but Priapus routs them, using not his traditional threat
of rape with his enormous erection, but, symbolizing H.'s brand of satire, the
less aggressive, more comic expedient of an enormous fart.

2 *Priapus*: a fertility god, originally from Lampsacus in the Hellespont,
whose statues were regularly placed in gardens to act as scarecrows and as
deterrent to thieves. There is a whole genre of poetry about or spoken by
the divine statue, much of it collected in the so-called *Priapea*.

5 *red stake . . . crotch*: a brightly coloured erect phallus was the standard
attribute of Priapus, reflecting both fertility and, as here, the threat of
rape against thieves and intruders.

6 *reed*: to scare birds when it waves in the wind, suggesting the scarecrow is
alive and dangerous.

7 *new gardens*: built by Maecenas on the Esquiline Hill.

11 *Pantolabus*: in Greek, 'one who takes everything'; apt for the *scurra* who
lives off his patron in return for entertainment.

Nomentanus: see note on *Sat.* 1.1.101.

13 *'the monument not to pass on to heirs'*: a common inscription protecting a
burial site from being sold by one's heirs and hence disturbed. There is a
double irony in its use at a mass paupers' grave and in its being ignored
by Maecenas, who built his gardens there anyway.

14 *These days*: a symbolic transformation from death to fertile rebirth in the
new gardens, particularly significant in a time of civil war.

15 *Mound*: the *agger* strengthened the wall of Servius Tullius where it had to cross the low-lying area between the Porta Collina and Porta Esquilina.

19–20 *hags . . . potions*: Priapus' main enemy is revealed. Their magic, like much of that in the ancient world, seems to be love-charms, but symbolizes a more general force of disorder, irrationality, and destruction.

21 *wandering moon*: essential for gathering ingredients for spells, while the hint of personification suggests the identification of Diana with both the moon and the goddess of witchcraft, Hecate.

24 *Canidia*: this witch appears in several of H.'s *Epodes* and very briefly at the beginning and end of *Satires* 2. Some attempt to identify her, but she is clearly a type, though also a symbol of broader negative forces in Roman life. Her name evokes her grey hair (*canities*).

25 *Sagana*: another stock witch, who also assists Canidia in *Epode* 5, and whose name (despite the short first -a-) evokes *saga*, 'witch'.

27 *black lamb*: black animals were traditionally sacrificed to the gods of the Underworld. The use of teeth is partly a gruesome perversion of ritual, but also in accordance with the avoidance of iron tools in magic rites.

30 *One effigy . . . the other of wax*: representing Canidia and the lover she wishes to influence. The wax figure's potential to be moulded and melted fits the lover's role. Wool is often used in spells for binding the beloved, and seems to have been associated with female flesh (C. A. Faraone, *Ancient Greek Love Magic* (Cambridge, Mass., 1999), 51–3).

32 *as a slave would*: a hint of the 'slavery of love' embraced by Roman elegists, but here enforced by Canidia.

33 *Hecate*: see note on line 21 above.

34 *Tisiphone*: one of the three Furies, also associated with the Underworld.

34–5 *snakes and hell-hounds*: Tisiphone's hair and Hecate's entourage, respectively.

blushing Moon: a humorous interpretation of the moon's reddening, but perhaps hinting that the witches are causing an eclipse, one of their regular spells.

37–9 *No, if I'm telling . . . top of me*: a typical oath amusingly adapted to the speaking statue. The figures are unidentifiable (despite the scholiasts) but Julius is striking immediately after the mention of regicide in *Sat.* 1.7; the effeminate Pediatius (the Latin even uses the feminine form *Pediatia*) may suggest *pedicare*, 'I bugger'; and the thief's name may suggest his voracity. Inscriptions show that micturition and defecation on statues were real concerns.

40 *What need . . . manner*: the common technique of *praeteritio*, claiming to pass over what one describes anyway.

42 *wolf's beard . . . snake*: the aim of this magic ritual is unclear.

43–4 *the waxen image . . . higher*: as the image is held over the fire to melt it (and the lover), the drips kindle flames (and perhaps flames of passion).

46–7 *For I farted . . . bursting*: Priapus' fart is a comical but gentle alternative
to his habitual threat of violent anal rape, symbolizing H.'s approach to
satire, using humour rather than violent Lucilian invective.

48–50 *you'd have laughed . . . from their arms*: laughter is the appropriate
response to Priapus' fart and H.'s gently comic satire, but it is still effect-
ive in dispelling the dark forces represented by the witches. The loss of
false teeth and wig represent a typically satiric stripping away of appear-
ances to reveal the sordid reality underneath, but, in combination with the
loss of their magic apparatus, also marks satire's ability to disarm these
negative forces.

SATIRE 1.9

H. narrates how, on a walk through Rome, he was accosted by a loquacious
social climber who would not leave him alone and who was determined to use
H. to enter the circle of Maecenas, about which he held numerous cynical
misconceptions. After many failed attempts, H. is 'delivered' when the 'chat-
terbox' is hauled away by his opponent in a legal case.

1 *Sacred Way*: the *Via Sacra* linked the Velian Hill with the Forum
Romanum.

7 *literary*: lit. 'learned' (*doctus*), particularly associated with Roman follow-
ers of the Alexandrian school of poetry, which valued scholarly knowledge
of other poetry and the display of that knowledge in one's own.

11 *Bolanus*: unknown, but clearly a type of an angry man, who would give the
chatterbox the short shrift he deserves.

18 *Caesar's gardens*: on the west bank of the Tiber, where Caesar entertained
Cleopatra in 44 BC, and which he left to the Roman people.

22 *Viscus*: linked with Varius among H.'s ideal readers in *Sat.* 1.10 and among
Nasidienus' guests in *Sat.* 2.8, but otherwise unknown.

23 *Varius*: see third note on *Sat.* 1.5.40.

23–5 *for who can . . . envious*: rapid composition links the chatterbox with
shoddy writers like Lucilius and Crispinus condemned in *Sat.* 1.4, while
Hermogenes Tigellius' singing is ridiculed in *Sat.* 1.3. Effeminate dan-
cing, though not explicitly condemned in *Satires* 1, would fit well among
its targets.

26–7 *Do you have a mother . . . health?*: perhaps either a threat of violence or a
reference back to the danger of contagion from H.'s sick friend.

29 *Sabine*: ancient Italian people living north-east of Rome, whose women
were famously raped by Romulus' Romans. The Latin *Sabella* could also
refer to the Sabelli, or Oscan-speaking people of southern Italy.

31–4 *'This youth . . . begun'*: another mock-heroic touch, as the stylistically
convincing prophecy mixes lofty, epic language with lower references to
gout and, of course, the threat of the chatterbox. The dangers of exces-
sive and unguarded speech are, however, a serious and pervasive theme
of *Satires* 1.

35 *Vesta's temple*: at the eastern end of the Forum Romanum, and hence its entrance for those approaching by the Via Sacra.

36–7 *at that time . . . case*: evidently the chatterbox is the defendant in a civil case, on the terms H. describes.

38 *support*: the chatterbox importunately asks H. to be his informal legal adviser.

43 *'How do you get on with Maecenas?'*: the chatterbox here reveals his misconceptions about the nature of Maecenas' circle.

59–60 *"On mortals . . . untold"*: the moralizing platitude in the chatterbox's mouth is the more jarring since it refers to social climbing rather than any worthwhile enterprise.

61 *Aristius Fuscus*: the addressee of *Odes* 1.22 and *Ep.* 1.10; his being a writer of comedies might contribute to his depiction as a joker here.

69 *a thirtieth Sabbath*: whether an actual festival or, more probably, a fabrication as part of Fuscus' deliberately feeble excuse, it is not one he would be expected to observe, even if he showed more reverence to Judaism than in his crude allusion to circumcision.

70–1 *religious qualms*: H.'s Epicureanism is put to desperate use.

74 *executioner's blade*: the *culter* might suggest that H. is like a sacrificial animal, but the image of impending doom is the same.

75 *legal opponent*: although the chatterbox would have forfeited the case by failing to appear, presumably the plaintiff still wishes to see justice done and have his day in court.

76 *May I call upon you as a witness?*: a legal formula for requesting a witness to the arrest of a defendant who refused to respond to a summons.

77 *extended my ear*: the witness's ear, as the seat of memory, was formally touched by the plaintiff; H. proactively volunteers himself.

78 *Apollo*: a Latin translation of Lucilius' quotation (in Greek) of *Iliad* 20.443, presumably in a broadly comparable context. The refusal to quote Greek puts into practice the principles espoused in the next satire. The reference to Apollo has added wit, since it refers to the statue of Apollo in the Forum which, like that of Marsyas at *Sat.* 1.6.120, is associated with the legal cases it 'hears' argued near it (see especially Juvenal 1.129).

SATIRE 1.10

H. returns to the theory of satire and 'responds' to some alleged reactions to his criticisms of Lucilius in *Sat.* 1.4. He reflects further on Lucilius' use of Greek words as well as his speed and carelessness of composition. More generally, H. asserts the importance of careful revision and of aiming, not for mass appeal, but for the discerning approval of those whose opinion matters, before giving a list of his ideal readership. A brief coda ends the book.

1 *I said*: in *Sat.* 1.4. As in that poem itself, H. looks back at 'earlier' satires and the alleged reaction to them.

6   *Laberius' mimes*: Decimus Laberius (*c.*106–43 BC), along with Publilius Syrus, produced a literary form of the southern Italian genre of mime, but evidently not literary enough for H.

16 *Old Comedy*: see note on *Sat.* 1.4.1.

18 *Hermogenes*: see note on *Sat.* 1.3.129.

    that ape: unclear whether a specific imitator of the neoterics (see next note) is alluded to; 'training' translates *doctus*, an ironic application of the neoteric ideal of learnedness.

19 *Calvus and Catullus*: friends and members of the so-called 'neoteric' school of late-Republican poetry, following Alexandrian aesthetic principles of polish and erudition. C. Licinius Calvus, whose work only survives in fragments, was probably best known for his short epic, *Io*.

20 *'But his blending . . . achievement'*: the fragments of Lucilius do show considerable use of Greek words.

21 *late learners*: H. immediately puts his principle into practice, giving a Latin version of the Greek word *opsimatheis*.

22 *Pitholeon*: perhaps the same as the Pitholaus mentioned in Suetonius' life of Julius Caesar as attacking him with abusive poems and the M. Otacilius Pitholaus whose ridicule of a consul Caesar appointed for one day Macrobius preserves.

24 *Falernian . . . Chian*: famous Italian and Greek wines respectively.

26 *Petillius*: see note on *Sat.* 1.4.94.

28 *Pedius Publicola and Corvinus*: the latter is probably M. Valerius Messalla Corvinus, later patron of Tibullus and Ovid; Pedius cannot securely be identified but may be the brother of Messalla referred to at line 85 below.

30 *Canusian*: on Canusium, see note on *Sat.* 1.5.91–2. Ennius and Lucilius call the Bruttii of nearby Calabria *bilingui*, presumably speaking native Oscan and the Greek of the many colonies in Magna Graecia.

32 *Quirinus*: the deified Romulus and hence the quintessentially Roman god. His insistence that H. write in Latin is a variation on Apollo's appearance to Callimachus in prologue of his *Aetia* insisting that he write fine-honed poetry rather than epic, a scene much imitated by, among others, Virgil, Propertius, and Ovid.

36 *Alpman . . . Rhine*: probably the Furius whose description of the Alps is mocked at *Sat.* 2.5.39–41, and whose identification with Furius Bibaculus is much disputed. Whether this notorious line or his birthplace makes him Alpine is also uncertain. The death of Memnon, an Ethiopian king, son of the Dawn and ally of Troy, was the subject of the cyclical epic *Aethiopis* and presumably of another by Furius. As often, a poet is presented as doing what he describes, but with the added implication that Furius makes a mess of the poem, perhaps even by using the unpoetic word *iugulat*. The description of the Rhine probably came from Furius'

epic on Caesar's Gallic campaign, but the muddy river again evokes Callimachean imagery for bad poetry.

38 *Tarpa's verdict*: according to one of Cicero's letters, Pompey appointed Sp. Maecius Tarpa to choose plays to be staged at his new theatre, and he hence represents official, public critical judgement.

42 *Fundanius*: only mentioned here and as the narrator of Nasidienus' dinner at *Sat.* 2.8, but, from the character names and plot situations, evidently a successful writer of New Comedy in the manner of Plautus and Terence.

   Pollio: C. Asinius Pollio, distinguished historian, among other accomplishments, but celebrated here as a great tragedian, writing in iambic trimeters.

44 *Varius*: see note on *Sat.* 1.5.40. His mastery of epic is only attested elsewhere in *Odes* 1.6, unless *epos* is taken broadly as 'hexameter poetry', so including his *De morte*.

45 *Virgil*: at this date, author only of the pastoral *Eclogues*.

   Muses: H.'s choice of *Camenae*—Italian goddesses whose name the first Latin poet, Livius Andronicus, used to translate Homer's *Mousa*, before Ennius naturalized it as *Musae*—is particularly appropriate in the context of celebrating Latin poets using the Latin language.

46 *Varro of Atax*: known for his *Bellum Sequanicum* on Caesar's Gallic wars, his Latin version of Apollonius' *Argonautica*, and other poems, but not otherwise of satires; presumably his attempts were so much in vain that they were never published.

48 *its inventor*: Lucilius.

50 *muddy stream*: referring back to *Sat.* 1.4.11.

53 *Accius' tragedies*: youngest of the three great Republican tragedians (170–*c*.86 BC) and a frequent target of Lucilius' hostile literary criticism.

54 *Ennius' verses*: 239–169 BC, writer of tragedies, comedies, and other genres, but probably targeted by Lucilius as author of the epic *Annales*, as at fr. 413 *ROL*.

59 *six feet per line*: i.e. a hexameter.

61–2 *Cassius . . . a river in spate*: an unknown poet, also criticized using river imagery.

77 *Arbuscula*: an actress mentioned in one of Cicero's letters. The parallel with H. is not entirely clear: the knights could represent a discerning elite or, if we take the singular *equitem* literally, perhaps even Maecenas. H.'s list of those whose opinion of his work he does and does not value alludes to Lucilius (fr. 635 *ROL*).

78 *Pantilius*: unknown, but the Greek etymology of his name suggests a critic who picks at everything.

79 *Demetrius*: also linked with Tigellius in line 90 below, but otherwise unknown.

80 *Fannius*: see note on *Sat.* 1.4.21.

81 *Plotius and Varius*: see second and third notes on *Sat.* 1.5.40.

82 *Valgius*: C. Valgius Rufus, writer of elegies, addressed in *Odes* 2.9.
    Octavius: Octavius Musa, a historian.

83 *Fuscus*: see note on *Sat.* 1.9.61.

85 *both Viscus brothers*: see note on *Sat.* 1.9.22 for one Viscus. Of his brother
    even less is known.

86 *Bibulus and Servius . . . Furnius*: uncertain, though a Bibulus fought for
    Brutus at Philippi, a Servius is mentioned by Ovid as a love poet, and
    Plutarch refers to an orator called Furnius.

92 *Off . . . this little book of mine*: H. orders a slave to add this final satire to
    the other nine. That the collection is a 'little book' (*libellus*) fits with H.'s
    principles of Callimachean satire, but 'lose no time' (*citus*, lit. 'quickly')
    smacks of Lucilian haste.

SATIRES, BOOK 2

SATIRE 2.1

H. defends his decision to write satire in dialogue (the dominant form of this
second book) with the lawyer Trebatius and in the face of alleged complaints about
its abusive content. In the process, he justifies not writing epic in praise of Octavian
and again invokes the model of Lucilius. This influential poem became the tem-
plate for the so-called 'programmatic satire' imitated by Persius and Juvenal.

4   *Trebatius*: C. Trebatius Testa (*c.*84 BC–AD 4), distinguished lawyer and apt
     source of advice on the legality of H.'s satires. Many of his responses to
     H. are couched in legal language.

11   *the deeds of unvanquished Caesar*: Trebatius suggests H. write a panegyrical
     epic about Octavian.

12–13 *my strength fails me*: Augustan poets frequently excuse themselves for
     not writing such an epic, disingenuously claiming they are incapable of it,
     a strategy known as *recusatio*.

13–15 *columns of men . . . horse*: typical epic motifs, with a particular Roman
     colouring, as the Gauls recall Julius Caesar's campaigns and the Parthians
     (ruling an area roughly corresponding to modern Iraq and Iran) being
     Rome's continuing *bêtes noires*, against whom an expedition by Octavian
     was repeatedly mooted.

17   *Lucilius . . . scion*: Trebatius suggests that, if H. cannot write epic, he
     could praise Octavian in satire, as Lucilius did his contemporary Scipio
     Aemilianus.

18   *Flaccus*: a rare use of H.'s *cognomen*, sometimes thought to suggest
     poetic impotence by alluding to a limp penis. More probably its meaning
     'droopy-eared' contrasts with the 'attentive' ear of Octavian.

22   *'Pantolabus . . . Nomentanus'*: a quotation of *Sat.* 1.8.11, reflecting on H.'s
     satiric practice in *Satires* 1.

24 *Milonius*: a contemporary *scurra*, according to Porph., but this would be odd behaviour for one.

26–7 *Castor . . . boxing*: Castor and Pollux were sons of Jupiter, disguised as a swan, and Leda, who hence bore them in an egg.

28–9 *rounding off words in feet as Lucilius did*: i.e. writing verse satire in metrical feet.

33 *votive tablet*: such as a survivor of shipwreck might dedicate to a god, depicting his sufferings.

34–9 *Apulia's sons or the fiery men of Lucania*: H.'s home town of Venusia was on the border of these two regions in southern Italy. It was originally a Samnite settlement but was resettled as a Roman colony in 291 BC. H. identifies himself as a satirist with the warlike Italians rather than the colonists and proceeds to develop the parallel between satiric invective and martial violence.

47–9 *Cervius . . . judge*: further parallels for H.'s threat of reprisal against his enemies, but also incidental targets of satire. None are known. Cervius' name suggests a timid deer, perhaps undercutting his reputation for anger; the urn is that in which jurors would place their votes. On Canidia, see note on *Sat.* 1.8.24. Albucius is probably the supplier rather than the victim of the poison, though both scholiasts take him to be Canidia's father. There was a judge called Turius in the 70s BC.

52 *the wolf . . . the bull with his horns*: the first of many allusions to and uses of beast fable in this book.

53 *Scaeva*: meaning 'Left-handed' and so punning with 'dutiful right hand'.

62 *deadly chill*: 'a frosty reception' from his patrons, but following the concern for H.'s life there must be a suggestion of the chill of death.

65 *Laelius*: C. Laelius (190–c.129 BC), close friend of Lucilius' 'high-placed friend' Scipio Aemilianus and hence analogous to Maecenas.

65–6 *man . . . Carthage*: P. Scipio Aemilianus took the *agnomen* Africanus after sacking Carthage in 146 BC.

67–8 *Metellus . . . Lupus*: Q. Caecilius Metellus Macedonicus (d. 115 BC), prominent general and statesman, enemy of Scipio, and target of Lucilius. L. Cornelius Lentulus Lupus (d. 125 BC) was likewise a prominent opponent of Scipio, whose death prompts a council of the gods to discuss the destruction of Rome in Lucilius 1.

70 *Virtue*: Lucilius defines and praises *virtus* in one poem (fr. 1196–1208 *ROL*).

74 *vegetables*: simple food, exemplifying a simple lifestyle, as in *Sat.* 1.6 and especially in the next satire.

80–3 *be warned . . . bad verses against another*: there were defamation laws at Rome from the Twelve Tables onwards, but it is unclear how serious was the threat of prosecution for satire.

83 *bad verses*: H. puns on the double sense of 'malicious' and 'poor quality'.

84 *Caesar's judgement*: again playing on legal and literary judgement, with the suggestion of an appeal to the *princeps* against a verdict.

85 *barked*: the common image of the satirist as an aggressive but vigilant guard-dog.

86 *the case . . . scot-free*: laughter, as often in H.'s satire, resolves the situation.

SATIRE 2.2

The morality of food is the theme of this satire, as the simple fare associated with the countryside both symbolizes and reflects simple but honest values, while an obsession with luxurious gastronomizing epitomizes the vice and folly of the modern city. H. cites the rustic Ofellus as his authority but, unlike the speakers of the subsequent satires, Ofellus' actual words are not given until the very end; rather, H. provides his own synthesis of Ofellus' teachings.

2 *Ofellus*: a genuine Oscan name, but one which suggests *ofella*, 'small cutlet', an appropriately moderate meal.

9 *Every judge*: referring to the stomach 'bribed' with luxurious food, in contrast to being honestly hungry.

15 *Hymettus*: mountain in Attica famous for its bees and honey.

Falernian: see note on *Sat.* 1.10.24.

19–20 *greatest pleasure*: the Epicurean ideal, as well as applicable in its more straightforward sense.

26 *a fine show*: the contrast between outward appearance and inner reality is a common motif of satire.

31 *pike*: or possibly a bass. The point is that expensively imported and locally caught fish are indistinguishable in taste.

32–3 *between the bridges*: it is uncertain which are meant, but clearly the fish is caught in a stretch of the Tiber within Rome.

Tuscan river: the Tiber's source is in Etruria (modern Tuscany).

34 *mullet*: an expensive and luxurious fish; the notion that one can only eat small portions of even the largest amount recalls *Sat.* 1.1.

40 *Harpies*: monstrous bird-women sent to punish Phineus by devouring the feast daily set before him, and hence types of gluttony.

41 *winds from the south*: the hot sirocco will make the food go off.

47 *Gallonius*: an allusion to a poem by Lucilius (fr. 203–5 *ROL*) in which Laelius criticizes Gallonius for his gluttony.

50 *praetor*: the scholiasts offer various possibilities, including Plotius Plancus, Asellius, and Sempronius Rufus.

51 *roasted gulls*: not a delicacy at Rome, and hence an appropriately absurd extreme to which dedicated followers of fashion might be led.

54 *pointless . . . weakness*: chiming with H.'s own general emphasis on moderation, and especially on avoiding extremes in *Sat.* 1.2.

55–6 *Avidienus . . . 'Dog'*: the name suggests *avidus* ('avaricious'), apt for a miser, while the nickname suits a scavenger with no regard for civilized values, and perhaps a Cynic (Gk.: 'canine') like Diogenes.

64 *a wolf . . . on the other*: broadly 'a rock and a hard place' but perhaps in the context a more specific antithesis between the ravenous wolf and the stingy 'Dog', Avidienus.

67 *Albucius*: perhaps with white (*albus*) hair; the point is that his excessive concern that everything be in order for his guests leads him to mistreat his slaves.

69 *Naevius*: possibly the same as at *Sat.* 1.1.101, if the latter is a miser rather than a spendthrift (see note), though the main point here is his lack of attention to his guests' needs (in contrast to Albucius) rather than stinginess. The water is for washing hands rather than drinking.

75 *bile . . . phlegm*: two of the four humours, central to ancient medical thought.

79 *nails . . . a portion of the divine spirit*: a blend of Pythagorean, Platonic, and Stoic philosophy. Stoics believed the soul was part of the divine spirit, while Plato describes the soul being made part of the body by various physical experiences.

84 *holiday*: one of Rome's many annual religious festivals. Allowing oneself occasional treats is part of the message of moderation.

89–93 *Our forefathers . . . heroes!*: a puzzling section, mixing conventional Roman nostalgia for the rustic good old days with ironic satire of their boorishness. The connection with the argument is unclear, but perhaps the late guest corresponds to the old man, so that the host (like the man in his youth) should not enjoy the feast prematurely.

97 *uncle*: proverbially strict.

99 *Trausius*: unknown.

101–5 *Is there, then . . . that great heap?*: public benefactions or euergetism were an important part of civic life in the classical world. The mention of collapsing temples adds a religious note; one of Octavian's most trumpeted achievements was the restoration of derelict temples and of the religious observance associated with them.

106–10 *You alone . . . required in war?*: a change of tack from morality to self-interest, combining several different strands of argument: the common ancient fear of enemies' ridicule, the danger of a change in fortunes, the associated need for prudent preparation, and the contrast between a reliance on luxury and the ideal of self-sufficiency (*autarkeia*).

112–14 *Ofellus . . . pruned back*: Ofellus' life, as opposed to his ideas, now validates the argument, especially the most recent one about prudence and self-sufficiency. Evidently, he lost much of his farm in the land confiscations of the civil war period, when land was seized to be given as rewards to veteran soldiers.

114–15 *plot . . . their work*: the small parcel of land left to Ofellus after his farm had been divided and assigned to veterans.

tenant-farmer: no longer owning his farm.

116 *account*: Ofellus' speech closes the satire.

120 *fish*: an expensive luxury, as can be seen earlier in this satire.

123 *forfeit*: difficult, and emendations have been suggested, but perhaps the forfeit automatically dictates what the revellers must drink, taking the place of the *arbiter bibendi*.

124 *Ceres*: the goddess of grain, but also a metonymy for the grain itself which they pray might 'rise'.

126 *Fortune*: a capricious and random force. Ofellus' reflections match his general outlook, but are also typical of the drinking-party or symposium, so common in the *Odes*, of which this is a rustic variation.

131 *he in turn*: the motif of changes in fortune becomes a consolation rather than a threat.

133 *Umbrenus' name*: the name might suggest he is as transient as a shadow (*umbra*) or an interloper from Umbria some way to the north of Venusia.

SATIRE 2.3

The bankrupt dealer in luxury goods, Damasippus, has been saved from suicide and converted to Stoicism by the philosopher Stertinius. He recounts this to H. before reproducing a very long diatribe by Stertinius on the Stoic doctrine that everyone except the Stoic wise man (*sapiens*) is mad. The satire ends with a brief and inconclusive skirmish of words between H. and Damasippus. As with *Sat.* 2.7, the tone and some of the content of the 'satirized' diatribe is strikingly similar to that of H.'s own diatribes, especially *Sat.* 1.1–3.

1–4 *You write . . . mention*: Damasippus ascribes H.'s small output to laziness, aligning himself with Crispinus and others in *Satires* 1 who value rapid and prolific composition. The web suggests Penelope's ruse of refusing to marry her suitors until she had completed Laertes' shroud, which she unpicked nightly.

5 *Saturnalia*: festival of Saturn held for a week from 17 December, marked by revelry, and temporary licence (especially for slaves) and inversion of social hierarchies. H. implicitly denies Damasippus' charge of drunkenness since he shuns this festival's opportunities.

10 *country house*: probably the Sabine villa given to H. by Maecenas. The rural setting, in contrast to the bustle of the city, is significant.

11–12 *Plato . . . Archilochus*: Plato is included partly as a philosopher, partly as a writer of dialogues akin to those in *Satires* 2; Menander (*c*.344–292 BC) was the undisputed master of New Comedy, which was acknowledged as related to satire at *Sat.* 1.4.48–52; on Eupolis, see note on

Sat. 1.4.1; Archilochus was a seventh-century writer of *iambos*, or abusive poetry, H.'s main model in the *Epodes*, and a significant presence in the *Satires*.

16 *Damasippus*: may well be the man referred to in several of Cicero's letters as a dealer in luxury goods.

17 *barber*: because Damasippus, as a convert to Stoicism, has the beard which was the mark of the philosopher.

18–19 *central Janus*: the *Ianus medius*, an arch probably near the Basilica Aemiliana and a gathering place for bankers and speculators.

21 *Sisyphus*: mythical trickster, and object of divine punishment in the Underworld; Damasippus exaggerates his wares' antiquity but, since Sisyphus was also founder of Corinth, there is a connection with the popular Corinthian bronzeware.

25 *"Mercury's pal"*: god of deceit and trade.

33 *Stertinius*: a Stoic philosopher, whose presence on the bridge may (or may not) suggest he preached on street-corners. Mentioned (jocularly) along-side Empedocles at *Ep.* 1.12.20 and so maybe real, but his name does suggest that he causes listeners to snore (*stertere*).

36 *Fabrician bridge*: linking the island in the Tiber with the left bank.

42 *dying bravely*: suicide per se was not condemned by Stoicism, and was indeed an approved means of escaping an intolerable situation, most famously practised by Cato the younger, but Damasippus' reasons are not appropriate.

44 *Chrysippus' portico*: see note on *Sat.* 1.3.127. The portico (*stoa*) was the school's location and source of its name.

55 *a tail dragging behind him*: Ps.-Acro suggests a proverb, Porph. a children's game; both are plausible.

53–6 *One class . . . the other type*: note the similarity to H.'s condemnation of extremes, especially in *Sat.* 1.2 and 2.2.

60–2 *drunken Fufius . . . 'Mother, I implore you!'*: in Pacuvius' tragedy *Iliona*, the eponymous heroine's dead son, Deipylus, appears to her in a dream. Fufius and Catienus act Iliona and Deipylus respectively, the latter with a little help from audience participation.

69 *Nerius . . . Cicuta*: evidently both financiers who process the loan; their names suggest a sea-god (apt for dealings with Proteus) and hemlock (a deadly businessman).

71 *Proteus*: the old man of the sea, who could change into all the forms listed here, and did so to try to escape Odysseus.

75 *Perellius' brain*: if 'you' is Damasippus, then his creditor; if generalized, another type-figure of a moneylender.

82 *hellebore*: a herb believed to cure madness; Anticyra, a port in Phocis, was a famous supplier.

84   *Staberius*: evidently a miser whose belief that wealth was the ultimate good led him to prescribe in his will that his heirs display that wealth, either as a figure inscribed on his tomb, or through lavish public munificence.

86   *Arrius*: mentioned in Cicero as a rich man who gave a banquet for thousands at his father's funeral.

87   *Africa's harvest*: the province, covering modern Tunisia and some of the Libyan coast, rather than the continent of Africa; an important source of grain for Rome.

88   *uncle*: proverbially strict, ironic in the mouth of one addressing his heirs.

97   *he will also be a king*: Staberius (incorrectly, in Stertinius' view) assigns to the rich man all the goods Stoics assign to the wise man.

100 *Aristippus*: philosopher from Cyrene in North Africa, associate of Socrates, notorious for luxuriant living and extravagance, the opposite extreme from Staberius.

106 *cobbler*: Stertinius' parallels for the 'mad' amassing but failing to use wealth curiously echo Stoic doctrine about the wise man being a good singer or cobbler, even if he does not practise those skills; see 1.3.124–33 above.

115 *Chian . . . Falernian*: see note on *Sat.* 1.10.24.

128 *pelt the crowd with stones*: considered a standard sign of madness.

131 *hang your wife and poison your mother*: both typical female means of suicide, as which the murder is disguised.

137 *Orestes*: son of the Argive king Agamemnon and Clytemnestra, who avenged the former by killing the latter and was driven mad by the Furies; the classic mythical example of madness. Stertinius' point is that he was mad to kill his mother, not driven so afterwards.

139–41 *he didn't dare . . . bile*: alluding to a scene from Euripides' *Orestes*, with his devoted friend and sister respectively, though there is no insult to the former and Stertinius' vagueness may suggest he has misremembered the play. Black bile (*melancholia*) is one of the four humours, an excess of which causes madness.

142 *Opimius*: suggests wealth (*opes*) and the consul whose name marked the vintage year 121 BC.

143 *Veii*: Etruscan city 10 miles north of Rome, not noted for its wine.

144 *Capuan ladle*: see note on *Sat.* 1.6.114–18.

161 *Craterus*: a famous doctor, mentioned by Cicero and Galen.

165 *pig . . . Lares*: a standard sacrifice to the gods of the roads and crossroads (among other things), presumably in thanksgiving at a (premature) diagnosis of sanity.

166 *Anticyra*: see note on line 82 above—he is mad after all.

168 *Oppidius*: suggests a provincial (*oppidanus*) opposed to the values of the big city. On Canusium, see note on *Sat.* 1.5.91–2. The anecdote initially

reprises the danger of extremes of avarice and extravagance, before focusing on the new topic of political ambition.

171 *knucklebones and nuts*: common children's toys.

175 *Nomentanus*: see note on *Sat.* 1.1.101.

Cicuta: evidently a miser, just about consistent with the character at line 69 above.

180 *aedile or praetor*: specified since both had responsibility for putting on games, with the attendant expenses. Oppidius' veto on seeking political office goes against standard elite Roman values.

182 *chickpeas . . . lupins*: food which would be distributed to the people at games.

183 *Circus . . . bronze*: i.e. during chariot races at the Circus Maximus and as a statue memorializing your munificence.

185 *Agrippa*: M. Vipsanius Agrippa (*c.*63–12 BC), Octavian's right-hand man, who gave particularly munificent games when aedile in 33 BC. The contemporary reference might suggest that Stertinius resumed speaking at 'Would you squander . . . '.

186 *fox . . . lion*: imagery from fable, though matching no surviving example.

187 *Son of Atreus*: Agamemnon, leader of the Greek army at Troy. Stertinius imagines himself at Troy holding a dialogue with the mythical king.

Ajax: Greek hero of the Trojan War, embittered after the arms of Achilles were awarded to Ulysses rather than him, plotted to murder him along with Agamemnon and his brother Menelaus, but, driven mad by Athena so that he slaughtered livestock instead, he killed himself and was denied burial. The story is best known from Sophocles' *Ajax*, imitated by Ennius. Ajax is another exemplar of madness, but Stertinius again unexpectedly argues that Agamemnon is the true madman.

188 *'I am king'*: literally true, but not in the Stoic sense.

195 *Priam and Priam's people*: a phrase used several times in the *Iliad*.

199–200 *Aulis . . . a heifer's place*: Agamemnon sacrificed his daughter Iphigenia at the port of Aulis to gain fair winds for the expedition to Troy. Sacrificing a girl as though she were an animal inverts Ajax's 'madness' of killing sheep as if they were men.

203 *his wife and child*: Tecmessa and Eurysaces.

204 *Teucer*: Ajax's devoted half-brother.

216 *Rufa or Posilla*: common girls' names.

217–18 *the praetor . . . in their right mind*: the urban praetor was in charge of many legal matters, including decisions about rights and guardianship.

223 *Bellona*: goddess of war. The line has a mock-epic ring matching the mockery of martial glory.

228–9 *Etruscans' street . . . Velabrum*: the *Vicus Tuscus* was the main thoroughfare from the Forum Romanum to the Forum Boarium, famous for its shops, especially incense- and perfume-sellers. It formed the eastern boundary of the Velabrum, an area of low ground between the Palatine and Capitoline, noted as a commercial district and especially for its food-shops.

234 *Lucanian*: from a mountainous region of southern Italy, famous for its game.

237–8 *whose wife*: the mercenary complaisant husband is a common figure, and perhaps one of the targets of Augustan adultery legislation.

239 *Aesopus' son*: son of the actor M. Clodius Aesopus, whose extravagance with his massive inheritance is mentioned by Cicero and others.

Metella's ear: Caecilia Metella, daughter of Clodia, divorced wife of P. Lentulus Spinther.

244 *Quintus Arrius*: presumably the same as at line 84 above.

245 *nightingales*: not just expensive, but prized for their song rather than their flavour.

246 *chalk . . . charcoal*: imagery from the marking of auspicious and inauspicious days on a calendar.

249 *beard*: here a mark of an adult rather than a philosopher. Stertinius moves on to love.

252 *prostitute*: on the *meretrix*, see note on *Sat.* 1.4.111–12. They are common figures in New Comedy and the mistresses of Roman elegy share many of their features.

254 *Polemo*: philosopher of the fourth–third century BC and head of the Academy. When young he burst into a lecture on self-control by its then head Xenocrates and was converted.

255 *leg-bands . . . scarves*: the parallel between the physically ill invalid and the mentally ill lover is reinforced by the means they use to keep warm, one to recuperate, the other for spending cold nights outside his beloved's door as a locked-out lover (*exclusus amator*).

256 *garlands*: traditionally worn at drinking-parties (*symposia*).

259–60 *the locked-out lover*: a stock figure in Roman elegy, but H. here closely adapts a scene from New Comedy (one of elegy's influences), Terence's *The Eunuch*, which opens with the young man Phaedria soliloquizing outside the house of the courtesan Thais and receiving advice from his slave Parmeno. Compare also H.'s own attack on 'the thrill of the chase' at *Sat.* 1.2.96–110.

272–3 *when you squeeze . . . with one*: a game, not unlike that of throwing the dregs of a cup (*kottabos*), played at *symposia*, success at which was believed to augur success in love. Picenum (modern Marche) was a region on the central east coast of Italy whose apples are often mentioned with approval.

277 *Marius ran Hellas through*: evidently a Roman lover and his Greek (possibly courtesan) mistress, involved in a crime of passion showing how close the madness of love is to more widely acknowledged forms.

280 *applying . . . related*: i.e. since, to a Stoic, 'crime' and 'madness' are related concepts, the distinction commonly drawn between the two—as here in branding Marius a criminal not a madman—is false and purely linguistic.

281 *street-corner shrines*: to the *Lares Compitales*, tended by guilds of freedmen which were made illegal in the late Republic but restored by Augustus.

284 *easy task for gods*: a humorous application of a notion which goes back to Homer.

286 *warranty*: there was a legal obligation to declare any flaws when selling a slave.

287 *the prolific clan of Menenius*: evidently 'the mad', but the reference is obscure. The most famous Menenius persuaded the plebs to end their secession from Rome in 494 BC but any possible connection is unclear.

290 *quartan fever*: one recurring every three days, the fourth (*quartus*) day counting inclusively, and considered mild, hence the mother's actions are even more deranged.

295 *Fear of the gods*: Stertinius' lecture ends on a note closer to Epicureanism than Stoicism.

296 *eighth of the sages*: i.e. worthy to join the Seven Sages of archaic Greece.

297 *revenge*: Damasippus sees Stertinius' doctrine as a means and justification for petty reprisal.

299 *what hangs . . . notice*: Stertinius' reassurance at line 53 is turned into a basis for reciprocal name-calling.

303 *Agave*: another tragic type of madness, here from the final scene of Euripides' *Bacchae*; the mother of Pentheus, king of Thebes, driven mad by Dionysus, who tore him to pieces with the other Theban women and carried the head to her father Cadmus in the belief that it was a lion's.

308 *engaged in building*: as a sign of ambition and an attempt to 'get above himself'.

309 *your full height*: H. admits to being short in *Ep.* 1.20.

310 *Turbo's*: 'Whirlwind'; Porph. plausibly suggests a short gladiator, while Ps.-Acro adds a short soldier as an alternative.

314–20 *mother frog . . . large*: a fable found in Babrius and Phaedrus illustrating the dangers of the small imitating the great; some argue the details are inappropriate and show Damasippus' incompetence, but the meaning of fables tends to be based on the moral rather than the details.

SATIRE 2.4

A certain Catius is hurrying home from a lecture on gastronomy to write down what he has heard, but is persuaded by H. to recite it to him from memory. The speech absurdly treats the art of cookery and hospitality in terms more suited to natural and moral philosophy.

1   *Catius*: there is much debate over his identity, candidates including an Epicurean philosopher (playing on the misconception of that philosophy as advocating gourmandizing) and an Insubrian Gaul mentioned in Cicero's letters.

3   *Pythagoras*: sixth-century BC philosopher, whose advocacy of vegetarianism and abstinence from beans may add point to his inclusion here.

     the man Anytus put in the dock: Socrates; Anytus was among those who successfully prosecuted him for corrupting the young and introducing new gods in 399 BC.

11   *secret*: probably a deliberate tease on the part of Catius and H.

12   *eggs*: traditional starter of a Roman dinner and hence of Catius' lecture.

19   *Falernian*: see note on *Sat.* 1.10.24.

24   *Aufidius*: unknown. It is typical of didactic to correct predecessors, but the quibble here is trumped by Ofellus' ridicule of mixing honey and wine at all at *Sat.* 2.2.15–16.

29   *white wine from Cos*: mixed with sea water as a laxative and not necessarily from Cos.

32   *Lucrine*: coastal lagoon between Puteoli and Baiae, famous for its shellfish.

     Baiae: fashionable seaside resort on the Bay of Naples.

33   *Circeii*: modern Circeo, a promontory and colony on the west coast of Italy about 60 miles south of Rome.

     Misenum: town near the cape at the north end of the Bay of Naples.

34   *Tarentum*: see note on *Sat.* 1.6.59.

39   *elbow*: Roman diners reclined on a couch, propped on one elbow.

40   *Umbria*: a region in eastern central Italy.

42   *Laurentian*: from Laurentum, on the west coast, south of Ostia.

46   *no palate before mine . . . anyone*: a parody of the philosopher's claim to original discoveries.

51   *Massic wine*: a type of Falernian from the Mons Massicus in Campania.

55   *Sorrento's wine*: Sorrento, on the Bay of Naples, was noted for its lighter wine.

62   *cookshops*: popinae, low shops selling basic 'take-away' food to the poor. The prawns and snails are an elegant substitute for the ancient equivalents of kebabs craved by the drunk.

63   *It's worth your while*: see note on *Sat.* 1.2.37.

66   *Byzantium*: modern Istanbul, not yet of course the capital of the Eastern Empire, but presumably a processor of fish from the Black Sea.

68   *Corycian*: from Corycus in Cilicia, southern Asia Minor, source of the best saffron.

69   *Venafran*: from Venafrum in northern Campania, a famed source of olive oil.

70 *Tibur's*: modern Tivoli, ancient city north-east of Rome.

Picenum's: see note on *Sat.* 2.3.272–3.

71 *Venuculum's*: unknown, but source of a famous grain as well as grape.

72 *Alba*: the Alban hills in Latium produced fine wine.

73 *I was first*: identifying the first inventor (*prōtos heuretēs*) of skills is a common motif, but both the self-glorification and the triviality of the discoveries are parodic.

76–7 *a gargantuan error . . . in a narrow dish*: what starts like a moralizing condemnation of extravagant expenditure on fish in the manner of Ofellus bathetically concludes as a ruling on elegance.

84 *Tyrian purple*: Tyre in Phoenicia (modern Lebanon) was famous for its very expensive purple dye made from shellfish.

88 *learned*: *doctus* puns on the fact that Catius has been 'taught' all this and is merely parroting it. H.'s enthusiasm is ironic.

91 *interpreting*: suggests a priest or sibyl communicating the oracles of a god.

94 *sequestered . . . to drink deep*: an allusion to Lucretius, in keeping with the satire's odd relationship with Epicureanism.

SATIRE 2.5

The shade of the seer Tiresias continues his address to Ulysses where he left off in *Odyssey* 11 with advice on how to restore his wealth by the very first-century Roman practice of legacy-hunting (*captatio*), whereby people flattered and cultivated the childless rich in the hope of becoming their heirs. Much of the humour derives from the incongruity of the witty connections drawn between the world of heroic epic and that of contemporary satire.

1 *Tiresias*: blind Theban seer, featuring in numerous tragedies, but here in his Homeric role as a shade in *Odyssey* 11.

2 *lost wealth*: a recurrent motif of the *Odyssey* is the suitors' consumption of Ulysses' wealth by constant feasting.

3–5 *'Is it no longer enough . . . his ancestral home?'*: a metapoetic joke, since the aim of the Homeric epic hero is insufficient for his reimagining in Roman satire. The word for home, *penates* (lit. 'household gods'), helps to Romanize the scene.

6 *as you prophesied*: a tendentious reading of Tiresias' words in *Odyssey* 11 referring to Ulysses' disguise as a beggar. Again, note how Ulysses looks back to a prophecy uttered centuries ago in real time, but a moment earlier in dramatic time.

10 *thrush*: a deliberately anachronistic, Roman touch.

14 *Lar*: see note on *Sat.* 2.3.165. The offerings are probably the 'first fruits' (*primitiae*).

17 *on his outside*: to protect him from splashes and bumps from the road.

18 *Dama*: typical slave name; the juxtaposition with Troy is particularly (but still deliberately) jarring.

20 *I will bid . . . this*: an allusion to Ulysses' address to his soul in *Odyssey* 20, but 'this' turns out to be not poverty but the self-abasement necessary for legacy-hunting.

29–30 *make yourself the advocate*: defending someone in court was a common *officium*, or favour, in the reciprocal world of Roman elite relationships, and as such could be more cynically employed by the *captator*. The childless, of course, lack obvious heirs.

30–1 *have nothing . . . home*: having heirs or a wife capable of producing them makes the man who would otherwise be more deserving of no interest to the *captator*.

32 *first names*: the use of *praenomina*, the first of a Roman's 'three names', signals close friendship.

38 *attorney*: a *cognitor* had full authority to represent the plaintiff or defendant and present his case in court.

39 *Dog-star*: see note on *Sat.* 1.7.25–6.

40–1 *Furius . . . Alps*: i.e. it is cold and wintry. H. adapts a line later cited by Quintilian as an example of forced imagery, in which Jupiter spits snow on the Alps. H. makes the poet do what he describes, as he did with probably the same epicist at *Sat.* 1.10.36 (see note). Bramble argues that the poet bloated with tripe symbolizes the bloated rhetoric of the line, and he vomits the snow as a result (J. C. Bramble, *Persius and the Programmatic Satire* (Cambridge, 1974), 64–6).

44 *More tunny . . . swell*: picking up the fishing imagery of lines 24–6 above.

46 *acknowledged*: lit. 'lifted up', as a Roman father would to acknowledge that a son was his.

48–9 *second heir*: to inherit should the first heir die.
    Orcus: the Underworld, in grandiloquent epic language.

50 *this game*: the image is of a throw of the die (*alea*).

53–4 *second line*: containing the legatee's name; the first gave that of the will's maker.

56 *public clerk . . . raven*: respectively, the actual status of Coranus and a metaphorical description of Nasica, stressing the greed and rapacity of the *captator*. Tiresias speaks in the riddling language of oracles, since this anecdote from 30s BC Rome must be a prophecy of the future in the era of the Trojan War. The names suggest the small-town man from Cora and an aristocrat, perhaps fallen on hard times.

59 *Laertes*: Ulysses' father; the patronymic is another jarring epic touch.

60 *Apollo*: god of prophecy.

62–4 *a youth . . . by land and sea*: Octavian, in more riddling oracular language, with a hint of panegyric. On the Parthians, see note on *Sat.* 2.1.13–15.

Aeneas, as well as being the founder of the Roman people, was ancestor of the Julian *gens* through his son Iulus and hence of Julius Caesar and Octavian.

64–5 *stately . . . full*: clearly the marriage is an attempt by Nasica to ingratiate himself and become Coranus' heir; Nasica's debt is obscure, but probably not owed to Coranus and simply indicates his financial need and hence motive for legacy-hunting.

76 *Penelope*: Ulysses' wife; the suggestion of prostituting her is the more shocking since she was famous for her faithfulness during his twenty years' absence, despite many importunate suitors.

80 *frugal in giving a lot*: a cynical take on Penelope's demand in *Odyssey* 18 that the suitors bring gifts instead of eating up the palace's wealth. Tiresias implies that, if they had been more generous, she would have yielded.

83 *dog . . . hide*: based on a Greek proverb but translating the sound rather than the sense of the Greek *khorion* ('afterbirth') with the Latin *corium* ('hide').

84 *When I was old*: amusing variation on 'when I were a lad', relying on the two factors of Tiresias' being a ghost and his having a lifetime of seven generations.

89 *don't fall short . . . all proportion*: H.'s ideal of moderation, but perverted to immoral ends.

91 *Be Davus in the comedy*: a common slave name, especially in Roman comedy, where the cunning slave was a stock character.

106–9 *fellow heirs . . . pittance*: hence winning the favour of a new potential testator.

110 *Proserpina*: wife of Pluto and queen of the Underworld.

SATIRE 2.6

H. prays to Mercury for a simple life in the countryside and, from the quietude of his Sabine farm, contrasts the joys of rustic life with the bustle of the city and the business he has to conduct there. The comparison (*synkrisis*) is crowned by the description of a simple, rustic dinner-party at which Cervius tells the famous fable of the town mouse and the country mouse.

5 *O Son of Maia*: Mercury, son of Jupiter and Maia, one of the Pleiades. He is associated with property and transactions in general, as here, as well as trade specifically, as at *Sat.* 2.3.25.

13 *Hercules*: in Rome and Italy, a multi-faceted god who had a particular association with benefactions to individuals and communities.

14 *fat*: though we say 'fat-headed', it is hard to bring out the play on *pinguis*, which means 'plump' of livestock and 'dull' of wits.

16 *my citadel in the mountains*: a humorously incongruous designation for the Sabine farm, but one which does point to its remoteness and protection from the evils of the city.

17 *my Muse who goes on foot*: emphasizing the low subject matter and plain style of satire, in contrast to epic and other lofty genres, which might either soar or ride in chariots.

19 *unhealthy autumn*: season of fevers at Rome.

Libitina: goddess of funerals.

20 *Father . . . 'Janus'*: Pater Matutinus is otherwise unknown but may (actually or in invented wordplay) be related to the goddess Mater Matuta. Janus was the two-faced god of doorways and hence associated with beginnings (including that of the year, with January), but in the context of city life, there is probably also an allusion to the mercantile 'central Janus' (see note on *Sat.* 2.3.18–19).

27 *stated . . . what may do me harm*: either the promise to pay the debt if the friend defaults, or the terms of the oath stating what should happen to him if he breaks it.

32 *This . . . like honey*: i.e. the mention of Maecenas.

33 *Esquiline*: gloomy because of its former concentration of cemeteries, and the focus of H.'s visit because of Maecenas' house there (on both, see *Sat.* 1.8).

35 *Roscius*: unknown and a common name, but perhaps playing on *roscidus*, 'of the dew', since he wishes to meet at the (for H.) ungodly hour of 8 a.m.

the Well: the Puteal in the Comitium, near the Forum, was a common location for financial transactions.

36 *Treasury-officials*: such *scribae* were unelected public officials.

37 *Quintus*: H.'s *praenomen*.

44 *Chicken . . . Syrus*: gladiators. A Thracian was a type of gladiator, armed with a round shield and curved sword. 'Chicken' carries none of the modern connotations of cowardice, but the feminine *Gallina* is hardly complimentary.

45 *morning . . . care*: weather, the universal subject of small-talk.

46 *leaky ear*: meaning, not that Maecenas fears H. would let his words 'go in one ear and out the other', but that his indiscreet *mouth* would 'leak' what had been 'dropped' into his ear. Considering the depiction of their relationship elsewhere, this must be ironic.

48 *our friend*: H. himself, who continues to speak of himself in the third person in the next sentence where 'he' (H.) is at the games with 'him' (Maecenas).

49 *Campus*: see note on *Sat.* 1.1.91.

50 *Rostra*: the platform in the Forum from which orators spoke to the people, so called from the fixing of the beaks of ships (*rostra*) to it as trophies of war.

52 *closer contact with the gods*: sneering hyperbole for H.'s influential friends, probably with no reference to Octavian's future deification.

Dacians: a tribe from north of the Danube, best known from the much later expedition of Trajan commemorated on his column, but at this time hostile to Octavian's Rome owing to their allegiance to Antony.

55–6 *veterans . . . promised*: see note on *Sat.* 2.2.112–14.

63 *beans, Pythagoras' kinsmen*: a simple food suiting the simple life on the Sabine farm. Pythagoras forbade the eating of beans on the same grounds as meat, since human souls might have transmigrated into them. H.'s phrase humorously exaggerates the claim.

66 *house-bred slaves*: *vernae*, as opposed to bought slaves; they were often considered more loyal and more closely integrated into the household.

67–70 *well watered . . . with moderate ones*: Romans generally drank their wine diluted, and at symposia the level of dilution (as well as other arrangements) was determined by the *magister bibendi* ('master of drinking'). No such restrictions or sophistications apply at this relaxed, rustic party.

72 *Lepos*: evidently a dancer in pantomime, which bore no relation to its modern namesake, but was a sort of solo ballet on mythological themes accompanied by chorus. The name means 'Charm' or 'Sophistication'.

77 *Cervius*: unknown, but the name is attested.

77–8 *old wives' tales*: a felicitously literal translation of *aniles fabellas*, but the Latin lacks the English phrase's suggestion of superstition and traditions with no basis in fact; rather it marks this as a beast fable in the tradition of Aesop, appropriate for an old woman to tell by the fire, in contrast to the sophisticated repartee of an urban symposium.

78 *Arellius*: unknown, but presumably a city-dweller as well as a rich man.

106 *purple*: a mark of luxury, owing to expense of its production from seashells and of its importation.

109 *first . . . serves*: a murine variation on the slave 'first tasting' (*praelambens* as opposed to *praegustans*) the master's food to make sure it was not poisoned.

114–15 *Molossian hounds*: from the territory of the Molossi in Epirus, north-west Greece, noted for their strength.

SATIRE 2.7

H.'s slave Davus takes advantage of the licence granted slaves at the Saturnalia to speak freely to upbraid his master for his moral failings. In particular, he elaborates on ideas he has heard from the doorkeeper of the Stoic philosopher Crispinus to prove that, since by Stoic doctrine everyone except the wise man is a slave, H. is a slave to his passions for sex and food and hence no freer than he. H.'s response is to threaten Davus with hard labour.

2 *Davus*: a classic name for the crafty slave of Roman comedy and H. uses it to refer to the stock character at *Sat.* 1.10.40, 2.5.91, *AP* 237. H.'s slave is thus aligned with a theatrical type.

3   *bought slave*: such *mancipia* were considered less integrated into and hence less devoted to their master's household than house-bred *vernae* (cf. note on *Sat.* 2.6.66).

4   *the freedom December allows*: at the Saturnalia (see note on *Sat.* 2.3.5).

9   *Priscus*: the name means 'ancient', with connotations of old-fashioned morality, so is ironic for such a figure.

10 *change his stripe*: an allusion to the stripe on the toga, whose thickness differentiated senators, knights, and other ranks, but perhaps meant in a loose, metaphorical sense here.

13 *man of letters*: specifically a philosopher, for which Athens was famous and in contrast to the unethical philanderer.

14 *Vertumnus*: Etruscan god of change; the association with Priscus is obvious, but the reason for deducing his hostility is presumably that the latter does not benefit from his changeability.

15 *jester Volanerius*: on the *scurra*, see note on *Sat.* 1.4.87–9; Volanerius is unknown and his name has no obvious resonance.

    gout he had earned: traditionally through overindulgence.

20 *man . . . now slack*: a figurative phrase for one who has equal difficulties in dealing with contrasting conditions, perhaps an allusion to towing a barge or adjusting the rigging of a ship.

22 *con-man*: lit. 'fork-bearer' (*furcifer*), a common term of generalized abuse for a slave in comedy alluding to a form of punishment in which a fork-shaped yoke was attached to the victim's arms.

30 *carefree greens*: on the ethical connotations of simple food, see note on *Sat.* 1.6.114–16 and *Sat.* 2.2 as a whole; indeed Davus is alluding to H.'s praise of the simple life in precisely these passages and others like them.

36 *Mulvius*: evidently a *scurra* who, with the other parasites, is robbed of their expected dinner with H. now that the latter is going to Maecenas'.

43 *five hundred drachmas*: an average price for a slave; the Greek currency may be an allusion to the Greek settings of Roman comedy.

45 *Crispinus' doorkeeper*: like Damasippus and Catius, Davus is parroting someone else's argument, but here filtered through another intermediary (also a slave). Since the argument is based on the Stoic doctrine that 'all fools are slaves', Crispinus is probably the Stoic philosopher of *Sat.* 1.1.120, 1.3.139, and 1.4.14.

46 *You . . . by a whore*: the first part of Davus' argument is almost precisely that offered by H. in *Sat.* 1.2.

47 *cross*: see note on *Sat.* 1.3.82.

49 *tail's*: the male genitalia, rather than the female, as in US slang.

50 *ridden . . . horse*: sex with the woman on top was considered less respectable, since it gave her a symbolically dominant position and, according to Lucretius, impeded conception, thus rendering the act purely sensual.

The prostitute's nakedness in full light, as well as the crude language, all contribute to the lowness of the scene.

52 *piss*: i.e. ejaculate, a common but crude metaphor.

53 *knight's ring*: a gold ring was a mark of equestrian rank.

54 *Roman dress*: the toga, as opposed to the slave's tunic.

   juror: i.e. someone both eligible to serve on a jury and of suitably sound character.

   Dama: another typical slave name, like Davus, meaning here a 'slave' in the Stoic sense.

59 *gladiator*: bankrupts might be reduced to making a living by becoming gladiators, and hence slaves.

62 *lawful power over both parties*: i.e. the right to kill them, always true of slaves and also of adulterers caught in the act until Augustus' adultery law of 18 BC. A husband also had the right to kill his adulterous wife, which might be relevant to what follows.

63–7 *His power . . . reputation*: a difficult and controversial passage. In the context of Davus' overall argument and in particular the gladiator parallel, the comparison ought still to be between slave and adulterer; if so, the contrastive *illa tamen . . . non* ('*she* doesn't, after all . . .') must compare the adulterous matrona with the slave's prostitute, which would fit the contrast in sexual positions, though the sentence as a whole probably reads more naturally as contrasting the wife with the *adulterer*, the latter being more to blame, and that is how this translation renders it. The relationship of the wife's fear and mistrust to the lover's self-enslavement is not entirely clear either, and line 65 may be an interpolation, though it could make sense meaning 'although' the wife feels like this, and hence does not surrender to her emotions, the adulterer does. In any case, there is a double meaning in the lover's risk of actual degrading punishment more appropriate to a slave while also becoming a 'slave' to the 'furious master' passion according to Stoic doctrine. The stocks relate to the *furcifer* of line 22. It may be foolish to try to make totally consistent sense out of Davus' garbled diatribe, but we should beware of giving up too easily.

76 *magistrate's rod of liberty*: the *vindicta* was used symbolically by a magistrate in the act of manumission to give a slave his freedom; in some texts, the *vindicta* is the ritual and the rod called *festuca*. Davus, of course, is using it metaphorically of the Stoic 'slave'.

79–80 *"deputy" . . . "co-slave"*: a *vicarius* was a slave owned by another slave, and hence subject to his orders, but either because he was also ultimately under the control of his owner's master or simply because both were slaves, he could be conceived of as a *conservus*. Since H. is a 'slave' in Stoic terms, his real slave Davus could fall under either of these headings.

82 *strings that other hands pull*: primarily the passions to which H. is enslaved, but in the years of transition from Republic to principate, this must have some political resonance.

83 *The wise man*: specifically the Stoic ideal of the *sapiens*.

86 *smooth and round*: Davus is either elaborating on or misunderstanding the Stoic notion of god as like a perfect sphere.

88 *Fortune*: the capricious, unpredictable element of chance which still existed within, but was quite separate from, the Stoic notion of a grand providential Fate, and to whose whims the *sapiens* was immune.

90 *A woman*: evidently a courtesan or at least a mercenary girlfriend.

93 *pitiless master*: erotic passion, figured as a horse-rider.

95 *Pausias*: fourth-century BC painter from Sicyon in the northern Peloponnese, famous for his paintings of boys and flowers; the main contrast between these and pictures of gladiators is the sophistication of taste and social rank to which they appeal, but there is also a contrast between effeminacy (is H. 'languishing' over the boys as well as the pictures?) and virility.

96–7 *Fulvius . . . Pacideianus*: gladiators.

105 *a beating*: a regular punishment for slaves, over whom their masters had rights of life and death, in real life but also a stock motif in comedy.

110 *body-scraper*: a *strigil* was used to scrape oil, sweat, and dirt from the skin in bath houses.

116 *stone . . . arrows*: respectively suggest chasing a dog and the weapons of Apollo.

117 *crazy . . . verse*: the association of poetry with inspiration is distorted into one with madness also at the end of *Sat.* 2.3 and of the *AP*. Fitzgerald ingeniously notes that *versus* is an anagram of *servus* in the poem's first line (W. Fitzgerald, *Slavery and the Roman Literary Imagination* (Cambridge, 2000), 24).

118 *or else . . . farm*: a common threat in comedy.

SATIRE 2.8

The comic poet Fundanius tells H. about a dinner-party (*cena*) held by the nouveau riche Nasidienus, attended by Maecenas, Varius Rufus, and other notables. Though it can be hard for a modern reader to be sure exactly which aspects of the *cena* betray Nasidienus' lack of taste and 'class', his main—perhaps only—fault is to describe in tedious and socially inept detail the exotic provenance of each dish and the gastronomically precise techniques of its preparation. After an accident with some tapestries, Nasidienus brings in yet more dishes with yet more descriptions, provoking his guests to leave suddenly.

3 *from midday*: an early start for a Roman dinner, allowing more time for luxurious ostentation and indulgence.

5 *angry stomach*: the Latin *iratus uenter* plays on the two meanings of *stomachus*: stomach and anger.

6 *To start with*: the hors d'oeuvres (*gustatio*) usually consisted of lighter fare than boar, an early sign both of luxury and misjudgement.

Lucania: see note on *Sat.* 2.3.234.

7 *the father of the feast*: Nasidienus, ironically expressed.

gentle . . . blowing: H., citing Ofellus, warned at 2.2.41 that the hot sirocco can make boar go off; evidently this wind was less fierce, but it sounds as if Nasidienus means that it has positively beneficial effects on flavour.

7–9 *sharp-tasting . . . Coan wine*: closer to the normal fare of the *gustatio*.

10 *tunic tucked up high*: to show off the legs of a beautiful slave-boy.

11 *wiped . . . cloth*: an allusion to Lucilius (fr. 598 *ROL*), which might suggest further parallels to the *cena* given by Granius in one of Lucilius' satires.

13–14 *like . . . Ceres*: ceremoniously, like the *kanēphoroi*, most famously associated with the procession at the Panathenaia, but evidently also associated with rites of Demeter (Ceres) such as the Thesmophoria.

Hydaspes: the expensively imported Indian slave is named after a river in the Punjab.

15 *Caecuban*: famous wine from southern Latium.

Alcon: evidently a Greek slave to bear the Greek wine.

Chian: famous Greek wine from the Aegean island of Chios.

without sea-water: too good for such dilution, but *maris expers* also means 'lacking in manhood'.

16 *Alban . . . Falernian*: see notes on *Sat.* 2.4.72 and 1.10.24 respectively.

Maecenas: the first indication that he is present.

19 *Fundanius*: see note on *Sat.* 1.10.42; the identity of H.'s interlocutor is at last revealed and his being a writer of comedies is clearly appropriate.

20–1 *Viscus . . . Varius*: see notes on *Sat.* 1.10.85 and third on 1.5.40 respectively. The three poets are seated together.

Servilius the Jester: taking *balatro* as a name or nickname, rather than as his role, though he clearly is a *scurra*; the name Servilius might also hint at his slavish role.

22 *Vibidius*: unknown.

extras: lit. 'shadows' (*umbrae*), hangers-on brought along uninvited by invited guests.

23 *Nomentanus . . . Hog*: Nasidienus' clients. There is no strong reason for differentiating the former from the recurrent spendthrift (see note on *Sat.* 1.1.101). The latter's name, Porcius, is clearly and immediately linked to his gluttony.

25–6 *point out . . . our attention*: Nasidienus' tedious and socially inept insistence on detailing the sophistications of the *cena* to his guests is compounded by his employment of Nomentanus to cover any points he omits.

31–2 *moon is on the wane*: more likely than 'not yet full' as the meaning of *minorem ad lunam*. The claim is over-fussy as well as absurdly superstitious.

34 *we'll die unavenged*: a vague assertion of determination, with mock-epic colouring.

35 *larger cups*: usually reserved for the symposium after the *cena*.

36 *caterer*: a *parochus* provided food and other necessities to travelling magistrates; by reducing Nasidienus to this level, Fundanius denies him the social role of host.

39 *Allifanian*: from the town of Allifae (modern Alife) in Samnium; the point is evidently that such cups were large, but this is the only evidence for that.

40–1 *guests on the bottom couch*: Nomentanus and Porcius, showing respect to Nasidienus' feelings.

42 *moray eel*: fish were a luxury and this is at the top end of the scale; there does not seem to be anything wrong with his choice of fish, dish, or accompaniment here.

45 *Venafran*: see note on *Sat.* 2.4.69.

46 *sauce . . . fish from Spain*: the *garum* so widely used in Graeco-Roman cooking, of which Pliny claims the best was made from Spanish mackerel.

    Methymna: city on Lesbos.

51 *I was first*: see note on *Sat.* 2.4.73.

    elecampane: a herb also known as horse-heal, recommended by Ofellus at 2.2.44 (there translated 'tart pickles').

52 *Curtillus*: unknown, but the citation of an authority recalls the pseudo-scientific tone of Catius in *Sat.* 2.4.

58 *Rufus*: evidently Nasidienus' *cognomen*.

65–74 *"These are the terms . . . conceals it"*: in contrast to Nomentanus' phil-osophizing consolation, which is ironically absurd to Fundanius and H., but sincerely meant by the sycophantic client, Jester is clearly mocking the aggrandizing application of such ideas to the trivialities of the *cena*. Nevertheless, Nasidienus takes him at his word.

77 *slippers*: a sign that he is about to leave the dining room.

79–80 *I'd have preferred . . . after these*: H.'s first words *in propria persona* for a while and his last in the *Satires*.

84 *back you come*: the apostrophe, or address of a character, could be a mock-epic touch or, conversely, add to the informal vividness of Fundanius' narrative.

86–92 *carrying . . . real delicacies*: the luxury and excess are part of the absurd-ity, but Fundanius makes it clear that the guests would have enjoyed them were it not for their host's pedantic and inappropriate description of every detail of their provenance and preparation, a description which Fundanius himself mimics here.

92–3 *origins and properties*: ironically evoking the language of natural philosophy.

95–5 *off we ran . . . them*: an abrupt ending to the *cena*, the poem, the book, and H.'s satiric corpus proper (though the *Epistles* are close kin), without even the unsatisfying comments of H. himself which close 2.3 and 2.7. On Canidia, see note on *Sat.* 1.8.24, though the emphasis is on her as poisoner rather than witch (albeit the two were related) as at 2.1.48. The snakes of the province of Africa (roughly modern Tunisia) were proverbially venomous.

EPISTLES, BOOK 1

EPISTLE 1.1

H. writes to Maecenas to explain that he has 'retired' from the writing of trivial lyric and is now concentrating on philosophy—though without strictly adhering to any one school—and the question of how to live well. He provides some preliminary thoughts, stressing the superiority of virtue over wealth and political power, and that it is possible to improve a little, even if perfection is unattainable.

1 *my earliest Muse*: i.e. in *Satires* 1.

2 *wooden baton*: given to a gladiator when he retired, as H. has from writing lyric.

5–6 *Veianius . . . temple*: a gladiator who, like tradesmen, has marked his retirement by dedicating his 'tools' to a god; cf. *Sat.* 1.5.65–6. The Roman Hercules was particularly associated with gladiators.

7 *I have someone*: an allusion to Socrates' similar claim to hear an admonishing voice.

10 *verses*: i.e. the lyric of the *Odes*; the *Epistles*, as a form of satire, do not claim to be real poetry; see note on *Sat.* 1.4.42.

14 *there's no master . . . loyalty to*: H. denies being a doctrinaire adherent of any philosophical school, using military and gladiatorial imagery from the swearing of oaths to generals and trainers respectively.

16–17 *I become active . . . virtue*: i.e. as a Stoic.

18 *Aristippus*: see note on *Sat.* 2.3.100. He is prominent in *Ep.* 1.17 and his adaptability contrasts with the rigidity of Stoic ethics.

28 *Lynceus*: preternaturally and proverbially keen-sighted watchman of the *Argo*.

29 *blear-eyed*: the imagery of sight and conjunctivitis continues from the *Satires*.

30 *Glycon's physique*: a contemporary athlete competing in the *pankration*, a combination of boxing and wrestling.

33 *fever*: the medical imagery shifts from parallel to metaphor.

34 *sayings*: philosophical maxims acting like magical incantations.

37 *read the booklet three times*: as in rituals, but using a philosophical treatise rather than a book of spells.

38 *the slave*: this word is not in the Latin, but is consistent with the wider imagery of this epistle.

49 *villages and crossways*: alluding to the festivals associated with them (Paganalia at *pagi*, villages, and Compitalia at *compites*, crossways) at which prizefights would be held.

52 *Silver . . . gold*: the connection to modern Olympic medals is coincidental.

54 *Janus*: the two-faced Roman god of gateways and new beginnings, here imagined as Rome's schoolteacher, but also alluding to the trading district of the *Ianus medius* (see note on *Sat.* 2.3.18–19).

58 *four hundred . . . nonentity*: in order to be a member of the equestrian order (above the people but below the senatorial order), property of 400,000 sesterces was required. Moral probity was also a criterion, though less examined and unsuited to H.'s argument. The Latin's *plebs* puns on 'nonentity' and the narrower sense 'of lower than equestrian rank'.

60 *rules . . . ruler*: H. hears in the boys' chant the deeper truth that if you act 'rightly' (*recte*), you will be 'king' (*rex*), in the philosophical sense of free and in control, the opposite of a 'nonentity'.

62 *Roscius' law*: see second note on *Sat.* 1.6.40.

64 *Curius*: Manius Curius Dentatus, third-century soldier and politician, a representative of the simple morality of old Rome; more specifically relevant to this context, he was famous for rejecting silver offered as a bribe by the Samnites, asserting that he preferred turnips!

    Camillus: M. Furius Camillus, early fourth-century conqueror of Veii and restorer of Rome after its sack by the Gauls.

67 *Pupius' . . . plays*: unknown but evidently a tragedian whose plays provoke tears (*lacrimosa*) through both their pathos and their abysmal quality.

71 *use . . . colonnades*: an elaborate way of saying 'frequent the city', though there may be a play on *portico/stoa*, as a place where mercenary Romans espouse a very different 'philosophy' from Zeno's Stoics.

73–5 *the cunning fox . . . from it*: beast fables are common in *Epistles* 1 as in *Satires* 2. This one is paralleled in Babrius and others, but its precise application here is slightly obscure, since the Roman people seem to be represented both by the tracks (warning against following the herd) and the lion's den (the inescapable destruction of their avarice).

76 *beast . . . heads*: most probably alluding to the Lernaean Hydra, slain by Hercules and, like other monsters defeated by him, often allegorized.

77 *state-contracts*: for collecting taxes in the provinces.

77–9 *others . . . game reserves*: legacy-hunting, the theme of *Sat.* 2.5; the hunting imagery is extended to keeping the prospective testators on game-reserves (*vivaria*).

80 *interest*: a sign of discreditable usury rather than of a savings account in the modern fashion.

83 *Baiae's*: see second note on *Sat.* 2.4.32.

84 *lake . . . to their cost*: the building of moles out into lakes and seas is a common focus of moralizing against luxury and, as a violation of nature,

could be depicted as something which the personified water-bodies suffered.

85 *Teanum*: probably the city of that name in northern Campania, rather than that in Apulia, though the latter would increase the building enthusiast's capriciousness.

87 *marriage bed . . . in his hall*: the *lectus genialis* was a symbolic wedding bed positioned in the *atrium* marking the union of the couple's *genii* or attendant spirits.

90 *Proteus*: see note on *Sat.* 2.3.71, but here an image of fickleness rather than elusiveness.

103 *praetor*: see note on *Sat.* 2.3.217–18.

106–7 *wise man . . . kings*: Stoic doctrine, gently undercut, but far from dismissed as at the end of *Sat.* 1.3.

EPISTLE 1.2

H. writes to his young friend Lollius Maximus, extolling the potential of Homer's *Iliad* and *Odyssey* as sources of ethical models far superior to actual philosophers. He proceeds to show that the urgency and energy with which material gain and physical desires are usually pursued would be better devoted to the pursuit of living well.

1 *Lollius Maximus*: also the addressee of *Ep.* 1.18; identity uncertain, but possibly the son of M. Lollius, consul in 21 BC and addressee of *Odes* 4.9.

2 *Rome, Praeneste*: also juxtaposed in Latin, pointing the antithesis between city and country; the latter is in Latium, about 23 miles east of Rome.

poet . . . War: Homer, as poet of the *Iliad*, though his *Odyssey* emerges as equally enlightening about ethics.

4 *Chrysippus*: see note on *Sat.* 1.3.127.

Crantor: Greek philosopher (340–275 BC), representing the Academic school founded by Plato.

6 *Paris' love*: the Trojan prince eloped with Helen, wife of Menelaus of Sparta, sparking the Trojan War.

9 *Antenor*: old and wise Trojan counsellor, who proposed returning Helen in *Iliad* 7.

11 *Nestor . . . Atreus*: the old and wise *Greek* counselor Nestor tried to resolve the conflict between Achilles (son of Peleus) and Agamemnon (son of Atreus), notably in *Iliad* 1.

13 *the first . . . anger*: the wrath of Achilles is the *Iliad*'s stated theme, but Agamemnon is equally enraged in Book 1; 'love' is a slightly romanticized interpretation of Achilles' feelings for Briseis, the 'prize' of which Agememnon deprives him.

19–22 *subdued . . . adversity*: a close paraphrase of *Odyssey* 1.1–5.

23 *Sirens' songs*: monsters with the faces of beautiful women who lured men
   to their deaths using their beautiful song; Ulysses stopped his crew's
   ears with wax and had himself bound to the mast, so he could safely hear
   them. They are allegorized here as femmes fatales.

   Circe's cups: semi-divine sorceress who transformed Ulysses' crew into
   swine using a magic potion. Drunkenness is added to the femme-fatale
   motif in this allegorization, turning men into beasts. In fact, Ulysses did
   drink the potion, but was rendered immune by the herb *moly* through the
   advice of Mercury.

25 *mistress*: more pointed in Latin than in English, retaining the metaphorical
   sense that the man is her slave, rather than neutrally connoting 'female lover'.

28 *suitors*: the youths of Ithaca who demanded Penelope's hand during
   Ulysses' absence and in the meantime feasted at his expense in his
   house.

   Alcinous: king of the Phaeacians, with whom Ulysses sojourns after escap-
   ing Calypso's island before returning to Ithaca. The Phaeacians are only
   mildly criticized in the *Odyssey* itself, but became types of indolence in
   moralizing interpretations of the epic.

42 *countryman*: although the Romans idealized the hardy, simple morality of
   the countryside, they could also characterize them as dim-witted hicks.

58 *Sicily's tyrants*: notorious for cruel and elaborate tortures, such as the red-
   hot bull in which Phalaris of Acragas placed victims.

EPISTLE 1.3

H. writes to another young friend, Julius Florus, who is part of the entour-
age of the future emperor Tiberius on his expedition to Armenia in 21 BC.
He enquires about the poetic pursuits of the young men in the entourage,
before advising Florus to give some thought to philosophy and especially to
burying a quarrel with a friend.

1 *Julius Florus*: in addition to what can be deduced from this epistle, Porph.
  claims that he was a public clerk (*scriba*) and a writer of satires.

2 *Claudius*: Ti. Claudius Nero, the future emperor Tiberius, son of
  Augustus' wife Livia and not adopted by the *princeps* himself until AD 4.

3 *Thrace . . . Hebrus*: proverbially cold, Thrace was a Roman province and
  area covering parts of modern Bulgaria and north-eastern Greece; the
  Hebrus was one of its rivers, hyperbolically claimed to be frozen.

4 *straits . . . towers*: the Hellespont, dividing Europe and Asia, and more
  specifically the towers from which the star-crossed lovers Hero of Sestos
  and Leander of Abydos looked out.

5 *Asia's*: not the modern continent, but the Roman province in the west of
  modern Turkey.

9–11 *Titius . . . streams*: Titius is otherwise unknown, though Ps.-Acro adds
  the name Septimius, but evidently he composed grand, choral lyric in the

manner of the Greek Pindar (*c.*518–446 BC). H.'s own lyric *Odes* align themselves more with the sympotic poetry of Alcaeus (odes on love and wine, performed at drinking parties), but, in spite of claims to the contrary, Pindar was an important influence. Water commonly symbolizes poetic inspiration and the unfrequented springs here evokes Callimachean aesthetics, the opposite of the muddy Euphrates (see note on *Sat.* 1.1.57).

13 *Theban metres*: i.e. those of the Theban Pindar. H. faced comparable challenges writing Latin odes in the metres of Alcaeus and Sappho, but Pindar's 'triadic' metres are more complex still.

15 *Celsus*: the addressee of *Ep.* 1.8.

17 *whatever writings Palatine Apollo . . . charge*: i.e. books in the public library in the temple of Apollo on the Palatine; Celsus is straying across the line between imitation and plagiarism.

18–20 *flock . . . laughing stock*: another fable, with parallels in Phaedrus and Babrius.

21 *beds . . . round*: H. uses the same image of his poetic dilettantism as like the browsing of a humble bee in *Odes* 4.2, both of which may allude to Pindar's *Pythian* 10.54.

31 *Munatius*: probably the son of L. Munatius Plancus, consul in 42 BC and, following many changes of side, a supporter of Octavian at Actium and thereafter.

EPISTLE 1.4

H. gently upbraids his friend Albius for not enjoying the many gifts the gods have bestowed on him.

1 *Albius*: also addressed in *Odes* 1.33 and often thought to be the love–elegist Tibullus. H. plays on his name's suggesting 'white' (*albus*) by calling him 'genial' (*candide*, also 'white').

2 *Pedum*: ancient Latian city, east of Rome, with territory between Tibur and Praeneste.

3 *Cassius of Parma's pen*: one of Caesar's assassins; this is the only reference to his writings.

15 *Epicurus' herd*: H. plays on the common misconstruction of Epicureans' emphasis on 'pleasure' as entailing hedonism. The Latin *grex* means both 'herd of animals' and 'school of philosophers'.

EPISTLE 1.5

H. invites his friend, the advocate Torquatus, to a simple dinner-party, where the food, crockery, and furniture will be plain but the wine carefully chosen for quality and appropriateness, and the company good. Torquatus is urged to find time away from his legal duties to enjoy relaxation and companionship.

1 *Archias*: unknown but evidently a producer of non-luxurious couches.

2 *modest . . . vegetables*: on the ethical connotations of such simple food, a recurrent motif in H., see especially *Sat.* 2.2.

3 *Torquatus*: unknown, but the name suggests an aristocrat.

   end of the day: Romans usually dined in the late afternoon; the late start here both contrasts H.'s *cena* with those beginning early to fit in a long, luxurious, and ostentatious menu (like Nasidienus' in *Sat.* 2.8), and allows Torquatus to finish his legal business for the day.

4 *Taurus' . . . consulship*: 26 BC, the consul being the great general T. Statilius Taurus. It was standard Roman practice to identify a year by the name of the consul(s).

5 *Minturnae*: town on the Appian Way in southern Latium, near Campania. Petrinum is unknown, but between Minturnae and Sinuessa (see first note on *Sat.* 1.5.40) lay the Mons Massicus, so this is an elaborate way of saying the wine is Massic. The quality of the wine contrasts with the humble food and furniture.

9 *Moschus' case*: Volcacius Moschus was a declaimer from Pergamum, who was convicted of poisoning and went into exile in Massilia (modern Marseilles). The Elder Seneca mentions that the distinguished Asinius Pollio (see second note on *Sat.* 1.10.42) defended him, so the reference is a compliment to Torquatus, rather than a jibe at his failure.

   Caesar's birth: we might expect a reference to Augustus' birthday (23 September); it is not known to have been an official holiday, so the point may be that H. is using it as an excuse to lure Torquatus from his workaholic lifestyle. However, Julius Caesar's birthday (13 July, celebrated on the 12th) *was* a holiday from 42 BC on and makes more sense as a 'summer night'.

13 *worrying . . . heir*: ironic; the point is not that the miser actually cares about his heir, but that only the heir will enjoy the benefits of his self-denial.

14 *drinking . . . flowers*: as at a symposium.

20 *free*: plays on the wine-god Bacchus' name *Liber* and in its literal sense (*solutum* 'released') on his Greek title *Lyaeus* ('the looser of bonds').

26–7 *Butra's . . . Sabinus'*: unknown, which may be the point at this intimate, unpretentious dinner.

31 *client*: not someone whom Torquatus is defending in court, but a humble man to whom he is a 'patron' and who evidently tends to accompany him to dinners uninvited.

EPISTLE 1.6

H. starts by telling Numicius to make an idol of nothing and then shows why such common objects of idolatry as wealth, political success, food, and love are unworthy of it. Detached moderation is preferable.

1 *'Make . . . nothing'*: a sentiment common to many philosophies, but there is a particularly Epicurean colour to much of what follows.

Numicius: unknown, barely characterized, and even the commentators do not speculate.

7   *shows . . . people*: both theatrical and circus shows were a common means of gaining and parading popular support; the word for Roman people used here, *Quirites*, stresses their civic and hence electoral identity.

18 *Tyrian dyes*: Tyre in Phoenicia (modern Lebanon) was famous for purple dye extracted from shellfish, a proverbially expensive and luxurious product.

22 *Mutus*: suggest he both is silent (*mutus*) and engages in trade (*muto*).

24 *Agrippa's colonnade*: more usually called the Colonnade of the Argonauts, after a series of paintings on its walls, located in the Campus Martius, and built by Augustus' right-hand man in 25 BC.

    Appius' highway: H. again avoids the usual name (Appian Way) to produce an effect of defamiliarization. In these two cases, we are made to focus on the great men who are immortalized in their monuments but remain mortal in their bodies.

27 *Numa and Ancus*: the second and fourth kings of Rome. Ancus was used as an example of how even the mightiest die by Lucretius, adapting Ennius, and H. later joined him with Aeneas and Tullus in this context at *Odes* 4.7.15.

31–2 *sacred . . . firewood*: chopping down sacred groves is a classic act of atheism and impiety, particularly associated with the mythical Erysichthon in Callimachus' *Hymn to Demeter* and (later) in Ovid's *Metamorphoses* 8.

33 *Cibyra and Bithynia*: a city in Phrygia (north-west central Turkey) and a region to the north, on the Black Sea coast, both representing mercantile trade in the East.

34 *a thousand talents*: a deliberately vague and hyperbolic sum.

37–8 *Cash . . . Persuasion*: personifications did have divine status in Rome, but these are cynical parodies.

39 *Cappadocian king*: probably Archelaus, last ruler of this client kingdom (from 36 BC to AD 17) in eastern central Turkey, favoured by Augustus, who expanded his kingdom. His alleged impecuniousness seems to be based on this passage and the point may rather be that even the fabled wealth of an Oriental king is not enough for the greedy man.

40 *Lucullus*: L. Licinius Lucullus (d. 56 BC), great general of the late Republic, especially renowned for his role in the war against Mithridates, but also notorious in later life for his wealth and luxurious living.

41 *cloaks . . . theatre*: presumably for costumes; the use of the Greek *chlamydes* for 'cloaks' adds an extra suggestion of foreign luxury.

45–6 *impoverished . . . pilferers*: ironic, of course, like all the exhortations to avarice in this passage.

47 *make . . . happy*: linking back to the theme as set out at the start of the letter, using exactly the same words.

50 *slave . . . ear*: a *nomenclator*, enabling his master to greet those he meets by name, especially when electioneering, as well as providing further relevant information.

52 *tribe*: one of thirty-five ancient divisions of the Roman people (including those named), still used in H.'s time for voting and certain other purposes.

53–4 *bundle of rods*: emblems of elected magistracies, the fasces or rods were carried by the magistrate's attendants (*lictores*), while the ivory curule chair (*sella curulis*) was used by consuls and praetors.

55 *adopt*: emphasizes the hollowness of the candidate's use of the familial terms by facetiously suggesting that it constitutes a legal adoption.

58 *Gargilius*: unknown.

62 *wax of Caere*: another defamiliarizing phrase for the more usual 'Tablets of the Caeretans' (*tabulae Caerites*) on which were listed the names of those whom the censors had deprived of civic rights. The connection with Caere, an Etruscan city about 29 miles north of Rome, is disputed.

63–4 *wicked crew . . . birth*: a moralizing interpretation of the *Odyssey* (cf. *Ep.* 1.2 above); in the context of gluttony, this must refer to the crew's killing and eating of the cattle of Helios (*Odyssey* 12), even though Homer stresses that they were starving and acted with extreme reluctance.

65 *Mimnermus*: seventh-century BC Greek elegist from Smyrna, but adopted by Colophon; his output was varied but he was celebrated as a love poet by Propertius and others (H. here alludes to fr. 1 West).

EPISTLE 1.7

H. writes to Maecenas to explain why he is still on his Sabine farm and has not returned to the city, despite his promise. He proceeds to muse on the relationship between patron and client, especially the gifts which the former bestows and the obligations they incur from the latter. An extended anecdote on the disastrous patronage accepted by the auctioneer Mena from the advocate Philippus illustrates his point.

6 *funeral marshal . . . togas*: a *dissignator* was a lictor in charge of funerals; dark clothing was worn in mourning. The period H. refers to is the autumn.

9 *unseal wills*: because the testator has died.

10 *Alban hills*: 13 miles south-east of Rome.

11 *bard*: H. uses *vates* here with self-deprecating irony, but adopts its connotation of a prophetic, public poet in the *Odes*.

13 *west . . . swallow*: in the spring.

14 *Calabrian*: from the Salentine peninsula in the 'heel' of Italy, not the 'toe', which is modern Calabria but ancient Bruttium.

23 *lupine seeds*: used as stage money.

26 *lungs*: the Latin *latus* evokes the orator's powerful lungs but, in context, also the stamina of the lover's loins.

28 *Cinara*: the name, as well as the context, suggests a courtesan. She recurs in *Ep.* 1.14 and in *Odes* 4.1, and in both places she likewise represents a past life which H. has left behind, even though she does not actually appear in *Odes* 1–3.

25–8 *But if . . . lover*: H.'s point is complex. He no longer has the stamina of youth to sustain the demanding pleasures of Maecenas' lifestyle, but age has also brought a change of attitude so that he no longer wants such pleasures, or at least not unremittingly. The apparently autobiographical sketch of his past self and life is also related to his literary *persona* in and the sympotic scenarios of the *Odes*. All of this recalls the opening of *Ep.* 1.1.

29 *It happened once*: another beast fable, of clear applicability to the patron–client relationship; in Babrius 86, both characters are foxes.

40 *Telemachus*: another moralizing use of the *Odyssey* in the manner of *Ep.* 1.2; H. closely paraphrases *Odyssey* 4.601–8, but crucially omits Telemachus' request at 4.600 for treasure (*keimelion*) instead, in keeping with Homeric codes of gift-exchange but not Horatian morality.

43 *son of Atreus*: here, Menelaus.

45 *Tibur . . . Tarentum*: see notes on *Sat.* 2.4.70 and 1.6.59 respectively, though the provincial seclusion of both, not the latter's luxuriousness, is evoked.

46 *Philippus*: often identified with L. Marcius Philippus. consul in 91 and praised as an orator by Cicero, but without certainty. His name, which translates as 'Horse-lover', provides a connection with the previous section.

48 *Carinae*: the western end of the southern spur of the Esquiline, so named from the resemblance of certain buildings on it to ships' keels. It is not far from the Forum Romanum, except in the mind of a tired old man.

50 *close-shaven*: Mena's neat appearance contrasts with his later transformation into a rough-hewn rustic and especially his unshaven state at the climax.

55 *Vulteius Mena*: the name suggests a freedman, Menas, who has taken his *nomen* from his former master.

56–9 *of modest means . . . Campus*: many of the simple virtues of moderation espoused in the *Satires* and *Epistles*. 1. On the Campus Martius, see note on *Sat.* 1.1.91.

61 *invite him to come to dinner*: one of the standard *officia* (favours/duties) offered by a patron to his client, marking that Philippus wishes to make Mena his.

68 *visited . . . morning*: on the *salutatio*, see note on *Sat.* 1.6.101.

68–9 *in short . . . first*: the man of lower social status ought to greet his superior first.

73 *mid-afternoon*: the usual time for dinner.

75 *morning . . . table*: Mena's day is now bookended by the *salutatio* and the *cena*, both marking him as Philippus' client.

76 *Latin Festival*: held in honour of Jupiter Latiaris on the Alban Mount in spring, marking the kinship of the Roman and Latin peoples.

77 *Sabine*: area north-east of Rome and location of the estate which Maecenas gave to H.

84 *elms*: for supporting the vines.

94 *Attendant Spirit*: the *genius* was a sort of double and guardian spirit.

96–8 *Let . . . standard*: the moral is drawn very briefly, but the relationship between the story and H. and Maecenas' situation, while mainly contrastive, is left somewhat ambiguous.

EPISTLE 1.8

H. addresses, not his friend Albinovanus Celsus, but the Muse with a request to address him. Celsus has been appointed secretary to Tiberius and, after a tactful reflection on his own moral failings, H. gently advises him not to become arrogant because of his elevation.

1 *Celsus Albinovanus*: unknown, but perhaps related to the poet Albinovanus Pedo. H. plays, especially at the end of the epistle, with his *cognomen*'s literal meaning, 'lofty, elevated'.

2 *Nero*: not, of course, the emperor now known by that name, but the future emperor Tiberius, Ti. Claudius Nero (cf. note on *Ep.* 1.3.2).

1–2 *Muse . . . good wishes*: H. plays with epistolary and poetic conventions by having the Muse as an intermediary.

4–6 *hail . . . pastures*: H. is evidently on his Sabine farm, but his troubles are not the practical ones which faced Mena in the previous epistle.

12 *Tibur . . . Tibur*: compare Davus' accusation at *Sat.* 2.7.28–9. On Tibur, see first note on *Sat.* 2.4.70.

16 *drop . . . ears*: there may be a hint of the slave whispering in the triumphator's ear to remember that he is mortal.

EPISTLE 1.9

H. writes a letter of recommendation to Tiberius, as he has been asked to by Septimius, and after much explanation of why he *shouldn't* be writing it, recommends him briefly, conventionally, and ironically.

1 *Septimius*: unknown, but also addressed in *Odes* 2.6.

   Claudius: Tiberius again (cf. *Ep.* 1.3.2), as is the Nero of line 4.

13 *fine, brave fellow*: conventional and non-committal.

EPISTLE 1.10

H. writes to Aristius Fuscus in praise of the countryside and all the moral advantages it represents, in contrast with the city.

1 *Fuscus*: see note on *Sat.* 1.9.61.

6 *nest*: i.e. the city.

10–11 *slave . . . cakes*: the simple life of the countryside is linked with freedom, while the luxuries of the city both accompany and enforce a sort of slavery.

16 *Dog-star*: see note on *Sat.* 1.7.25–6.

Lion's motions: the sun is at its hottest in late July and August, when it is in the constellation of Leo.

19 *mosaics of African stone*: African marble was of high quality, but it is its exoticism and import value which are contrasted with Italian grass.

25 *break through*: perhaps evoking vegetation breaking through paving or stonework.

26 *Sidonian*: from Sidon in Phoenicia; see note on *Ep.* 1.6.18.

27 *Aquinum's dye*: town in south-east Latium, not otherwise attested as a producer of dye, which fits with H.'s characterization of it as inferior to Sidon in this respect.

33 *grandees*: lit. 'kings', perhaps evoking the Homeric phrase 'Priam and the people of Priam', who were likewise doomed.

34–8 *The stag . . . from his mouth*: Aristotle reports that the lyric poet Stesichorus used this beast fable to dissuade the citizens of Himera in Sicily from increasing the power of the tyrant Phalaris, though there the man does not even take action against the stag but immediately enslaves the horse, so the emphasis is on trickery and naive misjudgement rather than, as here, the trade-off between prosperity and freedom.

49 *dictating*: presumably to a personal scribe.

Vacuna's: a Sabine goddess (thus marking H.'s location as near his farm) of uncertain attributes. Varro claims she is the goddess Victory, but the scholiasts offer numerous alternatives.

EPISTLE 1.11

Bullatius has been sightseeing in Asia Minor, which prompts H. to reflect on the irrelevance of place, or change of place, to the production of happiness, since one can never escape from oneself.

1 *Bullatius*: unknown; the name may suggest that he is childish (*bullatus*) enough to wear the traditional protective amulet (*bulla*).

1–2 *Chios . . . Lesbos . . . Samos*: islands in the eastern Aegean, off the west coast of Asia Minor.

Sardis . . . Croesus: the first of three cities in western Asia Minor to match the three islands, former capital of Lydia, whose last, most famous and proverbially wealthy king was the sixth-century Croesus.

3 *Smyrna*: modern Izmir, at the head of the Hermaic gulf.

Colophon: north-west of Ephesus.

4 *Mars' Field*: see note on *Sat.* 1.1.91.

5 *Attalus' cities*: the name of three kings of Pergamum, the last of whom bequeathed his kingdom to Rome in 133 BC. Of the kingdom's many famous cities, Pergamum itself and Ephesus stand out.

6 *Lebedus*: city north-west of Colophon, with a prosperous past but in decline since its sacking by Lysimachus in the early third century B C.

7–10 '*You know . . . rage*': Bullatius' apparent interjection, though typical of satire, feels odd in a letter, and some argue that H. himself expresses a short-lived desire for a change of scene before pulling himself up short.

7–8 *Gabii . . . Fidenae*: cities in Latium, apparently declined, though Gabii was (again?) prosperous under Hadrian.

11 *Capua*: principal city of Campania, from which one would travel to Rome along the Appian Way. H.'s point in this and the following two examples is that one should not give short-term relief in response to immediate circumstances a disproportionate importance.

13 *bakehouses*: see note on *Sat.* 1.4.37; here, a source of warmth.

baths: public baths, including the *caldarium*, or hot-room.

17 *Rhodes and Mytilene*: another eastern Aegean island and the main city of Lesbos.

28 *busy idleness*: the oxymoron stresses the futility of such a lifestyle.

30 *Ulubrae*: small town in Latium by the Pomptine marshes, a proverbial backwater, and hence the extreme example of the irrelevance of location to happiness.

EPISTLE 1.12

Iccius has a good job as steward of Agrippa's estates in Sicily but is evidently complaining about it, perhaps because it distracts him from his beloved natural philosophy. H. advocates contentment with one's lot, and perhaps hints that both ethics and politics need to be given attention alongside physics.

1 *Iccius*: the addressee of *Odes* 1.29; his excited anticipation there of the wealth and glory to be gained on his first campaign contrasts with his ascetically philosophical attitude here.

Sicilian . . . Agrippa: Iccius is evidently the steward (*procurator*) of Agrippa's estates in Sicily.

12 *Democritus*: Greek atomist philosopher from Abdera in Thrace, who lived in the second half of the fifth century BC. Cicero more vaguely states that he left his fields uncultivated.

13 *swift . . . abroad*: a common image for the natural philosopher's mental exploration of the cosmos.

20 *Empedocles*: Greek philosopher (*c.*492–432 BC) from Acragas in Sicily, a point of contact with Iccius, and author of *On nature*. His 'madness' probably alludes to his claim to divinity and his suicide by jumping into Mt. Etna, as described at the end of *AP*.

Stertinius: the Stoic philosopher quoted at length by Damasippus in *Sat.* 2.3 (see note on 2.3.33) on the doctrine that everyone except the Stoic wise man is mad.

21 *fish . . . butcher*: a dismissive allusion to philosophical restrictions on diet, such as Pythagoras' ban on meat and beans because they might be reincarnated humans.

22 *Pompeius Grosphus*: addressee of *Odes* 2.16, which makes it clear he was a wealthy man with land in Sicily.

26 *Cantabrian . . . valour*: Agrippa made an expedition to Spain in 19 BC to finish the long task of pacifying the peninsula. Cantabria in the north-west was among the last regions to succumb.

26–7 *Armenian . . . Nero's*: a laudatory description of Tiberius' expedition to set Tigranes III on the throne of Armenia, though he was accompanied by an army. The two theatres of action mark the western and eastern edges of Roman power.

27–8 *Phraates . . . Caesar*: considerable spin is put on the diplomatic agreement of 20 BC whereby the Parthian king returned the legionary standards lost by Crassus at the battle of Carrhae in 53 BC.

28–9 *golden . . . horn*: an allusion to the cornucopia or horn of plenty; images of fertility and abundance are common in Augustan poetry and art.

EPISTLE 1.13

H. gives instructions to Vinius on how—and how not—to deliver to Augustus the three books of his *Odes*.

2 *Vinius*: Nisbet suggests he may be the remarkably strong centurion Vinnius Valens, whom the Elder Pliny mentions as having served in Augustus' praetorian guard (R. G. M. Nisbet, 'Notes on Horace, *Epistles* 1', *Classical Quarterly*, 9 (1959), 73–6, at pp. 75–6).

8–9 *turning . . . joke*: 'Asina' suggests *asinus*, 'donkey'.

9 *talk of the town*: lit. 'fable' (*fabula*), perhaps a hint at the beast fables in which donkeys often feature and which are so common in the *Epistles*.

14 *Pyrria*: the name is corrupt in the manuscripts and the allusion obscure.

15 *a fellow tribesman . . . dinner*: also obscure, but the reference to tribes might suggest an electioneering dinner and the invitation of a potential voter who would not be used to such social events.

EPISTLE 1.14

H. writes to the bailiff on his Sabine farm praising the countryside in response to the latter's grumbling about being stuck away from the city, but admits at the end that his attitude has changed since the pleasure-loving days of his youth.

1 *Bailiff*: a *vilicus*, though a slave, oversaw all business on an estate.

3 *heads . . . to Varia*: the term *patres* suggests Roman senators as well as fathers of their household, so they might go to the local market town to sit on a municipal council.

6 *Lamia*: unknown, but perhaps one of the addressees of *Odes* 1.26, 1.36, and 3.17.

9 *shatter . . . racetrack*: the point is not that H. longs for the very urban pleasure of the Circus but quite the opposite, that his mind and heart's longing to go to the countryside is like that of a racehorse's held back at the starting gate.

14 *factotum*: a *mediastinus* was a drudge of a slave, who could be called on for any task.

23 *the way . . . grapes*: an *adynaton*, or impossibility: the bailiff is imagined as complaining that the Sabine farm is as likely to produce the fruits of the Orient as the grapes it ought but fails to yield.

32 *The man*: H. himself when younger.

33 *Cinara*: see note on *Ep.* 1.7.28.

34 *Falernian*: see note on *Sat.* 1.10.24.

39 *my neighbours . . . stones*: in the context of H.'s argument, this is evidently meant to be a positive sign of frank, unmalicious amusement in antithesis to the snide carping whose absence in the countryside implies its presence in the city.

EPISTLE 1.15

H. writes to his friend Vala explaining why he is not at Baiae, and from this demonstrating his ability to adapt to changing circumstances; the unexpected figure of the spendthrift-turned-*scurra* Maenius provides a parallel.

1 *Velia*: the Greek Elea, modern Castellamare, city in Lucania, southern Italy, home of the Eleatic school of philosophy but a popular resort by Augustan times.

Vala: unknown, but his name suggests being healthy (*valere*).

Salernum: Roman colony south of the Bay of Naples.

3 *Antonius Musa*: Augustus' physician and evidently H.'s, particularly famed for his cold-compress cure.

Baiae: see second note on *Sat.* 2.4.32.

9 *Clusium's*: modern Chiusi in Etruria, not otherwise known for its springs.

Gabii: see note on *Ep.* 1.11.7–8.

11 *Cumae*: also on the Bay of Naples.

21 *Lucanian*: i.e. from the region in which Velia is located.

24 *Phaeacian*: see second note on *Ep.* 1.2.28.

26 *Maenius*: see note on *Sat.* 1.3.21; it is unusual for a Lucilian character to crop up in the *Epistles*.

28 *parasite*: for the *scurra*, see note on *Sat.* 1.4.87–9.

36–7 *bellies . . . iron*: hot metal plates (*laminae*) were applied as a punishment to the part of a slave's anatomy which had offended.

37 *reformed Bestius*: unknown, but evidently one who mercilessly condemns practitioners of his former vice, as Maenius does those who waste money on luxurious food.

39 *turn . . . ashes*: i.e. devour, continuing the metaphor of city-sacking from 'booty'.

EPISTLE 1.16

H. advises his friend Quinctius on the dangers of living one's life entirely based on the attitudes of others and of public opinion in general.

1 *Quinctius*: unknown, except possibly as the addressee of *Odes* 2.11, who is also an anxious figure urged to relax.

7 *chariot*: the sun god is usually imagined as driving a chariot across the sky.

11 *Tarentum*: city and holiday resort in (ancient) Calabria, the 'heel' of Italy.

13 *Hebrus . . . Thrace*: see note on *Ep.* 1.3.3, though the emphasis here is on pleasant coolness rather than bitter cold.

16 *September's season*: the time of fevers.

29 *praises of Augustus*: i.e. praise which only Augustus really deserves and hence inappropriately and sycophantically applied to Quinctius. H.'s point is that it is just as foolish to accept others' praise for one's wisdom and morality.

31 *with your own name*: as if in a roll-call at a levy, but also contrasting with the implied rejection of the military encomium, where one might say 'Not Quinctius but Augustus'.

34 *fasces*: see note on *Ep.* 1.7.53–4. 'They' are the Roman people, who can elect or reject a candidate.

36–7 *'Thief' . . . father*: extreme accusations of crime and vice were common in Roman politics.

38 *change colour*: i.e. blush or turn pale.

41 *the laws and privileges*: the phrase *leges iuraque* (or *et iura*) is a common one, notably featuring on an Augustan coin, and the two elements need not be clearly distinguished.

47 *flogging*: the standard punishment for slaves, over whose bodies their masters had complete rights.

48 *crows . . . cross*: see note on *Sat.* 1.3.82. The denial of burial, so important
     in the ancient world, adds to the punishment.

49 *Sabine owner*: by so describing himself, H. either alludes to his Sabine
     farm or, taking *Sabellus* more literally, to the Sabellan people of his native
     Venusia. In either case, he evokes the severe old-fashioned morality
     associated with both peoples.

58 *a pig or an ox*: i.e. for sacrifice.

60 *Laverna*: goddess of thieves, with a sacred grove on the Via Salaria.

64 *coin . . . crossroads*: a children's prank, performed then using molten lead,
     which is still practised today.

67 *loses . . . bravery*: metaphorically representing moral living in military
     terms, here the two most shameful acts a soldier could commit, resulting
     in capture and slavery.

68 *Since . . . him*: continuing the chain of imagery, the prisoner of war
     who has been 'enslaved' by avarice is put to work (both literally and
     metaphorically) in money-making activities.

73 *Pentheus*: H. adapts and radically reinterprets a scene from Euripides'
     Bacchae (and possibly the Roman tragedies on the same theme by Pacuvius
     and Accius), in which the tyrant Pentheus interrogates the disguised god
     Dionysus.

78 *The god himself . . . wish*: ironic in Euripides, where the disguised
     god himself is speaking and will indeed free himself. H.'s interpretation,
     playing on Dionysus as liberator (cf. note on *Ep.* 1.5.20) and the meta-
     phorical enslavement by avarice, is very different and speaks for itself.

EPISTLE 1.17

The first of two epistles focusing on how a client ought to behave towards a
patron. Scaeva is particularly advised to be accommodating to the wishes of his
patron (with a sideswipe at those who falsely pride themselves on their inde-
pendence) and to resist temptations to be grasping in the canvassing of gifts.

1   *Scaeva*: unknown, but his name means left-handed and hence perhaps
     awkward.

8   *Ferentinum*: there were towns of this name in Etruria and in the Hernican
     territory in Latium; whichever is meant, it evidently represents small-
     town quietude.

10 *passed . . . death*: lit. 'being born and dying has escaped notice', a Greek
     construction which paraphrases the Epicurean maxim *lathe biōsas*, lit.
     'living escape notice', more idiomatically, 'live without anyone noticing'.

14 *Aristippus*: see notes on *Sat.* 2.3.100 and *Ep.* 1.1.18.

18 *the Cynic*: Diogenes (*c.*412/403–*c.*324/321 BC), the first of the Cynics
     (it was neither a school nor he a founder), adopted the dog (Gk. *kuōn*;
     kunikos = canine) as emblematic of his advocacy of shamelessness and the

rejection of social norms. H. plays with the dog metaphor by imagining Aristippus chased by the biting Diogenes.

22 *inferior to the provider*: i.e. Diogenes is still a client, since his begging makes all those who give him anything his patrons.

30 *Milesian*: from Miletus, the great Ionian city on the south-west coast of Asia Minor, whose woollen products were renowned.

32 *ill-mannered life*: the Latin *ineptus* is hard to translate, suggesting broadly a failure to adapt or fit into normal society.

36 *It . . . Corinth*: a Greek proverb meaning that not everyone can attain the highest achievements or pleasures. Aulus Gellius derives it from the failure of all but the wealthiest to secure the favours of the famous Corinthian courtesan, Lais.

43 *king*: the Latin *rex* also means 'patron', but H. plays on its literal meaning throughout.

50–1 *crow . . . envy*: the language of fable again.

52 *Brundisium*: port city in (ancient) Calabria, Italy's 'heel', suggesting that patron and client may be going to Greece.

Surrentum: modern Sorrento, a Campanian city and resort on the Bay of Naples.

58–9 *The man . . . crossroads*: those stopping to help would be robbed.

60 *Osiris*: Egyptian god, whose cult (like that of his wife, Isis) was popular at Rome. An oath by the god who dies and rises again may be ironic in the mouth of the robber who feigns injury and springs up to mug his victim.

EPISTLE 1.18

Lollius appears to be of higher social status than Scaeva, but still in a (less economically dependent) patron–client relationship. The main focus is on the avoidance of falling into boorish incivility through a determination not to appear servile, but H. continues with various other recommendations about discretion, sexual continence, and the dangers of recommending unsuitable people to the patron.

1 *Lollius*: see note on *Ep.* 1.2.1.

frankest: significantly, *liberrime* also means 'most free'.

2 *hanger-on . . . friend*: a client could be depicted as a *scurra* (see note on *Sat.* 1.4.87–9) or as an *amicus*, with very different connotations.

9 *Virtue . . . extremes*: moderation is advocated throughout H.'s poetry, but this formulation particularly evokes Aristotelian thought.

11 *a mocker*: H. uses *derisor* instead of *scurra* here to stress how the man who ought to be mocking subversively is reduced to servile sycophancy.

14 *performing . . . mime*: the supporting actor would respond to and perhaps even parodically imitate the words and actions of the *archimimus* or lead.

15 *goat's wool*: i.e. trivialities; Porph. explains that it is a debate over whether goats' hair is bristles or wool.

19 *Castor or Dolichos*: Porph.'s guess of actors or gladiators is a good one. Of course, this and the next debate are also trivial.

20 *Minucian*: obscure but mentioned by Cicero as crossing Samnium. H. himself describes a journey to Brundisium along the Appian Way in *Sat.* 1.5.

31 *Eutrapelus*: P. Volumnius Eutrapelus, patron of, among others, the actress Cytheris (Volumnia), who became the lover of Antony and Gallus. His name in Greek means 'changeable', 'witty', or 'tricksy'.

34 *whore*: H. here uses *scortum*, a low streetwalker, rather than *meretrix* (courtesan).

36 *Thracian*: a type of gladiator, armed with a round shield and curved sword; bankrupts might be reduced to making a living by becoming gladiators, a mark of disgrace.

41-2 *Amphion and Zethus*: twin sons of Jupiter and Antiope, and founders of Thebes. Amphion the musician and Zethus the farmer famously debated the merits of their trades, and of the contemplative versus the active life more generally, as dramatized in the *Antiope* of Euripides and of Pacuvius (both now lost).

46 *Aetolian*: obscure. Possibly an allusion to the mythical hunt for the Calydonian boar in Aetolia; H.'s native Apulia is often called Aetolian through its connection with Diomedes, but the link with nets is unclear. Some suggest *Aeolian*, i.e. from Cumae, which the Augustan didactic poet Grattius praises (calling it the Aeolian valley) for its flax for making nets; although a Euboean colony, Cumae was often associated with Cyme in Aeolis (north-west Asia Minor).

54 *Mars' Field*: see note on *Sat.* 1.1.91; Lollius has undoubtedly been involved in contests related to military training, rather than in the Circus Flaminius.

55 *Cantabrian wars*: in north-west Spain under Augustus (the 'leader' who is incidentally praised here), 26–25 BC.

56 *Parthians' temples*: see note on *Ep.* 1.12.27–8, where it also forms an east–west pair with Cantabria.

61-4 *your forces . . . commanders*: a private, small-scale version of the sea-battle re-enactments (*naumachiae*) popular in public games at Rome, here enacting Octavian's great victory over Antony at Actium in 31 BC. The casting of Lollius' brother as Antony, Octavian's brother-in-law and brother Roman in civil war, is striking.

66 *both thumbs*: an allusion to the indication of whether a gladiator should live or die; it is unclear whether both thumbs were ever actually used or whether this is hyperbole to intensify the approval.

75 *enriches . . . worth*: the oxymoron reinforces the point that the patron would otherwise have owed you a more valuable gift.

82 *Theon's*: unknown, and the scholiasts seem to be guessing, but evidently an informer.

91 *Falernian*: see note on *Sat.* 1.10.24.

102–3 *What creates... unnoticed?*: calmness and freedom from care was an ideal of both Stoicism (*apatheia*) and Epicureanism (*ataraxia*), to be achieved in different ways. Politics would be consistent with, but not positively associated with, Stoicism, trade with neither, but the 'life unnoticed' is very Epicurean (cf. note on *Ep.* 1.17.10).

104–5 *Digentia ... Mandela*: evidently a river and a village near H.'s Sabine farm, but not mentioned elsewhere. The phrase 'which *x* drinks' is an epic one applied here to very humble locations.

EPISTLE 1.19

H. writes to Maecenas in praise of the importance in poetry of inspiration (*ingenium*) as represented by wine, over the technique (*ars*) of 'water-drinkers'. In particular, poetic models should be used but not slavishly. H. sketches his own poetic career, before defending his work against its alleged lack of popularity.

1 *Cratinus*: see note on *Sat.* 1.4.1. The allusion is to a line from his comedy *Pytine* ('The wine jar') in which he himself was the main character, whose wife, Comedy, threatened to divorce him for drunkenness. As a response to criticism from Aristophanes, it is a pertinent model for this epistle.

4 *Liber*: Dionysus, the god of wine. His Greek entourage consisted of half-human, half-goat satyrs, who were connected or equated with fauns, similar Italian rural spirits.

6 *Homer's praises of wine*: Homer does call wine 'sweet' and 'like honey', though he does also warn of its negative effects, especially in the *Odyssey*.

7 *Ennius*: see note on *Sat.* 1.10.54. He is referred to here as the author of the epic *Annales* and, a few years before the publication of the *Aeneid*, as the Roman Homer. In his own satires, he claims never to write poetry except when suffering from gout.

8 *Libo's well*: in the forum, perhaps as the place for rhetorical prose rather than poetry.

13 *Cato*: see note on *Sat.* 1.2.32, though H. could be referring to Cato the younger, Stoic and staunch opponent of Caesar, who committed suicide at Utica in 46 BC.

bare feet ... short: signs of asceticism and hardiness in the face of cold.

15 *Timagenes*: Alexandrian orator and historian, who lived in Rome from 55 BC onwards. He fell from favour with Augustus owing to his candour, and this could be the quality which the unknown Iarbitas unsuccessfully and perhaps disastrously imitated.

Iarbitas: the scholiasts' stories smack of guesswork, but his name does sound Numidian.

21–2 *first . . . had set foot*: evoking the language of Callimachus' *Aetia* pro-
logue, often imitated, notably by Lucretius.

23–5 *iambics . . . Lycambes*: H.'s *Epodes* imitated the abusive *iamboi* of the
poets Hipponax (sixth century BC) and especially Archilochus of Paros
(seventh century). Several of the latter's poems were attacks on Lycambes
and his daughter Neobule, who had broken her engagement with the poet;
according to tradition, both hanged themselves as a result of his attacks.
H. returns to this story in line 30.

26 *crown . . . leaves*: evoking the garland for the victor in a poetic contest.

28 *Sappho*: seventh-century lyric poet from Lesbos, and one of H.'s main
models in the *Odes*. She is described as *mascula* (lit. 'masculine'), evoking
her skill in what was considered a male vocation.

29 *Alcaeus*: lyric poet of the seventh–sixth century from Mytilene on Lesbos
and H.'s most privileged model in the *Odes*, especially for his combin-
ation of erotic, sympotic, and political themes. Hence H.'s claim to have
brought him to the Roman public's attention, despite the influence of
Pindar, Sappho, and the six other canonical lyric poets on the *Odes*.

34 *read . . . gentlemen*: it is notable that H. thinks of the *Odes* here as poems to
be read, though in the *Odes* themselves he preserves a (fairly transparent)
fiction of sung performance.

40 *seek the approval . . . tribes*: continues the electioneering metaphor, as *ambire*
literally means 'to go round canvassing'; for tribes, see note on *Ep.*1.6.52.

teachers: specifically *grammatici*, for which see note on *Sat.* 1.6.76–8.

41 *'That's . . . tears'*: a quotation from Terence's *Andria* which became proverbial.

41–2 *give a reading . . . halls*: see note on *Sat.* 1.4.23.

43 *Jupiter*: i.e. Augustus, a grandiose panegyric, but safely put in the inter-
locutor's mouth.

EPISTLE 1.20

H. addresses the book of epistles as if it were a slave-boy about to be freed,
reflecting on its destiny as he 'releases' it for publication.

1 *book*: there is a play on *liber* and the book/slave's freedom from its
master.

Vertumnus: i.e. the statue of the shape-shifting Etruscan god in the *vicus
Tuscus*, where the book wants to be put up for sale.

Janus: see note on *Sat.* 2.3.18–19.

2 *Sosii*: booksellers also mentioned at *AP* 345. Pumice was used to polish
any rough areas of a papyrus scroll, but, as with almost everything in this
poem, could be applied to a slave-boy, removing hard skin.

3 *keys and seals*: of the locked book-box or the locked house.

6 *Once . . . world*: a reflection on the author's lack of control over the fate or
even interpretation of his work once published.

13 *Utica*: city in the Roman province of Africa, now Utique in Tunisia, where the book hopes perhaps to find a new reading public.

bound . . . Ilerda: the slave is put in chains and sent to Spain (perhaps to its many mines), the book packaged with others and sent to a provincial market. It is striking that both Utica and Ilerda were sites of significant battles in the civil war, though the implications of this are unclear.

14–16 *like . . . cliff*: the final beast fable in the book, from Aesop; the master tries to stop the donkey from walking towards the cliff, but when it persists, pushes him towards it.

17 *teaching . . . streets*: the slave as a teacher, the book as a school text.

20–1 *be sure to say*: the ends of poems or collections often include a *sphragis* or seal, in which the poet identifies himself either by name or description.

freedman's son: see *Sat.* 1.6.

28 *in the year . . . colleague*: 21 BC, a typically Horatian variation on the Roman naming of the year by the names of the consuls, 'when *x* and *y* were consuls'.

EPISTLES, BOOK 2 AND ARS POETICA

EPISTLE 2.1: TO AUGUSTUS

H. explains why he has not written an epistle to Augustus before (in response to a jocular complaint from the *princeps*) and proceeds to criticize the contemporary preference for old literature over new, despite the former's lack of polish, technical expertise, and even care. He concludes with a further apology for not writing an epic in praise of the *princeps*, in which he manages to include all the elements of such a panegyric.

5 *Romulus . . . Pollux*: the founder of Rome, the god of wine, and Pollux were all sons of gods (Mars, Jupiter) by mortal women (Ilia, Semele, Leda); all acted as civilizing culture heroes and became gods, though Dionysus is usually considered divine from birth and Castor, the mortal son of Tyndareus, is not deified in all versions. However, the flattering parallels with Augustus in all three aspects are clear.

10–11 *He who . . . fate*: Hercules, the ultimate civilizing culture hero. Killing the Hydra of Lerna, a many-headed serpent, was among the Labours imposed on him by Eurystheus. H. probably hints at an allegorical interpretation of the Hydra as representing envy.

23–4 *Tables . . . men*: the so-called 'Twelve Tables', a legal code traditionally claimed to have been drawn up in 451 BC at the insistence of the *plebs* by two sets of *decemviri* ('ten men') with consular power.

24–5 *treaties of our kings*: even older documents, as underlined by the mention of kings, the last of whom was expelled in 510 BC, and by the equality of terms with cities long since dwarfed by Rome. However, a treaty between Gabii and Tarquinius Superbus was claimed by Dionysius of Halicarnassus to have survived to Augustan times at the temple of Jupiter Fidius.

24–5 *books of the Pontiffs*: the *libri pontificales* were records and prescriptions kept by priests of sacrificial procedures.

27 *Alban Mount*: see note on *Ep.* 1.7.76; as a sacred mountain, it is ironically proposed as the Italian equivalent of the Greek Helicon, where the Muses initiated Hesiod and other poets.

29–30 *Roman . . . balance*: i.e. we think the earliest Roman writings are the best.

31 *olive . . . outside*: an example of the absurdity of drawing parallels between dissimilar things.

32–3 *we have come . . . Achaeans*: a further example, closer to the current issue; just because Rome is dominant over Greece militarily and politically, it does not follow that she also surpasses her in these decadent and quintessentially Greek activities. 'Achaeans' evokes both the Roman province of Achaea and Homer's heroic Greeks, from whom contemporary Hellenes had so declined.

45 *horse's tail*: citing the argument about the point at which, as hair after hair is plucked, it ceases to be a horse's tail.

47 *dwindling heap*: likewise with stones removed from a heap.

49 *Libitina*: goddess of funerals.

50 *Ennius*: see notes on *Sat.* 1.10.54 and *Ep.* 1.19.7, though here he is emphatically *not* the Roman Homer.

52 *Pythagorean dream*: in the proem of the *Annales*, Ennius claimed, in accordance with Pythagorean doctrine, to be the reincarnation of Homer. H.'s precise point is obscure, perhaps that he had no need of further reincarnation since he is so widely read anyway.

53 *Naevius*: third-century BC writer of tragedies and comedies, but in combination with Ennius here must be included as author of the *Bellum Poenicum*, an epic in Saturnian metre on the First Punic War, the first epic on a Roman theme, and one already criticized as old-fashioned by Ennius.

56 *Pacuvius*: tragedian (*c.*220–130 BC), considered 'learned' (*doctus*) for his use of obscure myths for plots.

Accius: tragedian (*c.*170–80 BC) and younger contemporary of Pacuvius.

57 *Afranius' toga*: L. Afranius was a second-century BC writer of *comoediae togatae* ('comedies wearing the toga'), set in Italy, unlike the *palliatae* ('wearing a Greek cloak') of Plautus and Terence which retained the Greek setting and characters of Menander and other Greek models. H.'s point seems to be that Afranius' *togatae* were considered as good as Menander's New Comedies.

58 *Plautus*: third/second-century BC writer of *palliatae*, often considered less polished but more vigorous than Terence's.

Epicharmus: sixth/fifth-century BC Sicilian writer of comedy, probably akin to Attic Old Comedy, and an odd parallel to Plautus.

59 *Caecilius*: Caecilius Statius, second-century BC writer of *palliatae*, usually ranked with Plautus and Terence but, unlike them, surviving only in fragments.

   Terence: second-century BC writer of *palliatae*, famed for his pure style and subtle characterization.

62 *Livius*: Livius Andronicus, author of the first Roman tragedy in 240 BC and of the first Roman epic, a version of the *Odyssey*. From him to 'our own time' hence means the whole of Roman literary history.

71 *Orbilius*: the career of L. Orbilius Pupillus as a teacher at Rome is described by Suetonius.

79 *Atta's*: T. Quinctius Atta, second/first-century BC writer of *togatae*.

   saffron and flowers: scattered on the stage during *ludi scaenici*.

81 *Aesopus . . . Roscius*: famous and much-loved actors of the late Republic.

86 *Numa's Salian hymn*: the notoriously obscure (and, of course, very ancient) hymn sung by the leaping priests of Mars (*Salii*) at the festival of the Lupercalia, and ascribed to the second king of Rome, who reformed many of Rome's rituals.

101 *What likes and dislikes . . . changed?*: an odd line in the context, and perhaps misplaced or interpolated.

112 *Parthians*: not usually depicted as liars as such (though this line has been used as authority to generalize), but this probably alludes to their famous ruse of shooting arrows while apparently fleeing.

114 *southernwood*: a medicinal plant.

131 *famous examples*: the use of *exempla* to be followed or avoided was a key mean of inculcating Roman values, and poetry played its part. Cicero is eloquent on this in the *Pro Archia*.

132 *unmarried . . . boys*: H. must partly be alluding to his own *Carmen Saeculare* (Secular Hymn), performed by such a choir at the Secular Games of 17 BC.

138 *poetry*: H.'s point is reinforced by the further meanings of *carmen*, including 'hymn' and 'spell'.

143 *Earth*: Tellus was the Roman earth-goddess.

   Silvanus: god of the forest (*silva*) and of uncultivated land, which had to be kept within its appointed bounds.

144 *Genius*: see note on *Ep.* 1.7.94.

145 *Fescennine*: crudely and jocularly abusive verses performed most notably at weddings and triumphs; the etymology is uncertain but may reflect the city of origin or an association with the evil eye (*fascinum*).

146 *alternate verse*: dialogue in dramatic form, one speaker alternating with the other.

156 *Conquered . . . conqueror*: the famous line expresses the paradox of Rome's military conquest of but cultural submission to Greece over the course of the third and especially the second century BC.

158   *Saturnian*: a native Italian metre based on stress rather than quantity, unlike the Greek metres adopted by Roman poets, and used by Livius and Naevius in their epics before Ennius forged a Latin version of the dactylic hexameter for the *Annales*. On river metaphors for poetry, see note on *Sat.* 1.1.57.

161   *he*: the 'rough conqueror' of line 156, a collective embodiment of Roman poets in general.

162   *after the Punic wars*: ambiguous. Livius staged the first Roman tragedy to celebrate victory in the *First* Punic War in 240 BC; the plural could be explained as plural-for-singular, but the apparent parallel with the preceding potted history of epic might suggest that H. classes Livius' and Naevius' tragedies with their epics and sees Ennius as heralding the new age of both genres. In that case, the reference would be to the end of the *Second* Punic War (though the Third was still to come) in 201 BC.

163   *Thespis*: semi-legendary sixth-century inventor of Greek tragedy, who first separated a speaker from the chorus. His inclusion at the expense of Euripides, probably the most influential of the tragedians on Roman tragedy, is because the latter did not 'bring a benefit', i.e. introduce an innovation, unlike Aeschylus who introduced a second actor and Sophocles a third.

171–3   *helpless young lover . . . parasites*: stock characters of *palliatae*, whom the author Plautus is imagined as enacting. Dossenus was a stock character of Atellane farce, so that Plautus is depicted as acting like someone from a primitive, rustic genre when dealing with sophisticated, Greek characters.

174   *comic sock*: the *soccus* worn by comic actors was a generic marker, as the buskin was for tragedy; H. further exploits the image to suggest that Plautus 'doesn't fit' the genre, isn't 'big enough to fill its shoes', and that as a result his plays metaphorically 'fall flat'.

185   *knights*: as well as a separate social and, here, critical body, they had reserved seating under the *lex Roscia*.

186   *bear or boxers*: rival attractions at the theatrical games, appealing to a lower audience; Terence complains of these in the prologues of his comedies.

189–93   *For four hours . . . bronze*: Cicero criticized such an empty spectacle when Pompey paraded his Eastern spoils during a tragedy performed at the opening of his theatre in 55 BC. Corinthian bronze was so famous (cf. note on *Sat.* 2.3.21) that we need not think of games following the city's sack in 146 BC.

194   *Democritus*: see note on *Ep.* 1.12.12, but he was also renowned as the laughing philosopher for his detached and amused perspective on human affairs.

202   *Garganus' woods*: a promontory in Apulia jutting into the Adriatic.

      Tuscan sea: the Tyrrhenian sea (both words mean 'Etruscan') off the west coast of Italy.

207   *Tarentine*: see note to *Ep.* 1.16.11.

213   *Thebes . . . Athens*: common (and paradigmatic) settings respectively of Attic tragedy and Menandrian New Comedy, though Athens does feature in some tragedies.

216   *Apollo*: as god of poetry.

218   *Helicon*: home of the Muses and common scene of poetic initiation.

225   *fine thread . . . spun*: the language of Callimachean aesthetics and its Roman reception.

233   *Choerilus*: of Iasos, a proverbially bad poet, paid to write verse in praise of Alexander.

234   *Philips*: gold coins from the reign of Alexander's father, Philip II of Macedon.

238   *Apelles*: of Ephesus, the most renowned painter of classical antiquity, who painted both Philip and Alexander.

240   *Lysippus*: of Sicyon, famous sculptor, who likewise depicted Alexander.

244   *Boeotia*: region in central Greece including Thebes, proverbial in antiquity for its slow-witted and uncultivated inhabitants. Cicero ascribes this to the atmospheric conditions.

245   *your judgement*: Augustus', whose role as addressee may have been forgotten.

247   *Virgil and Varius*: see notes on *Sat.* 1.5.40; there is anecdotal evidence of Virgil's wealth, presumably in reward for his poetry, and for Augustus' generous payment of Varius for the *Thyestes*.

250   *'talks'*: H.'s *sermones* include all his hexameter works, including the *Satires* but here specifically the *Epistles*; in response to Augustus' complaint, he justifies not having written one to him.

251   *crawl along the ground*: H. continues the claim that his *sermones* are not really poetry, that their Muse goes on foot (cf. *Sat.* 2.6.17), here particularly contrasting them with the 'soaring' of panegyrical epic.

255   *bars . . . peace*: the gates of the Temple of Janus were opened when Rome was at war, closed when she was at peace. Augustus famously closed them three times, as bringer of peace.

256   *Parthians*: see notes on *Sat.* 2.1.13–15 and *Ep.* 1.12.27–8, and on line 112 above.

      emperor: H. uses the standard term *princeps* ('first citizen') and it is hard to be sure how far it had already by this time acquired the monarchical associations of 'emperor'.

257   *abilities . . . desires*: H. combines *praeteritio* ('passing by' topics he will not cover) with *recusatio* (polite 'refusal') on the conventional grounds of incapacity, while equally conventionally managing to include panegyrical references to all the things he 'cannot' describe.

264 *annoying attentiveness*: oxymoronic, since *officia* ('favours, benefits') ought to aid, not annoy or burden (*gravat*).

265 *wax*: a humbler equivalent of the bronze or marble in which a great ruler *should* be represented.

269–70 *street . . . paper*: the *Vicus Tuscus*, for which see note on *Sat.* 2.3.228–9.

EPISTLE 2.2: TO FLORUS

H. writes to Florus explaining why he has not written back (as he warned him he would not) and more particularly why he has not produced any more lyric poetry like the *Odes*. His series of reasons for the latter reflect on his life, the role of the poet, and the need (as in *Epistles* 1) to devote himself to philosophical pursuits rather than the trivialities of lyric.

1 *Florus . . . Nero*: see notes on *Ep.* 1.3.1 and 1.3.2.

3 *Tibur or Gabii*: small towns in Latium, a little to the east of Rome.

5 *eight thousand sesterces*: hard to judge the going rate, but this is probably relatively expensive.

6 *house-bred*: see note on *Sat.* 2.6.66.

16 *running away*: it is a little extreme, but not unparalleled, to refer to the shirking and hiding as *fuga*, which reinforces the seller's honesty.

17 *a penalty*: by law, sellers were required to declare any defects in the slave on offer.

26 *Lucullus*: see note on *Ep.* 1.6.40.

30 *king*: almost certainly Mithridates VI of Pontus, against whom Rome waged a protracted war including a long campaign by Lucullus, but Tigranes I of Armenia is also possible.

42 *Achilles' anger*: i.e. he studied Homer's *Iliad*, whose opening lines this paraphrases.

43 *Athens*: after the three levels of education listed in the note on *Sat.* 1.6.76–8, many elite Romans completed their education studying philosophy in Athens.

45 *groves . . . Academus*: the Academy, a gymnasium in Athens built on a site traditionally associated with the legendary Academus, site of Plato's philosophical school, and synonymous with Platonism in general.

46–8 *harshness . . . Caesar Augustus*: H. fought for Brutus at Philippi in 42 BC against the victorious forces of Antony and Octavian (anachronistically termed Augustus).

52–3 *doses . . . bile*: i.e. he would be mad, elaborately expressed by stating that the excess of the humour black bile (*melancholia*) could not be remedied by any amount of hemlock (emphatically in its role as medicine rather than poison).

59–60 *lyric . . . wit*: the three genres in which H. wrote, the lyric *Odes* (*carmina*), the abusive *Epodes* (*iambi*), and the conversational *Satires* (*sermones*) with elements of the Cynic diatribes of Bion of Borysthenes.

68–9 *Quirinal . . . Aventine*: two of Rome's seven hills.

70 *reasonably convenient*: hard to take either literally or ironically in the context, and the conjecture 'not very convenient' may well be correct.

71 *your*: i.e. 'one's' rather than 'Florus' '.

77 *whole . . . city*: a witty combination of Bacchus' association with poetic inspiration and the rather different abandonment of the city for the country by his followers in myths such as that depicted in Euripides' *Bacchae*.

80 *narrow tracks*: more imagery from Callimachus' *Aetia* prologue representing learned and obscure subject matter, but wittily recontextualized in relation to the impact on the poet of Rome's very literally bustling streets.

87 *lawyer*: a *iurisconsultus* was an expert on the law, closer to a modern solicitor than trial advocates like Cicero.

89 *Gracchus . . . Mucius*: clearly superlative examples of an orator and lawyer respectively, though the precise individuals meant is not clear. Gracchus is probably one of the brothers Tiberius and Gaius, who were great speakers as well as causing much political turmoil in the late second century BC.

94 *temple . . . bards*: the temple of Palatine Apollo contained two libraries, one devoted to Greek literature, one to Roman.

98 *Samnites*: a type of gladiator, armed in the manner of the central Italian people of that name.

99 *Alcaeus*: see note on *Ep.* 1.19.29.

100 *Callimachus*: a reincarnation of the third-century BC Alexandrian poet from Cyrene, who was the proclaimed model for elegant, small-scale, finely wrought poetry; the identity of the elegiac poet is much debated, but Propertius seems the strongest candidate, since he cites both Mimnermus and Callimachus among his privileged models.

101 *Mimnermus*: see note on *Ep.* 1.6.65.

110 *censor*: not in the modern sense of one who suppresses anything considered politically or morally undesirable, but a metaphor from Roman political life, where the censors would judge who was morally and economically fit to be a senator or knight, and expel those who fell short. The words to be 'expelled' from the poem are unfit on aesthetic, rather than moral, grounds.

114 *Vesta's precincts*: possibly an actual temple of Vesta, but more probably meaning a house, as centred around its sacred hearth. The general sense of expulsion is clear, but whether this is still linked to the censor or more generally ejecting someone from one's home is uncertain.

117 *Cato*: see note on *Sat.* 1.2.32, though cited here as an early example of great oratory, as well as author of the historical *Origines* and agricultural handbook *De agri cultura*, and as a source of archaic diction.

Cethegus: M. Cornelius Cethegus (d. 196 BC), commander in the Second Punic War and praised for his eloquence by Ennius.

119 *Need*: coinages and neologisms are figured as children begotten by the personified necessity of having a word for a new concept.

125 *dancer . . . Cyclops*: i.e. agile at one moment and lumbering the next.

128 *Argos*: city in the eastern Peloponnese.

137 *hellebore*: see note on *Sat.* 2.3.82.

143 *music . . . lyre*: i.e. the metres of Greek lyric used for Latin poetry, as in H.'s *Odes*.

144 *rhythms . . . life*: philosophy. The move from 'trivial' lyric to serious philosophy echoes *Ep.* 1.1.

158 *balance and bronze*: an allusion to an archaic ritual for selling property.

159 *ownership . . . possession*: the Roman legal concept of *usucapio*, that continued possession and use of land could constitute ownership, underpins this whole section. H. is showing how futile and meaningless the rich man's 'ownership' of the farm is, since the man who 'uses' the land effectively owns it, and the produce which the rich man thinks he owns he had in fact bought when he originally bought the land. This undermining of the meaning of 'ownership' leads into reflection on its transience, since death ends all ownership and thus renders it temporary hire.

167 *Aricia or Veii*: see notes on *Sat.* 1.5.1 and 2.3.143 respectively.

177–8 *Lucania . . . Calabria*: regions in south-west and south-east Italy.

180 *Tuscan figurines*: bronze figurines from Etruria.

Gaetulian purple: dye produced in North Africa.

184 *Herod's*: 'the Great' (*c*.73–4 BC), king of Judaea.

187 *Genius*: see note on *Ep.* 1.7.94.

197 *Minerva's holiday*: the Quinquatrus was a spring festival, originally of Mars, later of Minerva, held 19–23 March, and constituted a school holiday.

206–7 *ambition . . . death*: from a more general praise of moderation and living for the day, H. moves into areas more specifically associated with Epicureanism, and accordingly echoes the language of Lucretius.

209 *Thessalian miracles*: Thessaly in north-east Greece was associated with witches and magic of all kinds, but this may be an allusion to the so-called 'Thessalian trick' of drawing down the moon from the sky. Superstition (and indeed aspects of traditional religion akin to it) was a particular target of Epicureans.

212 *thorn*: i.e. moral failing.

213 *make way*: Lucretius in *DRN* 3 argues that those reluctant to die need to make room and free up atoms for the generations to come.

214–16 *You have . . . door*: a further allusion to *DRN* 3 and the depiction of life as a banquet which the sated reveller should leave contentedly.

EPISTLE TO THE PISOS: THE ART OF POETRY

See Introduction, pp. xxvi–xxvii.

1–4 *join . . . fish*: H. partially evokes various hybrid monsters of mythology (centaurs, sirens, Scylla), not with any regard to their depiction in art or poetry, but because their literal monstrosity corresponds to the aesthetic grotesqueness which he is attacking.

11–12 *savage . . . tigers*: impossibilities (*adynata*) were often used rhetorically in poetry (like the modern 'when hell freezes over'), and again H. exploits the incongruity to exemplify the evils of writing which lacks unity.

15–16 *purple patches*: in the metaphor of poem as robe, showy but incongruous additions.

16–18 *description . . . rainbow*: such showpiece descriptions (*ecphrases*) are common in ancient poetry and rhetoric. Diana had numerous groves and altars, but that at Aricia is the most likely.

24 *you father and you young men*: Lucius Calpurnius Piso and his two sons.

31 *desire . . . error*: an aesthetic variation on H.'s ethical advocacy of moderation; the dangers of rushing from one extreme to the other are most explicitly discussed at the start of *Sat.* 1.2.

32 *school of Aemilius*: unknown, even as to whether it was for teaching children or (as the scholiasts claim) gladiators.

nails: fingernails.

47–8 *clever combination*: the *callida iunctura* is a particular feature of H.'s own style, using relatively plain words but in striking combinations which give them a new force and even meaning.

50 *kilted Cethegus*: see second note on *Ep.* 2.2.117. The *cinctus* was an old-fashioned garment wrapped around the thighs and hips.

54 *Caecilius and Plautus*: see notes on *Ep.* 2.1.59 and 58 respectively.

55 *Virgil . . . Varius*: see notes on *Sat.* 1.5.40.

56 *Cato . . . Ennius*: see notes on *Ep.* 2.2.117 and *Sat.* 1.10.54 respectively.

59 *mint-mark*: the metaphor from currency persists in the modern term 'coinage'.

63–5 *Neptune . . . work*: i.e. a harbour is dug. The sea and its god are thus given a 'welcome' by being brought into the shore and show their gratitude by protecting ships (more prosaically protected by the harbour wall). The significance of the king is obscure.

65–6 *marsh . . . weight*: i.e. is drained and reclaimed as farmland.

73–4 *Homer . . . written*: epic should be written in hexameters. Metre was a key marker of genre and, though the relationship between the two could also be subverted, H. opposes such transgression here. For the identification of inventors, see note on *Sat.* 2.4.73.

75–8 *Verses... decided*: elegiac couplets, the 'joining' of 'unequal' hexameters and pentameters, were associated with lament (*e legein*, 'to say "alas"'), dedicatory and other epigrams, and eventually love.

79 *Rage . . . weapon*: for Archilochus and iambic poetry, see note on *Ep.* 1.19.23–5; there is a play on the etymology of *iambos* from a weapon one could throw (*iaptein*).

80–2 *this foot . . . action*: the iambic trimeter was also used for comedy and tragedy, designated as often by the footwear of their actors (see note on *Ep.* 2.1.174 on the comic sock), though with an added play here on literal and metrical 'feet'. For 'alternate speech', see note to *Ep.* 2.1.146.

83–5 *To the lyre... wine*: lyric included a range of sub-genres including hymns, epinician odes (celebrating victories in games), and sympotic poems (on love and wine).

89 *tragic verse*: since H. has just noted that both genres used iambic trimeters (even though the comic version was less strict), this must refer to style rather than metre.

90–1 *Thyestes' banquet*: Atreus served the flesh of his brother Thyestes' sons to him in revenge for the latter's seduction of his wife and attempted usurpation of his throne; a classic tragic plot, treated by Sophocles, Ennius, Accius, and most recently Varius.

94 *Chremes*: a stock father from New Comedy, eponymous character of Terence's *Self-Tormentor*, though the name may have been used in other lost plays; also named at *Sat.* 1.10.40.

96 *Telephus*: king of the Mysians, wounded by Achilles in a skirmish before the Trojan War, and reduced to ragged beggary; a classic tragic beggar and hence transgressor of the norms of tragic grandeur, especially in Euripides' *Telephus*, notably referenced in Aristophanes' *Acharnians*.

Peleus: son of Aeacus and father of Achilles, was exiled for the murder of his half-brother Phocus, took refuge with King Acastus of Iolcus (the subject of Euripides' *Peleus*), and was again exiled by Acastus in old age (in Sophocles' *Peleus*).

97 *words . . . length*: i.e. grandiloquent compound words, with a further play on foot as unit of metre and of distance.

113 *horse and foot*: a common phrase for 'the entire Roman people', originally conceived of in military terms as either cavalry or infantry, but with particular point here alluding to the division of theatrical audiences by rank (equestrians and *plebs*).

118 *Colchian . . . Assyrian*: the antithesis is probably between the under-civilized savages of the Caucasus (including Aeëtes and Medea) and the over-civilized decadents of Mesopotamia (though the latter is home to no obvious dramatic characters).

Thebes . . . Argos: there ought to be a similar antithesis, in which case it is obscure, but H. may simply be referring to two of the cities in which so many tragedies were set.

120 *Achilles*: son of Peleus and Thetis, greatest of the Greek warriors at Troy, most famous from the *Iliad* but also featuring in a number of tragedies; H.'s characterization is, as his argument requires, typical.

123 *Medea*: Colchian princess and sorceress who betrayed her father Aeëtes for love of Jason, but later killed her children when abandoned by him, as well as committing many other crimes; an archetypal tragic heroine.

Ino: wife of King Athamas of Thebes, who was driven mad by Juno and killed one of his children; Ino leapt with the other child into the sea, where they became marine divinities. Sophocles wrote an *Athamas* and Euripides an *Ino*.

124 *Ixion*: king of Thessaly who killed his father and, when purified by Jupiter, treacherously attempted to rape Juno; Jupiter substituted a cloud in her shape which gave birth to the centaurs, and Ixion was punished by being strapped to a wheel of fire in the Underworld. Tragedies of this name by Aeschylus, Sophocles, and Euripides.

Io: nymph raped by Jupiter and transformed into a heifer to hide her from Juno, who nevertheless drove her across the world, employing first the giant Argus and then a gadfly; the latter drove her mad, so the 'wandering' is both physical and mental. The *Prometheus Bound* attributed to Aeschylus memorably features her.

Orestes: see note on *Sat.* 2.3.137.

125 *entrust . . . character*: a very rare undertaking in tragedy, but the late fifth-century tragedian Agathon did invent an original plot and characters for his *Antheus*.

128–30 *It is difficult . . . unsung*: difficult indeed. The 'themes common to all' cannot refer to plots, since what H. says next argues precisely the opposite. He must mean that, since it is hard to explore such universal themes (life, death, morality, etc.) by means of 'individual' characters, the difficulty might be lessened by employing plots and characters (such as those associated with the Trojan War) which are themselves universal and the 'common' property of all, rather than unfamiliar, invented ones.

136 *cyclic poet*: one of those who wrote poems which were part of the 'epic cycle', treating events at Troy and elsewhere in the mythical tradition not covered in the *Iliad* and *Odyssey*. Callimachus singled out the cyclical poets for particular scorn.

140–1 *'Tell . . . cities'*: a translation of the first two lines of the *Odyssey*.

145 *Antiphates . . . Cyclops*: monsters encountered by Odysseus in his tales (*apologoi*) of his own adventures, respectively the king of the man-eating Laestrygonians, the sea-monster and whirlpool between which he had to sail, and the one-eyed giant Polyphemus, who ate a number of his crew and whom he blinded in revenge.

146 *Diomedes' . . . Meleager*: the *Nostoi* or 'Returns' of the various Greek heroes from Troy were part of the epic cycle, including that of Diomedes

to Argos, where he found his wife unfaithful and had to flee to Apulia. Beginning this story with the death of his uncle Meleager following the Calydonian boar-hunt would indeed involve excessive and extraneous back-story.

147   *Trojan war . . . twin egg*: likewise, beginning this story with the birth of Helen (twinned with Clytemnestra) from an egg laid by Leda, who had been raped by Jupiter in the form of a swan, would provide too much background to the main narrative.

148   *the middle of his tale*: the famous phrase *in medias res*, referring to the *Odyssey*'s beginning near the end of its hero's wanderings and relating them retrospectively.

162   *Campus*: see note on *Sat.* 1.1.91.

184   *an actor's . . . before our eyes*: in tragedy, violent actions and others which were hard to represent on-stage were conventionally narrated in a 'messenger speech'.

187   *Procne . . . bird*: an Athenian princess, who avenged her husband Tereus' rape and mutilation of her sister Philomela by serving her own and Tereus' son Itys in a meal to his father; she was then transformed into a nightingale, Philomela into a swallow (in some versions vice versa), and Tereus into a hoopoe. There were famous versions entitled *Tereus* by Sophocles and Accius.

   Cadmus . . . snake: founder of Thebes punished many years afterwards for killing the serpent who guarded the site by being transformed into a snake himself. No tragic version is known but this is predicted at the end of Euripides' *Bacchae*.

189   *five acts*: a development which postdates the fifth-century heyday of Attic tragedy, but clearly emerges from its series of 'episodes' divided by choral odes.

191   *No god . . . deliverer*: the so-called *deus ex machina* ('god [appearing] from the crane') often appeared at the end of tragedies to resolve crises, but excessive or inappropriate use of this device was the object of criticism.

192   *fourth actor*: a convention already observed in the fifth century and rarely broken.

193   *chorus*: H. reflects many criticisms of the use of the chorus, even as early as the later plays of Euripides.

202   *double-pipe*: the *tibia* was used to accompany the singing of the chorus and also lyrics sung by actors. Its inability to be heard in large theatres provides a transition to a contrast between the humble origins of Roman drama and its current luxurious decadence.

219   *Delphi*: in central Greece, home of Apollo's most famous oracle.

220   *goat*: alludes to one etymology of tragedy (*tragōdia*) from 'goat-song' (*tragos* + *ōdē*) and the aetiology (origin myth) which goes along with it.

satyrs: Attic tragedies were traditionally performed in a trilogy (linked or not) followed by a 'satyr play' featuring mythological burlesque and the low antics of a chorus of Dionysus' troupe of satyrs.

231–2 *Tragedy . . . actions*: Tragedy is here personified to reinforce the parallel with the respectable *matrona*. There is some evidence that Attic satyr plays dealt with myths related to those treated in the preceding tragedies, but H. deprecates too close a connection. Despite what he says, there is no evidence for satyr plays being written or performed at Rome.

237–8 *Davus . . . Pythias . . . Simo*: stock names for a New Comedy slave, slave-girl, and old man respectively, each appearing in Plautus and Terence.

239 *Silenus*: the leader of the satyrs and of their chorus; H. differentiates the style of satyr plays from that of comedy, even though both differ from tragedy.

244 *fauns*: see note on *Ep.* 1.19.4, here the precise Roman equivalent of satyrs.

248 *horse . . . wealth*: knights and senators; 'father' means a distinguished man, perhaps with a play on *patres* as 'senators'; 'wealth' means the 'census' needed to maintain the rank of knight or senator.

249 *one who buys . . . nuts*: the lower orders.

252 *he*: the personified Iambus.

'*trimeters*': so-called from the three 'metra', each containing two iambic 'feet'; H. playfully explains this terminological oddity on the grounds that Iambus' six feet were so quick that they only took the space of three.

256 *spondees*: feet consisting of two long syllables, which could replace most, but not all, the iambs in a trimeter.

258 *Accius*: see second note on *Ep.* 2.1.56; too many spondees in the trimeter is not desirable, so 'noble' is clearly ironic, perhaps suggesting too close a resemblance to the weighty 'nobility' of the epic hexameter.

259 *Ennius' verses*: see note on *Sat.* 1.10.54, but it is only his tragedies which are alluded to here.

270 *Plautus*: see note on *Ep.* 2.1.58 and the criticism of him at *Ep.* 2.1.170–6. His *senarii* are indeed governed by less strict rules than tragic trimeters, but H. unjustly ignores the metrical virtuosity of his sung *cantica*.

276 *Thespis*: see note on *Ep.* 2.1.163; the wine-lees make a connection with rustic festivals of Dionysus.

Aeschylus: oldest of the three great Athenian tragedians (*c*.525–456 BC).

281 *Old Comedy*: see note on *Sat.* 1.4.1.

282–4 *freedom . . . removed*: a theory found in ancient writers but largely disbelieved by modern critics. For whatever reason, however, the chorus plays a markedly smaller and less integrated role in the 'middle comedy' of late Aristophanes and in New Comedy.

286–8   *courage . . . themes*: for 'comedies wearing the toga' (H. uses the word *togatae* here) see note on *Ep.* 2.1.57; 'plays wearing the fringed toga' or (*fabulae*) *praetextae*, as H. calls them here, seem to have been very like tragedies, but on themes from Roman myth and history; we know of examples featuring Romulus, the expulsion of Tarquinius, the *devotio* of Decius, and even contemporary events such as Fulvius' siege of Ambracia in Ennius' play of that name.

290   *Latium*: the region surrounding Rome, effectively meaning Rome itself here.

292   *you . . . veins*: a circumlocution for the Pisos, members of the Calpurnian *gens*, descended from Calpus, son of Rome's second king, Numa Pompilius.

294   *test . . . nail*: see note on *Sat.* 1.5.32–3.

295–7   *Democritus . . . sanity*: a tendentious interpretation, with its roots in Plato, of Democritus' (see note on *Ep.* 1.12.12) emphasis on the importance of poetic inspiration, here recast as madness. For Helicon, see note on *Ep.* 2.1.218.

297–8   *sizeable . . . berth*: H.'s point may be that these men feign madness in order to appear 'poetic', but there is also a parallel between their slovenliness and the rough-hewn poetry which he has just criticized, and which is the result of too much emphasis on inspiration (*ingenium*) over craftsmanship (*ars*).

300–1   *Licinius . . . cure*: Ps.-Acro's story of the barber made a senator by Caesar because he said he hated Pompey may be fabricated, but at least is not deduced from the text. For Anticyras, see note on *Sat.* 2.3.82.

302   *bile*: see note on *Ep.* 2.2.52–3.

310   *Socratic corpus*: most famously Plato's dialogues, but Xenophon and others wrote about Socrates, and in any case H. seems more broadly to mean 'philosophical literature'.

325   *the as*: a copper coin originally equivalent to a pound, but repeatedly devalued.

327   *Albanus' son*: unknown, but the name ('from Alba Longa') emphasizes his Roman identity.

332   *smeared . . . chest*: i.e. preserved for posterity.

340   *Lamia's belly*: a female monster who devoured children.

341   *centuries*: divisions of the Roman people for electoral (and originally military) purposes, whose constitution tended to reinforce conservative values, as here where they only tolerate poetry which serves a didactic purpose.

342   *Ramnes*: one of the three original Roman tribes, and later the name of two of the six equestrian centuries, clearly meant to contrast with the conservative centuries just mentioned.

343   *vote*: continuing the electoral metaphor.

345 *Sosii*: see note on *Ep.* 1.20.2.

357 *Choerilus*: see note on *Ep.* 2.1.233.

359 *Homer dozes off*: certain inconsistencies in the *Iliad* and the *Odyssey* were noted by ancient critics.

371 *Messalla*: see note on *Sat.* 1.10.28, though here mentioned as a great orator.

   Aulus Cascellius: famous jurist, born in 104 BC.

373 *billboards*: Martial describes shops' doorposts on which some kind of publicity for authors was posted, and this may be the sense of *columnae* here, but they might alternatively have book-rolls tied to them for browsing, as at *Sat.* 1.4.71.

375 *Sardinian honey*: presumably unpleasant; Virgil calls Sardinian herbs bitter.

379 *Campus*: see note on *Sat.* 1.1.91.

383–4 *assessed . . . respectability*: see note on *Ep.* 1.1.58

385 *Minerva's approval*: goddess of wisdom and here almost its personification.

387 *Maecius*: see note on *Sat.* 1.10.38.

392 *Orpheus*: mythical Thracian poet and singer with the ability to charm beasts and inanimate objects. H. offers a rationalization of this myth.

394 *Amphion*: see note on *Ep.* 1.18.41–2.

402 *Tyrtaeus*: seventh-century BC Spartan poet, whose elegies encouraged men into battle and were regularly so used by later Spartans too. Homer, of course, is less explicitly hortatory but his praise of eternal fame won in battle could be used to such ends.

403 *verse oracles*: the Delphic and other oracles generally gave responses in hexameters.

404 *way . . . shown*: since the philosophical poems of the Pre-Socratics mainly dealt with physics rather than ethics, H. is probably referring to moralizing verse by figures such as Hesiod and Solon.

404–5 *by Pierian stains the favour of kings*: various poets are associated with the kings and tyrants of archaic Greece, including Pindar who wrote victory odes for the tyrants of Sicily. 'Pierian' refers to the Muses, after their birthplace near Mt. Olympus.

405–6 *entertainment . . . toils*: dramatic poetry to provide relief for the labouring masses, in antithesis to the kings' court poetry.

406–7 *in case . . . song*: refers to the whole of this section of the argument: because poetry has always been useful, there is no need to ashamed of it.

414 *Pythian piece*: evidently a number performed at the Pythian games in Delphi, though whether as part of a musical contest or in another capacity is uncertain.

426 *given . . . give one*: in Roman society this would put the receiver under an obligation, whether they were a 'client' of lower social status or an equal.

433 *servile mocker*: as the context shows, this *derisor* is a sort of sycophantic
    scurra (as at *Ep.* 1.18.11) who at this point is actually praising rather than
    mocking his patron's poetry.

437 *fox*: difficult, since one would expect a fox to hide inside a less threatening
    creature's skin rather than have something concealed inside it. Rudd's
    suggestion of an allusion to the Fox and the Crow rather strains what 'lies
    concealed inside' can mean. It may be that a note in the margin of a manu-
    script ('a fox was inside') has replaced the name of the animal in which the
    fox was hiding.

438 *Quintilius*: of uncertain identity, but perhaps the man whose death is
    mourned in *Odes* 1.24 and who is there praised for his 'unvarnished
    Truthfulness'.

450 *Aristarchus*: of Samothrace (*c.*216–144 BC), head of the library of
    Alexandria and famous editor of Homer and other poets, particularly
    noted for his marking of verses which he considered substandard.

453 *scab*: various ailments affecting the skin, including leprosy.

    king's ailment: jaundice.

454 *fit . . . anger*: probably related to Diana's identification with Luna, the
    moon, associated with 'lunacy'.

465 *Empedocles*: see note on *Ep.* 1.12.20, where his 'madness' is also stressed.

470–2 *It isn't . . . ground*: H. carries the equation of madness and poeticizing to
    the point of wondering whether the latter is caused (as the former could
    be) by an act of sacrilege. Urinating on statues was evidently practised, if
    we can trust inscriptions warning people not to. A *bidental* was a patch of
    ground struck by lightning and hence fenced off as sacred until a ritual
    had been performed to appease the gods.

INDEX

Index 203

Pindar 70, 116
Plato xi, 38, 47, 102, 114
Plautus 95, 98, 113
Plotius Tucca 18, 30
Polemo 45
Pollio, C. Asinius 29
Priapus xi, xvi, 25–6
Procne 111
Pythagoras 47, 54, 80, 95

Quirinus (Romulus) viii, 29, 94

river imagery xxv, 4, 14, 24, 29, 30, 68,
    98, 108

Sappho 91
Saturnalia 38, 56–9
Saturnian metre 98
satyr plays 112, 197
Scipio Africanus Aemilianus, P. x, xv, 32, 33
Servius Tullius 20
sex and love 7–10, 13, 20, 25–6, 45–6,
    57–8, 68, 74, 89–90
Sicily x, xv, 54, 69, 80, 118, 130–4, 175,
    186, 199
slaves and slavery xiv, 4–5, 9, 10, 12, 21,
    23, 25, 36, 45, 52, 54, 56–9, 68, 73,
    78, 81–2, 85–6, 89–90, 100–1, 123,
    125, 133, 134, 135, 139, 156, 157,
    159–62, 168, 179, 184–5, 197
Sophocles 98, 188, 194–6
    Ajax 151
speech and silence vii, x, xviii–xix,
    14–17, 24–5, 27, 32–4, 52, 54, 89,
    130–4, 137–8, 140, 144–6, 158
Stertinius 39–46, 80
Stoicism xxi–xxii, xxiv, 42, 46, 119, 120,
    124–7, 147, 148–53, 159–62, 165–7,
    183; *see also* Cato, Chrysippus,
    Stertinius

Tarentum xv, xvii, 22, 23, 48, 75, 84, 99,
    130, 134
Tarpa, Sp. Maecius 29
Telemachus 75
Terence 6–7, 95, 128, 130, 152, 184,
    188, 194
Thespis 98
Tiberius Claudius Nero xii, 69, 76,
    77, 80
Tibur 23, 49, 75, 77, 100
Timagenes of Alexandria 91
Tiresias x–xi, 49–52
town, *see* countryside
Trebatius Testa, C. x–xi, 32–4
Trojan War 13, 24, 28, 68, 102, 109–10;
    see also Achilles, Agamemnon, Ajax,
    Homer, Ulysses
Twelve Tables 94
Tyrtaeus 116

Ulysses (Odysseus) x–xi, 43, 49–52, 68,
    73, 75

Valgius Rufus, C. 30
Varius Rufus, L. 18, 20, 22, 27, 29, 30,
    59–60, 100, 108
Varro of Atax 30
Virgil xix, xxiii, 18–19, 22, 29, 30, 100,
    108
vision, poor, *see* conjunctivitis
visual arts 58, 100, 106

wine (*incl.* Caecuban, Chian, Falernian,
    Massic) 5, 18, 29, 32, 34, 36, 37, 38,
    41, 42, 47–50, 58–60, 66, 69, 71, 82,
    83, 89, 90, 91, 95, 97, 101, 104, 108,
    113, 117

A SELECTION OF   **OXFORD WORLD'S CLASSICS**

	The First Philosophers: **The Presocratics and the Sophists**
	Greek Lyric Poetry
ARISTOTLE	**The Nicomachean Ethics**
BOETHIUS	**The Consolation of Philosophy**
CAESAR	**The Civil War** **The Gallic War**
CATULLUS	**The Poems of Catullus**
EURIPIDES	**Bacchae and Other Plays** **Medea and Other Plays**
HERODOTUS	**The Histories**
HOMER	**The Iliad** **The Odyssey**
HORACE	**The Complete Odes and Epodes**
JUVENAL	**The Satires**
MARCUS AURELIUS	**The Meditations**
OVID	**The Love Poems** **Metamorphoses**
PETRONIUS	**The Satyricon**
PLATO	**Republic**
PLAUTUS	**Four Comedies**
SOPHOCLES	**Antigone, Oedipus the King, and Electra**
SUETONIUS	**Lives of the Caesars**
TACITUS	**Histories**
VIRGIL	**The Aeneid** **The Eclogues and Georgics**
XENOPHON	**The Expedition of Cyrus**

A SELECTION OF   **OXFORD WORLD'S CLASSICS**

THOMAS AQUINAS	**Selected Philosophical Writings**
FRANCIS BACON	**The Essays**
WALTER BAGEHOT	**The English Constitution**
GEORGE BERKELEY	**Principles of Human Knowledge** and **Three Dialogues**
EDMUND BURKE	**A Philosophical Enquiry into the Origin of Our Ideas of the Sublime and Beautiful** **Reflections on the Revolution in France**
CONFUCIUS	**The Analects**
DESCARTES	**A Discourse on the Method**
ÉMILE DURKHEIM	**The Elementary Forms of Religious Life**
FRIEDRICH ENGELS	**The Condition of the Working Class in England**
JAMES GEORGE FRAZER	**The Golden Bough**
SIGMUND FREUD	**The Interpretation of Dreams**
THOMAS HOBBES	**Human Nature** and **De Corpore Politico** **Leviathan**
DAVID HUME	**Selected Essays**
NICCOLÒ MACHIAVELLI	**The Prince**
THOMAS MALTHUS	**An Essay on the Principle of Population**
KARL MARX	**Capital** **The Communist Manifesto**
J. S. MILL	**On Liberty and Other Essays** **Principles of Political Economy** and **Chapters on Socialism**
FRIEDRICH NIETZSCHE	**Beyond Good and Evil** **The Birth of Tragedy** **On the Genealogy of Morals** **Thus Spoke Zarathustra** **Twilight of the Idols**